MW01712560

Arnie Patterson:
A Nova Scotian's Memoir

NIMBUS
PUBLISHING

Dedication

To my three girls

Nimbus Publishing Limited
PO Box 9166
Halifax, NS B3K 5M8
(902) 455-4286

Printed and bound in Canada

National Library of Canada Cataloguing in Publication Data

Patterson, Arnie, 1928-
Arnie Patterson : a Nova Scotian's memoir
Includes bibliographical references.
ISBN 1-55109-389-8

1. Patterson, Arnie, 1928- 2. Nova Scotia—Biography.
3. Businessmen—Canada—Biography. I. Title. II. Title: Nova Scotian's memoir.

FC2327.1.P38A3 2001 971.6'04'092 C2001-903326-5
F1038.P38A3 2001

Canada

The Canada Council for the Arts | Le Conseil des Arts du Canada

We acknowledge the financial support of the Government of Canada through the Book Publishing Industry Development Program (BPIDP) and the Canada Council for our publishing activities.

Contents

Author's Note

The chapters that follow will hopefully give you, dear reader, some insight into important, and not so important, events that were part of my life, which now at age 72 has been a relatively long one. The chapters follow my business and journalistic career in chronological fashion. Doubtless you will find that I have lived a varied, actually an episodic life, and if you follow it carefully you will conclude that I was a fellow who could not keep a job, or one who got bored easily. Neither thought is true but I did love the variety and the challenges that these widely diverse occupations offered.

The blame for this exercise should be placed with my daughter Carol, who last year suggested I chronicle the family history, or that part which at least involved the Patterson clan. I am afraid that once I started this visit to the past, it was like rolling downhill; I couldn't stop.

You will meet all sorts of interesting people in the pages that follow, and I trust and hope that you will find this read interesting.

For the most part the research involved has relied on my own recollections, old letters, documents, and reference to secondary texts: Greig Stewart's *Arrow Through the Heart: the Life and Times of Crawford Gordon and the Avro Arrow*; " D. M. Labourdais' *Sudbury Basin*; Dr. John Martin's *The Story of Dartmouth*; Nathan Phillip's *Mayor of All the People*; Harry Bruce's *The Story of R. A. Jodrey, entrepreneur* and *A Century at Central Trust*; Peter Newman's *Flame of Power*; and George Radwanski's *Trudeau*.

Arnie Patterson

Foreword

A friendship with C. Arnold Patterson is like a front-row seat on Atlantic Canada's most charmed life. On paper, in fact, it's as though he's had half a dozen lives: newspaper reporter (his one true calling, he will tell you); public-relations man; brewery manager; founder of two radio stations; tavern owner; press secretary to Prime Minister Pierre Elliott Trudeau; candidate for Parliament; newspaper columnist; and director of a shipyard, an airline, a university, a trust company, and a road-building company. And perhaps above all, he's been a blessedly matched husband and father.

Other than that (as Arnie might say, leaning over a beer in a Dartmouth tavern) there's more to it. Arnie Patterson was left fatherless at age two. His public-relations tasks included the Springhill Mine Disaster in 1958. He was twice defeated in politics. His businesses, as most do, saw their ups and downs. There was never a shortage of challenges. In the end, what has made the charmed life possible is Arnie himself. He takes his wins with humility and his losses with good-natured resilience.

Walk into that tavern with him, and the six-foot-two-inch millionaire ex-radio-station-owner becomes just another Dartmouth boy. Well, almost. Here in Atlantic Canada, where the mighty sit down with the other sports fans, he's a friend to one and all, remembering their names, recollecting great moments, and patting people on the back. This is where the kid who skated on Dartmouth rinks with the rest of them went on to create a community radio station, CFDR, that earned him the handle "Mr. Dartmouth." (There were always critics, of course. "If he's Mr. Dartmouth," a woman once asked me, "how come he lives in Bedford?")

Arnie's talent with people is a politician's gift, but also for him a genuine enjoyment. He does it with native charm and a sharp, ironic wit. Arnie is, as Senator Keith Davey once said, "one of the best raconteurs in the business."

And yet, the "hail fellow, well met" masks a subtle intelligence, one that takes the measure of people quickly and shrewdly. Arnie harbours a vast knowledge of business, journalism, and North American politics, to name only a few of his passions. So when he retired to Florida with his wife, Glo, to spend his winters golfing, it wasn't long before he distinguished himself at the Isla Del Sol Yacht and Country Club in St. Petersburg, becoming its first Canadian president. His golfing friends in the US found themselves just as charmed as the folks at home.

And now with this book, you, too, can have a front-row seat.

Douglas MacKay

Chapter One: Roots

Arnie, Bill, and Laurie Patterson, aged eight, thirteen, and seven. (1936)

After a lifelong habit of reading biographies I know it is largely custom to begin with childhood and work upward through the years. While this usual tabulation of fathers, mothers, grandmother, aunts and uncles, cousins, and so forth is often times boring, it is an essential part of the story. Our youthful years, especially those entwined around family, give formation to one's life and many of its values. As such, although tempted to do otherwise, I am going to begin this tale at the beginning.

My life began in early morning on July 2, 1928. I was born in our home at 11 Sinclair Street in Dartmouth, Nova Scotia. It was not unusual in that period for birth to take place at home. My parents were Charles and Mary Patterson, and I was the third of what was to be a family of four children. My sister Jeanne Marie was six when I born, my brother William Leonard (Bill) was five; brother Laurie Robert was born fourteen months later on September 16, 1929. I was named Charles Arnold; Charles, of course, for my father and Arnold for the husband of my mother's sister, Dr. Arnold Park, who lived in Montreal. Strangely I was never called Charles but rather have gone through life as Arnie. Only my sister Jeanne and grade one teacher have ever called me Arnold.

My mother, Mary Margaret (nee Sullivan) was born in Halifax in or near 1893. My father Charles Ardinald was born two years earlier in Dartmouth, the son and grandson of old Dartmouthians. They never met until they were in their early twenties, and this following a theatre party at Acker's Theatre on Barrington Street in Halifax. This movie house was later rebuilt and named the Capitol, and the massive Maritime Centre now

Charlie Patterson, a native of Dartmouth, was an outstanding athlete and served four years in the trenches during World War One.

occupies the site. While the date of their meeting is unknown to me, it had to be in 1912 or thereabouts for my father went overseas with the Canadian Army in 1914 and spent four years in the trenches in France, and during that period there were an incessant number of letters addressed to "Dearest Mary" and "My Dearest Girl." The caring and intimate detail indicated that a romance had ensued before his departure for war. While most of the correspondence has disappeared, through my sister Jeanne I was able to find ten surviving letters.

These were datelined "Somewhere [in] France" and later from army hospitals in England where he was recuperating after the war. I am able to reproduce certain parts here. The letters are remarkable, and for me personally a great joy. I never knew my father or heard him speak; he died when I was two. These letters give me a strong sense of him as a young man. He had a nice writing hand and he expresses himself well and grammatically. More meaningful were the sentiments he expressed for my mother, his girlfriend, and his sensitivity in general to the horrible events that surrounded him in the far-distant trenches.

Unfortunately many of the letters he wrote in the early years of the war were lost, and those that survive were written between 1917–1919. Here is a typical letter written from "Somewhere [in] France" and dated December 10, 1917—four days after the disastrous Halifax Explosion.

> My Beloved Mary,
>
> We received word yesterday of the awful disaster which has occurred in Halifax, and I have been sick with fear for you, my love, and your dear family; but God grant none of you have been hurt, and O! that I were only there with you in your trouble.
>
> I am also concerned very much about my dear old Dad, and those of my family in Dartmouth, but not so much as I am about you my own sweetheart: you are the world to me, and I would want to die if I thought you were among those killed. But something seems to tell me that you are safe, and I will keep up heart, and pray to hear that you are all right. But, O! it will be so long until I hear from you, my love, and days will seem like weeks.

Arnie Patterson's mother, Mary Margaret Sullivan, in her 1917 graduation photo from Sisters of Providence Hospital in Holyoke, Massachusetts.

Nothing in this awful war has made me so downhearted as what I have heard about this explosion. There must have been hundreds killed from what I have heard. I would send a telegram if I could, but there is no place to send one from here, so all I can do is to sit sadly and wait for news, but O! if I could only be there with you now.

Mary, my own, if you want any money to seek anyone who has suffered through this awful catastrophe, please let me know as I can send you two hundred dollars out of my book, and it would be good to help, and I will feel glad to know that I can do a little to relieve suffering.

Dear sweetheart, if it were not for you, I would have been killed long before this, as I have often thought it did not matter about me, where I died or not, but then I have always said to myself, perhaps Mary loves me, as I do her, and everything may come out right in the end. Then I would cheer up and be careful not to get into any more danger than I had to.

I am worried about Jack and Edie [Mary's brother and sister-in-law], as I understand from the English papers that the greater part of the damage is in the north end. My dear Mary, if any of your dear ones were taken away (God forbid!) be brave and bear up: but I know you will as I know you as a lovely brave woman: I only wish I could share all your sorrows, as I have shared your joys in times past.

You asked me in your last letter (which I received a few days ago, and which gave me great joy), if I remembered the show "Charlie's Aunt" which we saw the first night we met. Yes, dear girl, it is as fresh to me as the very night itself, as are all my memories of you, the only girl that I shall ever love.

I cannot realize the awful scenes which the explosion must have caused, and to think that you, my love, may be dead at this very moment. No, no, I know God will watch out for you as he has me.

Your Boy Ever,
"Charlie"

What a loving and thoughtful man he was, and what a difficult and anguishing position for him to be in, over in the trenches, thousands of miles away, and to learn of the explosion that killed more than 2,000 in his home area.

There is a much happier letter that followed and one with all doubts removed. This dated February 1917, two months after the disaster. I will excerpt from this.

Somewhere [in] France

> My Dearest Girl:
>
> O! How thankful I am that you and all of yours, and my folks, were spared in the awful explosion. I suffered more in the two months after the explosion than in all my life before, as I could get no word from home at all, but now that everything has come out right, I am praying and longing for the end of this nasty old war, and to be back home again with you. We will make up for all that we have missed, won't we, my darling.
>
> I have three Halifax Chronicles here tonight and all about the rebuilding of the city. I guess I won't know the dear old city when we come home, but I'm sure the dear old North West Arm will be in the same place, and we can go again on our grand little picnics for two. You remember those dear old days down at the Dingle and all round there. O! my, those days are so fresh in my memory as though only yesterday, and it is now that I realize what grand times we have had.
>
> Well, I am still looking forward to my next leave, but there is no sign of one coming yet: it is eight months since I was on my last leave. There is, however, something that I am looking forward to, and with greater expectation and longing than simply leave, and that is the time when I can put my feet on the Halifax pier.

This he signed, as he did in most instances, with "Your Boy Charlie."

It seems almost insane, criminal in fact, to think that young men like Charlie were to spend four years of their lives slogging through the muddy fields of Flanders. He came from a family of Scottish soldier boys though, and I suppose that service to King and Country was an honest if simple response. He was one of five Dartmouth Patterson brothers who answered the call to arms. When I was a youngster I always got a feeling of pride when I read the Patterson names on the old cenotaph in front of the Dartmouth post office.

For this dear Dartmouth boy caught in the trenches of France, there was no love for warfare. In many of his letters he refers to this God-awful conflict in critical terms: "My only desire is for me to see the end of this, most terrible war, and to be back home again with you, my sweetheart."; In another: "These are terrible days here, and many a poor fellow is going under in ferocious battles. I am sure though that we will soon see the end of it all, and the Boche will be beaten and I will come home." In a letter from France he wrote: "I feel more than content tonight as we are in a nice, clean billet with lots of new straw to lie on, and I hope to get a good night's sleep. I just wish I could stay here until the war is over: but I suppose someone else would have to do my bit if I did." In a letter written on May 4, 1917, somewhere in France, he wrote: "I received your letter and cards of the disaster a day or two ago, but was very busy the last few days. I think we were in a dozen different places (almost all at once), or at least it seemed so at the time: but now we are in a fine little town quite a way behind the line for a rest."

His thoughts were never too far away from home, and his love of skating got continual mention. In one letter, written while he was recuperating in an English army hospital in 1919, shortly after the armistice, he said: "How I would love to be going skating with you today, my sweetheart. But cheers! There are many winters coming." In another he wrote: "How I would love to be skating on the lakes (Dartmouth) leading about 50 boys up the lake and then putting on a spurt and leaving them well behind." He was a champion speed skater as were his uncles.

Mary, a tall, dark-haired young woman with striking brown eyes, and erect carriage, was not to be idle while her suitor was thousands of miles away. She went to Holyoke, Massachusetts and trained as a registered nurse at the Sisters of Providence Hospital in that city. She was the forerunner of a number of Halifax girls, all Irish Catholics, who made this migration. She returned to Halifax in 1917 following graduation and enlisted as a nursing sister, with the rank of lieutenant, in the Canadian army. As the war was then coming to an end she did not serve overseas but was attached to the Camp Hill Hospital for veterans in Halifax.

When Charlie returned from the wars the Imperial Oil Refinery was under construction in the Woodside area outside of Dartmouth. His cousin Johnny (Toughie) Patterson, with whom he played hockey for many years, was one of the company's early employees and through this connection he won employment in the processing operations. Imperial proved a benevolent and steady employer, and my father remained with the company until his early death of cancer at age forty in 1931. Imperial stock, which he bought in the twenties, was to help educate us many years later.

The courtship with Mary Sullivan renewed on his return from overseas. With the guarantee of a good and steady job they embarked on marriage in 1920. Their firstborn, my sister Jeanne, arrived the next year. They had rented an apartment in Halifax owned by mother's Uncle Will Adams but, with the arrival of a baby, bought a house at 11 Sinclair Street in Dartmouth. It was not a large house although comprised of three bedrooms. The lot was small but well-maintained with a lot of nice shrubs and bushes, and the backyard had a detached garage and raspberry bushes—my mother's pride and joy—which provided us with summer treats. One of the real delights of that house was its wonderful sun porch covered by hanging vines. As we grew up it became our summer encampment. I drove by 11 Sinclair just recently and the house remains intact and is well-maintained by the Connolly family. Alas, however, the sun porch has long since been removed, as was the large birch tree that stood as a sentinel in front of the property.

It was not a castle but a nice family house on a quiet, small street in a neighbourhood that abounded with boys and girls of our ages. I met the current owner, Jim Connolly, last year, and when he greeted me he said, "You should be nice to me for I live in your old house." I told him that it had been a happy house to grow up in and wished him and his young family the same experience.

In saying that it was a "happy" house I should add that it was not without tragedy. My father Charlie died in February 1931, when I was but two years old. My siblings were ages eight, seven, and nine months. I was never to know my father, although my mother kept his image alive by recounting stories of his various sports exploits. I have often thought what a devastating blow she must have felt in not only losing her husband, but in doing so in the depths of the Great Depression. She was widowed with four small children in a world adrift in its own woes.

As I am much older, and as I reflect on life, I think my mother was one of the most courageous and sensible people I have known. She was very strong and had a completely positive and happy outlook on life. I said to her one time, and I would have been an adult in my mid- or late thirties, "Mother I am always amazed at your ability to stand up to others. It shows great strength." She smiled and said that it was something she had to learn as a widow. I suppose it comes with being of Irish heritage but my mother was full of maxims: "If you are nice to others they will be nice to you," and "Don't be too critical of others. Rather be kind and considerate." Another golden rule is if you owe money and find it difficult to pay your debts, stay in touch with the person or persons you owe and pay fifty cents just to let them know you are honourable and recognize the debt.

I also think my mother was one of the early ecumenists. While we went to Catholic schools and had a fairly fervent religious upbringing, I never remember my mother making what I would judge today as a bigoted remark or comment. In fact, she was very liberal in a religious regard. Brother Laurie and I went to the St. James Presbyterian Wolf Cubs from ages eight to twelve. When we graduated from this we joined the Baptist Trail Rangers, and stayed on for Tuxis until we were about sixteen. I was even a member of the Bible Baseball team. I will admit that one of our initial attractions for the Trail Rangers was that they had one of the few basketball courts in town. Once, when confronted by the sister superior at our school about our intimate brush with Protestant institutions, my mother said, "When you have Wolf Cubs here the boys will come. In the meantime they are being well looked after." Personally I look back on those years with fondness. Victor Blenus was our cub master at St. James and he was a masterful leader and among other things a great teller of ghost stories. The Trail Ranger experience was just as satisfying and, I now believe as an adult, a great influence. I have often thought that I am more a natural Baptist than a Catholic in that I much favoured their hymns such as "Onward Christian Soldiers" and another favourite, "Church in the Wildwood." Our leader Walter Barss, the town solicitor, would bang away at the piano and we would sing as lustily as possible. I am sure the angels heard us. What was a good Catholic boy, or boys (Laurie too), doing in that renegade environment? Having a great time!

While my father's death was tragic, we as a family were able to survive without too much difficulty. There were several favourable factors in our situation. For one thing, we owned our own home, and it proved a solid and secure base for us growing up. In fact the house stayed in the family until Laurie gave up bachelorhood in the late 1960s, when he sold it. We also had the strong influence and help of our grandmother Elizabeth (Nan) Sullivan, who lived with us. Her presence allowed my mother to go back to nursing in 1935 when I suspect father's pension monies and savings were running low. One thing that truly amazed me, and this despite the tough times of the thirties and forties, was that when my mother died in 1967, at age seventy-five, she still held the shares in Imperial Oil that my father would have bought in the 1920s. As well she had a little money tucked into the St. Peter's Credit Union and a bank. That is quite an achievement for a widow left with four small children to rear.

Nan Sullivan, my mother's mother, was a wonderful woman who had a great influence on us in early life. As mentioned she was with us until her death in 1941, when she was eighty-one years of age. She was born in Halifax in 1860, one of three sisters. Her family name was Dunlay, and her Irish parents had immigrated to Canada some years earlier to escape the potato famines. Her husband, Maurice Sullivan, remains a mystery to us to this day. My cousin Charles Park of Calgary, who has laboured on a family history, tells me he can find no trace of the evasive Maurice. As children we were told that he was lost at sea, which seems plausible enough in that we lived on a seacoast. Anyway, dear Maurice was around long enough to father three children, the oldest of which was a son Jack, followed by my mother Mary and a daughter Lillian. Nan, like my mother years later, was widowed at an early age. Nan's spinster sister Johanna, Auntie Jo, lived with and helped support the young family as she was a skilled seamstress. Another of my grandmother's sisters, Auntie Kate, also gave strong support to the young Sullivan family. She was married to a highly successful Halifax north end grocer, William A. Adams, who operated a thriving business at the corner of Barrington and North Streets. They had two daughters, my mother's first cousins, Mary and May. We were close to Cousin Mary's family growing up as we exchanged visits with them on Sundays. Mary married John Campbell and they had two sons, Don, later a priest, and Jack, an engineer who we spent a lot of time with when we were young. We looked forward to Cousin Mary's visits because she brought coloured comics with her that for us constituted a major treat.

Cousin May caused a bit of a sensation in polite Halifax circles, and in fact mother's Auntie Jo, a zealous Catholic, called it a "scandal." In delicate health, suffering from bronchitis or something of that nature, May travelled with her mother to Arizona for a cure. They stayed on a ranch out in the wilderness. While there she fell in love with a cowboy, a legitimate, rope-twirling cowboy by the name of Fred Hoffman. I think she was in her late teens. Engagement followed and Fred arrived in Halifax sometime later with a Stetson, cowboy boots, and an Arizona drawl. With assistance from Uncle Will, the newlyweds set up housekeeping in Halifax, and Fred gained employment as a carpenter. While there were those who questioned the match, they brought up a family and remained happily married until they died both well into their seventies. Late in life when we had all left home mother spent a lot of time visiting with the Hoffmans in Lower Sackville. Although Cousin Mary had died in 1940, we remained in contact with our cousins Don, a priest, and Jack, who later lived in Dartmouth.

While mother had an Irish Catholic upbringing, went to Catholic schools, and trained at a Catholic hospital, she was undoubtedly a "liberated woman" for she questioned many of the tenets of the church. She was staunchly opposed to the Catholic Church's stand against contraception. I can remember her arguing with Cousin Don, a priest and a somewhat inflexible one at that. During the Depression she had worked as a VON nurse in Dartmouth and recounted stories in which the doctors and she would be paid, if paid at all, with eggs, butter, and produce. I remember her repeating a story to my grandmother about a woman who gave birth to her fourteenth child. The husband was unemployed and they lived in a shack. She said, "They have no right to bring more children into this world than to fly." Poor Father Don would always leave the house perplexed after mother gave her birth control speech.

She had a very outgoing personality and was not much given to anger or outbursts of any kind, yet she could stand up for what she perceived as her rights. Tradesmen or others who she thought tried to cheat her were usually taken to task. I can remember one instance that occurred after she had been on a nursing case and found herself with a few extra dollars. She bought new shirts and things for the four of us and a new dress for herself.

Apparently the dress didn't fit so she took it back to the store on Barrington Street where she had purchased it. One of the owners was a poker-faced woman who refused to refund her money since she had bought the dress on sale. The poor woman didn't know what she was up against. Mother said all right and she stood at the front of the store and warned everyone who came in not to buy anything as the people were untrustworthy. The owner threatened to call the police, but mother stood her ground. The refund was made.

She never remarried although she was widowed for a long time. Late in life, she would have been in her mid-sixties, she had a boyfriend, Billy Boak. "Boyfriend" may be an exaggeration. He and his wife Grace had been old friends, and Billy himself was a widower. As youngsters we had visited with the Boaks many times. Anyway mother and Billy, in their senior years, had weekly "dates." This consisted of dinner in Halifax at the Green Lantern on Barrington Street or the Lord Nelson Hotel, followed by a trek to the wrestling matches. I don't think my mother had ever been to a wrestling match before, but she became a fan. When I tried to tell her that the matches were fake, she got irate. Len Hughes and Dr. "Drop Kick" Murphy were on the up and up, she would contend in a dismissive way.

Billy had retired from a relatively senior position at Maritime Tel and Tel, and was quite well-off. He loved to come to the house as he was a sports nut, and he, Bill, Laurie, and I would hold our own Hot Stove league. We loved him and had great fun with him. We gave him the nickname "Sugar Daddy," which we all got a kick out of. Mother, with her Irish sense of humour, used to call him "Sugar" just for fun. Sadly he died in his late sixties from a heart attack after shovelling snow off his front walk.

I can't write as authoritatively about Charlie; as mentioned, he died when I was two years old. But we very much lived with his memory, which my story-telling mother kept alive. Further, he was an outstanding athlete, and we lived with boxes of medals, a roomful of silver trophies, silver plates, and assorted hardware that he'd won in speed skating, track and field, rowing, hockey, and other endeavours. And of course, growing up in Dartmouth, his home town, I heard hundreds of stories about his sports exploits from many of his friends. I have to this day a series of old, now yellowing press clippings highlighting his hockey abilities in play for the Halifax Crescents and the Windsor Swastikas (yes, Swastikas—this long before the emergence of Hitler). His older brother Arch, who lived nearby, and his first cousin Johnny, were also periodic visitors over the years and both were kind to our young family. While we had scores of Patterson cousins in Dartmouth (my father was from a large family), most of our time with relatives was spent with those on my mother's side.

The Pattersons were downtown Dartmouthians. My father was born in a small house on Church Lane. It was one of a small row of houses demolished and replaced by the eighteen-story Queen Square office tower. Ironically my own offices, those of CFDR and Q104 radio, of which I was the owner and president, had their studios and offices on the top of that building; I had advanced the family eighteen stories closer to heaven. My grandfather William was the manager of the Dartmouth rink, located at the top of Windmill Road, only a short distance from the Patterson home. In addition to running the rink, Bill, as he was known, was also the lighthouse keeper. It was situated, as it is today, just across the street overlooking the old St. Peter's graveyard. As a boy, it was my own father's role to run every morning to the light and extinguish the blaze. In the evening he saw that the light, obviously kerosene-fuelled, was lit. My mother said that, as a budding marathoner, he ran to and from with thoughts that he was taking part in a Boston Marathon.

My father was from a family of seven: five boys, two girls. He was the youngest of the boys and was named for his Uncle Charlie, who was an outstanding hockey player, figure skater, and speed skater. He and his brother Alexander (Sandy), stars of the Dartmouth Chebuctos and Maritime senior hockey champions from 1887 to 1893, are enshrined in the Nova Scotia Sports Heritage Hall of Fame. So too is my own father, who was referred to as Charles Patterson Second, although he was a nephew of the senior Charlie and not his son. The Chebuctos travelled to Montreal where they played the Wanderers, Canada's top hockey club of that era, and then on to Quebec to play a top Quebec City team. They lost to both teams while playing Montreal rules, but won all their games when playing the more familiar Halifax rules. They left one innovation, which was later used in hockey everywhere in Canada: that was the forward pass. Yellowing newspaper clippings in my possession also tell of my father's Uncle Charlie defeating the Quebec champion in a speed-skating exhibition.

One of the most fascinating people in our family tree, the original progenitor of the Canadian tribe, was John (Jock) Patterson, who came to Dartmouth around 1840. He was a piper in a Scottish regiment stationed in Halifax and became prominent in local circles as a piper for special occasions. On his death the North British Society, of which he was the official piper, awarded him a burial monument. In 1870, then in his sixties, he went with the Nova Scotia Regiment to fight in the Riel Rebellions. Jock and his wife, a Dartmouth Lennerton, had six children—two daughters and four sons—of which one was my grandfather William. He in turn married Elizabeth Warner, of a well-known Dartmouth family. I suspect this caused difficulties; the Warners were Catholic and, despite their Scottish roots, most of the Pattersons in that era were Anglicans. Given the suspicion and often disdain that prevailed between Catholics and Protestants in the 1880s, which was when the marriage took place, I would expect that their union in the then small town caused considerable debate and some anguish. Ironically while growing up my family had relatively close contact with several branches of our Warner cousins because we were brought up as Catholics, Charlie having converted when he married mother. We all went to the same schools and belonged to many of the same organizations.

My father apparently had a great sense of fun, and mother said that when he went to mass at St. Peter's Catholic Church after their marriage he would go to a pew at the front of the church. He would laugh saying, "I bet they're all saying, look at that Charlie Patterson! He never went to a church in his life and now he acts as if he is going to eat the altar cloth."

He too was a lively fellow. The late Bill Matthews, another Dartmouth boy, told me of running into my father when they were both in the trenches in France. He said that while they were forbidden to travel on the front, my father would walk and run hundreds of miles to visit with friends. They met one night at the front, and Charlie said he'd heard there were Dartmouth boys serving with a Canadian regiment a few miles from their own battlefront location. Charlie said, "Let's go look up the Dartmouth boys!" And so, Matthews recalled, "We set out at a run. When we came to the supposed location," he said, Charlie lifted up the heavy tarpaulin covering the sleeping quarters, and in a sing-song voice yelled, "Is there anyone in there from D-A-R-T-M-O-U-T-H?" He said they met up with a Creighton, a VanBuskirk, and a Behan from the north end.

St. Peters' basketball team, winners of the Dartmouth junior league, 1944. Arnie is front row centre wearing the DBC shirt, and brother Laurie is farthest left in the front row.

Dr. John P. Martin, the Dartmouth historian and a family friend, years ago sent me a note taken from a 1917 edition of the Dartmouth weekly. It contained excerpts from a letter my father had written to his father, William. In it he told of winning four track events at a Canadian army field day held in France; he'd been named the outstanding performer in the meeting. He ended his letter: "and father, there is life in the old boy yet."

Tone deaf, I have little musical ability, and yet mother told us that Charlie was fond of Scottish songs and could sing the words of all of the Harry Lauder tunes. Lauder, later knighted by the king, was the British Isles' most popular entertainer in the First World War era and beyond. Among the songs he made famous were "The End of the Road" and other great Scottish tunes of long ago. Sir Harry, as he was known, performed at the front for the Canadian troops and my father became a lifelong fan.

My father's four brothers were Arch, Bill, Harry, and Ern. His sisters were Ethel and Muriel. I never really knew his sisters, as they moved to the United States and married there. I do, however, have a faint remembrance of Ethel, who was my father's favourite, visiting us when we were very young. Uncle Arch was the only one of my father's brothers to whom we were close while growing up. Harry had moved to Boston as a young man and became the icemaker at the Boston Arena. He too had been an accomplished speed skater in his youth. While our Uncle Bill, a quiet man who worked at the shipyards, was not intimate with us, his sons David and Len became close friends in our teenage years. Uncle Ern lived in the Albro Lake area and was not close to our family, though his son Ed became a friend of mine in senior golf circles not so many years ago. Ed had been a caddy master at the Brightwood course in Dartmouth, and later had a distinguished career in the Canadian army. There were scores of other Patterson cousins in Dartmouth when we were growing up. Many with whom we had a close association remain today.

I don't think my father, being the youngest in his family and quite a bit younger than his brothers, was as close to them as he was to his cousins Doug and John, who were his age and both hockey players. In fact, as kids we called John "Uncle John" because he was a regular visitor and we often spent time at his summer camp at Chezzetcook. His brother Doug, an all-around athlete, moved to the United States in 1912 when he was a young man. While he was employed as a YMCA fitness instructor, he met and married a young woman whose father had a highly successful leather goods factory in up-state New York. He was later to become president of the firm and eventually its principal owner. He first came back to visit in the late 1930s and arrived at Sinclair Street in a big Cadillac. We viewed him as "our rich American cousin." Years later I met his only son, who had returned to Dartmouth to look up his own roots. We became close friends and have visited back and forth with one another over the years. In a visit a few years ago we took him on a tour of the sites, among them Christ Church (Anglican), which was his father's family church. The strangest thing happened. While I was giving some background on family names shown on various stained-glass windows, a young man, unknown to me, came up and said that he had a photo we might find of interest. It was the Christ Church boys' hockey team of 1908. Kneeling in the front row was my cousin Eugene's father, Doug. A remarkable coincidence, for the young man didn't know who I was, nor would he have known Eugene. But here, 85 or so years later, my cousin unexpectedly comes across a photo of his father while visiting his roots. Needless to say we were flabbergasted.

I was about nine or ten the day Cousin Doug visited us on Sinclair Street. He and my father had grown up together and played on all the same sports teams. While they were friends, my mother said they were also keen rivals. His visit was a big event, and I remember mother laying out a tea service for it; Doug was bringing his new bride, his first wife having died some years before. He arrived in this big blue Cadillac and parked it in the front of our rather modest house. Cousin Johnny (his brother and our favourite) and his wife Kit, were with the honeymooners. Laurie and I were "slicked up" for the occasion and allowed to sit in the living room as Doug, and to a lesser degree Johnny, recalled stories about my father.

Cousin Doug said that my father got his nickname "Donkey" when he was about ten years old. He used to play hockey with the British sailors and would apparently never give up. If one of the men took the puck from him he doggedly gave chase. He also talked about my father's exploits as a figure and speed skater and how he would always put on between-period exhibitions when they played hockey.

Cousin Eugene, who later ran the Puerto Rican branch of their leather goods manufacturing firm, told me that they were at one time the largest wallet manufacturers in the United States. The business was sold some years ago. On the day of the visit Doug, on leaving, presented Laurie and me each with a leather-encased photo album bearing a line drawing of a Mountie on the front cover.

While I never knew the details, years later when I was a teenager one of my father's aunts died in Louisiana. A sister of my grandfather William, she apparently had moved to the United States as a young woman and married a doctor who accumulated some wealth. Her husband predeceased her and when she died, she left a considerable amount of money. As she had no children, the monies were to be dispensed to her surviving relatives. Her brother Alexander (Sandy), the old skating champion, was then in his eighties and the chief beneficiary. As a branch of the family we too received a small share. I can remember the excitement in our house when my mother received a letter and a cheque (I never knew the amount) from a lawyer in Baton Rouge. To celebrate we had scallops that night, outrageously priced at ninety cents a pound.

I can recall meeting my grandfather William only once. I was about four. Apparently he was very ill and died shortly thereafter. My mother took Laurie and me to visit him on Commercial Street, where he was living with relatives. I have seen lots of photos; he always had a big mustache and dressed quite formally in a black suit and necktie. Uncle Arch always portrayed him as a dour, quiet man who had won local acclaim as an icemaker.

The Dartmouth rink on which so much of my father's life centred was quite a facility in its day. Constructed in 1884, it seated 2,000 people and measured 190 by 65 feet—slightly smaller than today's NHL rinks, which measure 200 by 85 feet. Among its many features was a lighted entrance, and this in the early days of the miracle of electricity. This quite imposing structure was built entirely of spruce and was situated atop a hill overlooking the harbour, its tower housing the original lighthouse. Adjacent to the rink, later the site for the old Park School, was the Chebucto Amateur Athletic Association's grounds for baseball and track and field sports. Today the Holiday Inn and an attached office tower occupy the site, which gained latter-day exposure as the Arrows ballpark—the home of the Dartmouth teams during the famed H and D baseball league of the 1940s and 1950s.

In winter the rink was the centre of activity in the Town of Dartmouth, which numbered no more than 4,500 residents. There was great community pride in its hockey teams. The Chebuctos were a dominant power, and their matches with rival Halifax teams drew capacity crowds. The Chebuctos remained a power in Dartmouth and provincial sports until the First World War, when most of its younger athletes left to serve king and country. The rink was demolished in the 1917 Halifax Explosion, although in the early 1920s two contractors, Marks and Cross, built a new arena across the road from the athletic field. While the Chebuctos were succeeded in the 1920s by the Dartmouth Amateur Athletic Association, the DAAA never achieved the same measure of success as did its predecessor.

The Pattersons were prominent players in all aspects of the Chebuctos sports agenda during its more than thirty-year existence. They excelled in many sports. Great-uncles Charlie and Sandy were the key players on their championship hockey teams, Grandfather William was usually the manager. Both brothers were also speed and figure skaters, and photos in the Sports Hall of Fame show them bedecked with medals. Sometime just before the turn of the century my father's Uncle Alexander (Sandy) toured Northern Europe, putting on skating exhibitions under the sponsorship of the Starr Manufacturing Company. Starr's skates were world-famous, and its huge plant on Prince Albert Road was one of the major employers in the old town. At peak, and for many years, the "skate factory," as we all called it, employed as many as 250 people. Founded by a hardware merchant, John Starr, in 1861, its primary function was the manufacture of nuts, bolts, screws, and assorted steel products. With the introduction of its skates in 1865, the other operations became secondary. It is estimated that between 1865 and 1938, after which skate production was abandoned, more than twelve million Starr skates were sold throughout the world. At one time the factory was producing a hundred thousand skates per year and the company had sales offices in the United States, Germany, France, Britain, Norway, Russia, and China. No one played a more important role in popularizing Starr skates than John Forbes, the factory's foreman. With the assistance of his deputy, Thomas Bateman, they invented a spring skate that allowed skaters to fasten skates securely to their boots.

Dr. Garth Vaughan's excellent book entitled *The Puck Stops Here* details the history of hockey in Windsor—which he claims as the birthplace of the game—and devotes considerable space to the history of the Starr works. Two old Starr advertisements are displayed on pages 119-120: one shows Dickie Boone, a Montreal Stanley Cup star, and Art Ross, the captain and later manager of the Boston Bruins, touting Starr skates. The Boone ad ran in newspapers and magazines in 1902, the Ross ad in 1926.

In a letter to the company, Art Ross said, "Your skates have stood the test and will be part of our equipment this season." Dickie Boone, in a much earlier endorsement, wrote, "I am most pleased to state that the hockey skates of your manufacture have proved by actual use to embody the features wanted for that purpose." He added, "I cheerfully endorse your claims for them after personally using them." Undoubtedly the Starr people were in the vanguard of those using personalities to endorse their products. I doubt that either Boone or Ross, heroes in their own day, received the multi-million dollar contracts now accorded sporting stars like Wayne Gretzky and Tiger Woods, but in their time they would have made effective ads.

In 1938 the Great Depression ended more than seventy years of skate production by Starr. Although competitors in the United States, Canada, and Germany cut into their market dominance, it was the worldwide financial collapse that felled this one-time industrial power. The company was reorganized in 1939 and carried on with the same Starr name in the same old premises. After the Second World War it operated under the ownership of Gordon (Pete) Stanfield of the Truro Stanfields, but there was no skate production and it was a much-diminished operation. The long, gray buildings stretching for several city blocks were finally demolished in the year 2000 although they had been empty for several years—a monument to passing glory.

Dartmouth had a strong manufacturing base throughout the nineteenth and well into the twentieth century. The Rope Works operated as Consumers' Cordage for many years. Founded by the Stairs family of Halifax in 1868, it was responsible for much of the development of the north end of the town. It ceased operations in the 1950s. John Mott's chocolate factory was another key industry in then sleepy Dartmouth. It was located on the shores of the harbour just east of the Dartmouth Marine Slips. The Mott family had begun manufacturing chocolate and related products in the 1830s. When John Mott died in 1896, he was regarded as one of the richest men in Nova Scotia, leaving an estate of close to a million dollars. His grand home on Pleasant Street was taken over by the Prince Edward Highlanders in the Second World War and turned into a massive series of barracks. Today it is the site of residential housing. Another key industry in the old town was the sugar refinery at Woodside. The first refinery was built in 1864, and rebuilt again in 1912 after the original buildings were destroyed by fire. It ceased operations in 1942. The Woodside ferry terminal occupies a part of the site of the refinery, which played a key role in the growth and development of Woodside and south Dartmouth. Also Dartmouth had a brewery as early as 1867. It was founded by the Oland family and operated for many years as the Army and Navy Brewery and later under the family name. It was located on Windmill Road just below Elmwood Avenue. Located on the site now are apartment buildings overlooking the harbour. The brewery received a direct blast and was shattered during the Halifax Explosion of 1917. The family rebuilt its facilities in Halifax, but for fifty years the brewery had been a major employer in Dartmouth. Interestingly a great grandson of Susannah, credited as Oland Breweries' founder, opened the Moosehead Breweries almost sixty years later. Little remembered is Dartmouth's rolling mill, which produced iron and steel products. The Dartmouth Rolling Works was a sizable industry. It employed several hundred men, and its facilities occupied a property on Canal Street that ran all the way to the harbour (a curling club is now located on a small part of this site). Founded in 1903, it later was absorbed by Starr Manufacturing and the buildings demolished. In the days of sailing ships and, to a lesser degree, steam vessels, Dartmouth was a centre for shipbuilding.

There were a number of yards, including Chappell's, Moseley's, and Lyle's, but the most ambitious project was the building of the Chebucto Marine Railway in the 1850s, still located at the foot of present-day King Street. The yard is now owned by the Irving group of companies and operates a major ship repair facility under the name of the Dartmouth Marine Slips. It has had a distinguished and successful history and remains one of the few industrial holdovers from the nineteenth century. Years back there was a score of smaller industries including a tannery, iron works, a distillery, grist mills, and other such operations, which contributed to the prosperity of the then small town.

While I suspect the Starr Manufacturing Company was probably the most important and best-known industry in the old town, special mention should be made of ice harvesting. The Dartmouth Lakes—both Banook, Mic Mac, and to a lesser degree smaller Maynard's—were the major sources for ice, both domestic and commercial, in Halifax–Dartmouth and its environs for more than one hundred years. Dr. John P. Martin, in his authoritative *The Story of Dartmouth*, said the harvesting of ice was started in or around 1830 by a man named Foster. In my own time growing up, there were five large ice houses on Lake Banook, two on Lake Mic Mac, and one at Maynard's Lake. Later there was a smaller operation carried out at Miller's Mountain. While the Glendenning, Lawlor, and Foster names had been identified with ice sales in earlier days, the four big companies in my era were Otto's, with three ice houses; Carter's, with two; Chittick's, with two; and Hutchinson's, with two. They employed hundreds of men during the winter harvesting season and, in the summer months and other periods of the year, had hosts of horse-drawn wagons, and later trucks, to cart their ice throughout the communities.

Chittick's horse barn was situated not far from our house on Sinclair Street, and in the days when horses were in vogue for transportation, which lasted throughout the war years, we would go down to the barn and talk to the horses, whom we knew by name. In the early hours on summer mornings we would be awakened by the rumble of the wagons and the pounding of hoofs, as the "icemen" set off on their daily rounds. Because we lived near the lakes and spent so much time there, we knew by name most of the key men in the ice business. One of our great favourites was Ted Hutchinson of Hutchinson's. My brother Laurie worked one summer as an assistant on Ted's truck. As well, as fourteen-year-olds, we both worked on the ice harvest for Hutchinson's, since the war made mature labour hard to find. Ted held hero status for us as a former star paddler and coach for our revered Mic Mac aquatic club. With refrigeration, the ice age in Dartmouth passed.

As mentioned earlier our growing up years were happy years. While we were certainly not well-off we had a good home and a good family. Laurie and I were a little luckier than our older siblings, who had to leave school at the high-school level. Sister Jeanne became a secretary while Bill, after a tough learning curve on a series of low-paying jobs, wound up as a salesman, for which he was well-suited. Jeanne had a happy and successful marriage to her high-school boyfriend, Carmen Moore, who for many years operated a pharmacy in the north end of Dartmouth. Brothers Bill and Laurie joined me at CFDR after we established the company in 1962. While Laurie went off on his own after a few years, Bill became the station's vice president of sales and a major contributor to its success. Jeanne has three children, Ian, Deanne and Valerie, all living locally. My nice brother-in-law Carmen died some years ago. Jeanne, now in her late seventies, continues to reside in Dartmouth. Sadly both of my brothers died, Bill eleven years ago at age sixty-six, and Laurie last year at age seventy. Bill and his wife, Mary, did not have children; but Laurie has a daughter, Lynne, and a son, Andrew. Lynne is a budding journalist here, while Andrew is a computer scientist and resides in Whistler, British Columbia.

I have always had a great respect for women, and I am sure much of that stems from my mother's training. My sister Jeanne had a special place in our household, and we were reminded regularly that she was to be treated with deference. That was not difficult for she was a kind and intelligent girl, and while I think she at times despaired of her younger brothers and their rough behaviour, she always showed us great affection. Tall and vivacious, she had an unending line of suitors during her teen years. My brother Bill—a handsome, blonde smiling boy—was a model big brother, always looking out for us and never complaining though we always tagged after him. He was strong support for my mother as he got older, and in some respects he assumed a father's role in relation to Laurie and me. He had to leave school early, I suspect to help with our survival, and in his teens he had a lot of low-playing and not so pleasant jobs, which was almost customary for the older boys in most families in the thirties. He worked on a delivery truck for Eaton's as a teenager. Later he worked catching rivets at the Dartmouth shipyards. Before joining the army he was a salesman for Boland's Limited, the local wholesale grocery distributor. On Friday night or Saturday he would bring home his pay envelope and give it to my mother. What an unselfish, conscientious, and loving fellow he was. His army stint was abortive. He was in the army less than a year when he contracted tuberculosis and wound up in the sanitarium at Kentville. He spent more than a year there.

I suppose in some respects it was payback time for me, but when we created the radio station, CFDR, I sought Bill out as sales manager. He spent the rest of his life in the employ of the station and retired with a substantial amount of money. Sadly he lived only a few years to enjoy his reward. I had a difficult time after he died. We had many differences in business and he was a very stubborn person, and yet he was a loyal and loving brother. I just couldn't dwell on the thought that he was gone and I chased those thoughts from my mind. He was a hard worker and a steadying force at the stations. He was much tougher on price than I was, and when he made a presentation there were no additional discounts other than that which showed in the initial tender. I, on the other hand, often frustrated when we had lots of time unbooked, would conceive of promotions offering big discounts. This was particularly true during the dog months of

January and February, or on weekends when we would have less than fifty percent of the station sold. If I made what I thought was a good sale, he would argue that I was giving the station away. Because it was my responsibility to meet the payroll on Friday and pay suppliers, I had to march to a different drummer. As well, I used to use a phrase denoting unsold time as DOS—dollars lost forever. Unlike in a grocery or car dealership, the unsold minutes at a radio station are not stored on a shelf, but evaporate. Bill and I got along well, although not without some battling. I thought he was too conservative and he thought I was far too liberal. Somehow we made things work.

Brother Laurie and I were closer to one another than our other siblings. This I suspect had much to do with age in that I was only fourteen months older. We went through school in the same grade (I started a year late), and both of us went on to college at Saint Mary's. He enrolled in Commerce and I in journalism. While our looks were somewhat different—he the pretty one—we were much the same size growing up; and in that we were inseparable, many people thought we were twins.

As a boy Laurie was exceedingly good-natured. He was always smiling, polite, and gentle, and not argumentative. He was not as competitive in sports as I was, although our talent levels were the same—pretty good at most but not special. We played just about everything. By grit and determination, as well as superior upper-body strength gained during two summers working on the ice trucks, he did become a top paddler in his era. Strangely, when he was an adult he developed a temper. While for the most part he was happy and smiling, he could explode.

As mentioned earlier we went to St. Peter's school from grade one through to high school. The school was only five minutes from our house, and we walked back and forth. Our teachers were the Sisters of Charity, and I look back on them and our experiences in that wonderful school with great warmth. I had a letter from my grade two teacher, Sister Leo Mary, just last year. She is eighty-seven, and living at the Motherhouse at Mount Saint Vincent. She commented on what a good student I was, but she never mentioned my conduct. While I always did well enough with most courses, the dear nun considered me a prankster, and my report cards, which shocked my mother, always reflected a "D" for conduct. I never considered myself unduly religious—I envy those who are—yet we went to church enough as youngsters to cover most people for a lifetime. The church was only a few hundred yards from the school, and the Sisters had us march there with regularity. Laurie was far more dutiful in that regard. On reflection, though, it was for me that very young period in one's lifetime that offers nothing but happiness and fun, save for the odd fight on the playground.

School was undoubtedly a major part of life but central to ours growing up were the Dartmouth Lakes. It was our playground, summer and winter. We lived only minutes away from Lake Banook and if we heard the crack of a gun signalling the start of a canoe, rowing, or sailing race, we were off like rabbits, running all the way to the lake to witness at least the finish. We had our heroes, mostly Mic Mackers, who in those days (and I suspect even today) were deadly rivals to Banook Canoe Club members who, by their very presence, sent a challenge from the northern side and down the lake to the Mic Mac A.A.C. on the southern side. Through the eyes of boys, the paddlers and oarsmen were giants: Elgee Lloy, the perennial Banook singles star; Dean (Buck) Leslie of the Mic Mac; Roy Myers and his Mic Mac tandem partner George Campbell; and so many others. What pure fun and excitement, and at no cost for little boys who thought a five-cent piece was akin to a gold brick.

Dartmouth in the 1930s, when we were youngsters and in our impressionable years was really small-town Nova Scotia. There were no more than eight thousand residents. There was little money, but we got by on revenues from our paper routes, and later caddying at Brightwood; for a time we even set pins at "Spud" Beazley's bowling alley on Portland Street. Later when we were fourteen or fifteen we worked at Charman's grocery store, our neighbourhood grocer—nothing as lofty as clerking but rather stocking the shelves. Our small town changed during the war years as military barracks grew up around us. The RCAF base at Eastern Passage, later Shearwater, quadrupled in size. The Prince Edward Highlanders moved into the Hazelhurst estate, and barracks sprouted up on that location. The army also built barracks on Faulkner's Field off Windmill Road in the north end and there was a major army facility built on the Cow Bay Road, now the A23. Later in the war, barracks and facilities were built just off Windmill Road at the foot of Albro Lake Road, and construction was completed on the massive Naval Armament Depot in the north end. Further, a score of bunker facilities continued expansion of the Magazine property, off what is today known as the Dartmouth Road. Our little town had, in fact, become almost an armed camp.

I mentioned earlier that, as boys, Laurie and I were almost inseparable. We did most things in tandem. He was quite complacent and good-natured while I was the more demanding. We had few real disagreements and certainly supported one another. When we were in grade eight, bowling, with an impetus from wartime service personnel, became a very popular sport. E.M. (Spud) Beazley, the only alley operator in town, was the big beneficiary. Laurie and I went downtown, alien territory, to see if we could get a job setting pins. Spud had played hockey with our father and said he would give us lots of work. So after school and on Saturdays we would go the alleys and make two or three dollars. As we were considered outsiders, we were often harassed. On one occasion, a big red-faced downtowner who was maybe a year or so older than me, started to hassle Laurie. I intervened and, the next thing I knew, I'd been challenged to a fistfight. There was a big, vacant field behind the bowling alley. I was scared to death but I couldn't back down because about ten of the pinsetters, all supporters of my opponent, were jeering at us.

The boy's name was Comer, and he kept shouting threats. If noise could kill, I was dead on the spot. But when we squared off, and to my continuing amazement as the fight progressed, he couldn't fight a lick, as they say in boxing circles. I knocked him down twice and the battle was called off. That was not the end of it, however. That night Comer arrived back at the bowling alley with a friend, a bigger boy by the name of "Rabbit." Laurie and I received a double challenge. Down we went to the field and I took on Comer, who again proved ineffective. Laurie took on the stranger. The first thing I knew Laurie was knocked into the bushes. I was a year older so I suggested we switch partners. I was in the fight only a few minutes when I realized I was in over my head—this guy could fight. So after one interchange in which I took two heavy blows to the head, I put my hand up and said, "What are we doing, fighting? We don't even know one another. Let's call this a draw and go get a milkshake." Much to my surprise he agreed, and the four of us, along with a few of their Woodside buddies, went to the local ice cream parlour. I bought milkshakes for the four participants.

I don't know whether it was ambition or simply need, but it seemed that Laurie and I had jobs from an early time in our lives. There was little money around, growing up in the thirties. We were dressed relatively well, ate regularly and were immersed in sports, but we always had a job. The first money I can remember earning was in hawking the Halifax papers down on Portland and Commercial streets in downtown Dartmouth. I don't think it was a brisk sale, but I can remember parading the streets with a bundle of both *Mail*s and *Star*s under my arm, shouting, "Extra! Extra! Read all about it!" Hardly original. The *Mail* was three cents, the *Star* only two, and I got paid a penny for each sale. I don't think anyone hawks papers in the downtown streets any more since newsstands have taken over. I graduated from this role to my own paper route when I was around eleven or twelve. I went into the office of the *Dartmouth Patriot*, the town weekly, looking for a route. The editor, a man for all seasons, was Hugh McGlashen, who later became the provincial assessor. He gave me the name and addresses of twelve customers, and I was to get a cent a paper. It had to be the most widely dispersed paper route in the world, for I had one customer on Gaston road, four miles south of downtown; another near the Brightwood golf course in the north end; and a handful not too far away. It was a long trek to make twelve cents a week.

I moved up a step within the next year when my friend Jack Regan hired me as his assistant on his big Halifax *Mail* route in the north end. He had more than one hundred customers, and I delivered a little more than a third. I think he paid me $1.50 a week.

I was usually the trailblazer, and then Laurie would follow. We both later assumed our own paper routes, which we kept for a few years. In the summer we both caddied, and for at least one winter we set pins at the bowling alley. And as mentioned earlier, we worked at a grocery store and later an ice company.

My first full-time summer job came when I was fifteen. The Imperial Oil refinery hired students in the summer months to help paint certain of their facilities. I went down with three other boys to apply. As I was the youngest and smallest of the four I really did not have great expectations. The personnel manager, A.G. Baker, did the interview himself. When I told him my name was Patterson he quickly asked, "Who is your father?" I told him, Charlie. "You stand over there," he said, separating me from the others. I got the job and wound up painting for the rest of the summer.

The next summer, and for two complete summers, I "ran" on the railway—the CN. I was first a pantry man and then a waiter. It was a heady life! Imagine going to glamorous Montreal and coming back each week throughout the summer months. It was also remunerative. I got $139 in salary but added at least another $250 a month in tips. I had great fun in Montreal, going to the Royals ball games and wrestling matches at the fabled Forum. I also had an opportunity to visit Uncle Arnold and Aunt Lil and to bring them greetings from home. The Royals, then the Brooklyn Dodgers' farm team, introduced two great rookies that year: Jackie Robinson and catcher Ray Campanella. The next year Robinson was the first Black to play in the majors, to be followed by Campanella.

Last summer I encountered my old dining car steward, Everett Landry, during a lunch at Brightwood. He was visiting with in-laws. It was the first time I had seen him in more than fifty years. We had a warm embrace and he said, "You were a very good waiter." I reminded him that on my early trips with his crew he had to wait on half my tables. They were good years.

I must bring this family tale to an end. I would be remiss though if I didn't mention two men who were influential in my life. These were Father Gerald Mabey and Fred M. Lahey. Father Mabey was a curate at St. Peter's and in his mid-to-late twenties when first I met him. A soft-spoken, actually terribly shy man, he came to St. Peter's when we were in grade eight. For we sports-crazed boys it was as if Knute Rockne had been dropped in our midst. In winter he turned the tennis courts below the church into a rink; in the warmer months it became a basketball court. He talked the St. Peter's Temperance Society into letting us use its hall, the old Majestic Theatre, as an indoor basketball court. He had come to us from St. Thomas Aquinas Parish in Halifax, which had been notable for its sports team. While we were in Dartmouth, and this was a first, he entered us into the Halifax schools hockey, baseball, touch rugby, and basketball leagues. We were so busy playing sports we hardly had time to go to school. What a marvellous man he was—so sacrificing. Many nights he would stay up until mid-morning, flooding the rink by himself.

While a very religious man himself, Father Mabey never pushed any of us in that direction. Perhaps he didn't have to, as the Sisters paraded us to church with regularity. He was one of the best men whom I have known in my life. And strangely enough, though he left St. Peter's, I was not to lose him as a friend. I wasn't sure what I was going to do after high school. I wanted to follow my friend Jack Regan to Saint Mary's and the journalism program, but it was going to be expensive. I had a summer job lined up as a counsellor at a children's camp, but it offered only modest reimbursement. That's where Father Mabey came in. By then he had been posted to a smaller parish at Terence Bay, but he remained in touch. One day he called me and told me he had made arrangements for me to go to St. Mary's, and that my tuition was paid for the full three years.

He died last year at age eighty-two. Sometimes you do the right thing in life, and although more than fifty years had passed since his days at St. Peter's, I stayed in touch. And delightfully we had lunch three times the summer before his passing. When I would start to tell him how appreciative I was of his support in my youth, he would shyly look away from the table and mutter a few words.

The late Fred Lahey, one of Dartmouth's most prominent businessmen and sportsmen, was another man who played an important role in my early life. He was in some respects a surrogate father, and I spent countless hours in his homes as both a boy and a man. It was largely through his influence that I got closely involved in harness racing, and I could listen to him for hours as he told tales of harness racing. His other passion was politics. While he was never a candidate himself, he was a lifelong fervent Conservative and a supporter of that party in good days and bad days. There were few sporting causes in Dartmouth that didn't get financial support from Fred Lahey. He was a great booster of the old town. He died in the late 1970s.

While the hustle and bustle of wartime subsided with the cessation of hostilities in 1945, growth in Dartmouth continued at a rapid pace. Although transportation to Halifax was by ferry or a long drive around the Bedford Basin, the town became in part at least a bedroom community for the expanding capital city across the harbour. In 1948, in my first experience as a newspaper reporter on the old Halifax *Chronicle and Daily Star* (absorbed the following year by the *Halifax Herald* papers), I covered many speeches given by then Dartmouth mayor Arthur C. Pettipas. One of his repeating themes was "Dartmouth, the future city of the east." He was a peppy trooper with great vision, although he turned out to be a one-term mayor. Growth had been steady through the late forties and early fifties, but the real mushrooming did not occur until after the construction and opening of the Angus L. Macdonald Bridge in 1956. There was a real population explosion. By 1961 the old town had a population of sixty thousand or more, and under the aegis of Mayor I. W. Akerley, for whom is named the major artery in Burnside Industrial Park and the vocational school, Dartmouth fought for and won both city status and the amalgamation of many of its suburban parts, including Woodside, Port Wallace, Tufts Cove, and Woodlawn. Overnight it became Nova Scotia's third city and the province's second largest municipality. Today, of course, my old home town is held within the embrace of the Halifax Regional Municipality, compelled and ordered by the Province in 1996. While I am a fourth generation Dartmouthian, I continue to have high hopes for the new amalgamated body. In this era when size is important I think having a bigger player on the national scene is of consequence. Further I think Halifax, and I include its many new parts, is a dynamic area with a bright future. I have a prejudice because as a young reporter more than forty-five years ago I saw the miracle of metropolitan Toronto and what the merged forces there did to spark both growth and prosperity in what is today Canada's most important city. With patience, faith, and the right leadership, Greater Halifax can be a major player in the Canadian swing of things.

Chapter Two: Newspaper Days

There never was a time from the fifth grade on that I didn't want to be a journalist. My real desire was to be either a sportswriter or a sports broadcaster. Foster Hewitt, broadcaster of the Toronto Maple Leafs games, was my hero, as he was of so many Canadian boys in those long ago years. I am afraid that I read the sports pages of the newspapers more diligently and thoughtfully than my school texts. In grade five I was named the sports editor of a class paper, a three-page mimeograph sheet. I wrote with more enthusiasm than my classmates, and my sports scribbling took up a full page. Maria Byrne, the editor and a very bright girl, bitterly complained that I was turning the project into a sports paper. More ambitious was an endeavour two of three years later, which was largely the inspiration of Chris Creese, who lived across the street from us. We undertook the publication of the *Sinclair Street News*. I again was the sports editor, and in a promotion squib (part of our paper), another neighbour Keith Barry wrote: "Arnie as sports editor is an ideal choice for he eats, sleeps and drinks sports." The life of this project was short-lived—I think two editions only. Later in life Chris Creese became a professional photographer of much repute.

Nevertheless my desire for journalism never left me. After high school I enrolled in the journalism faculty at Saint Mary's University. It was basically a three-year Arts course meshed with journalism lectures given by prominent local newspapermen and classes at King's College and Mount Saint Vincent University as well. I had an active time at Saint Mary's, then a small college with a total enrollment of less than three hundred. We were housed in a large relic of a building on Windsor Street, which had served as the city's male Catholic university for more than one hundred years. While it was the most modest of campuses, I did then and do now feel privileged to have had a Jesuit education. When I think back on my schooling, both with the nuns and later this elite body of priests, I sometimes think we were being trained for the religious life. It was rewarding in the long run, however, and I made the most of it as editor of the college newspaper, member of the intercollegiate debating team, intramural debating champion, secretary of the student council, and finally the life vice president of the Class of '50. It is hard to believe that last year was our fiftieth anniversary. The university today bears little resemblance to the struggling college that was our alma mater. I believe the enrollment is over eight thousand and the sprawling campus at Gorsebrook is modern and up-to-date in every respect. My brother Laurie had the distinction of being in the first class to graduate from the new facilities at Gorsebrook, this in 1952, with a Bachelor of Commerce degree.

During my sophomore and final years at Saint Mary's I already had jobs on newspapers. In 1948 my friend Allan Barry was named Dartmouth bureau chief of the *Chronicle* and the *Daily Star*, and he asked me to join him as a summer employee. We had a small staff at the bureau in a one-room office on Portland Street in Dartmouth's old downtown. If I had been paid by the hour I would have been the richest man going because I loved the job, and I worked not only on most days but just about every night as well. My beat was really the whole town. I covered the police beat, usually winding up driving around town at midnight in the paddy wagon. I covered the service clubs and their speakers, downtown commercial developments, and other community events. My major efforts, however, were reserved for sports coverage, and my mentor, Allan, let me go at this in full flight. While paddling was an old sport in Dartmouth I like to think that my coverage that summer set a pattern for the kind of coverage that paddling was to get in the years that followed; it is unquestionable in my mind that the extensive media coverage given the sport helped transform Dartmouth into the canoe capital of Canada. The senior softball league was another of my special coverage areas, and I wrote about golf as if I were covering the Masters. Because our paper, the *Daily Star*, had less advertising in it than the competing *Evening Mail*, I had the liberty of writing longer stories than my competitors. I really thought I was the new Damon Runyon. What I may have lacked in skills I made up for in zeal.

When Allan hired me, he apologetically told me that he could not guarantee me a salary but that I could work for what in those days were called "space rates." Allan was my boyhood idol and neighbour, and he knew how keenly I wanted to be a reporter. Anyway the space rate was eight cents an ingot line, and I was to be paid for whatever stories the paper published. Given the fact that I was to write the longest softball stories in history, a continuing commentary on paddling, and snippets from all aspects of life in Dartmouth, I made the princely sum of $41 in my first week as a part-time employee. This was in 1948 when there were many family men in Dartmouth earning less. The second week, my enthusiasm bounding, I made $44. Journalism was turning out to be a well-paying profession; the previous summer I had earned the great sum of $200 for ten weeks work as a counsellor at a Kiwanis Club camp for underprivileged children conducted at Cole Harbour beach. During my third week on the job as a roving reporter, I got a phone call from the secretary to the managing editor. I was to report to his office in the Chronicle Building, located at the corner of Prince and Grafton streets in downtown Halifax. Even Allan was mystified. On the ferry ride over (I interviewed the boat's captain en route) I wondered if I was going to be sacked. What had I done? I was a nervous young man, then nineteen, when I walked into the bustling newsroom. I had had no contact with the Halifax office up until that point, and I really didn't know anyone. But someone directed me to the managing editor's office which was in the corner of the large room. As I walked by the news desk I heard someone say, "That's Patterson." The person was Lou Zwerling, the news editor, who would become and remain a close friend and a mentor. His words further unnerved me. What had I done to receive such recognition?

On entering the managing editor's office, a tall, thin man, wearing an English-styled double-breasted suit, complete with vest and military striped tie, stepped from behind a big desk and extended his hand. "So you're Patterson," he exclaimed, flashing a wide smile. "What a pleasure!" And with that he shook my hand, giving me the thought that I must have won a sweepstake. My newfound friend was Leonard Tilley, the managing editor and a grandson of one of the Fathers of Confederation. He was a bit of an oilcan, and at his solicitous best he told me what a great job I was doing in Dartmouth, and that the editorial bosses were so impressed that he was pleased to offer me a full-time staff job. I was elated, and even after he told me the salary was $22 a week, I left as if on a cloud. I was a real reporter!

That fall in returning to Saint Mary's I learned that Brian O'Connell (the city editor of the *Daily Star* and the father of the late NDP member Eileen O'Connell) was going to conduct second-year journalism classes. I had never met him, but he had a reputation as a bit of a lion in the newsroom. When I met him at the door to the classroom he—a tall, very thin man—smiled and said, "You're Patterson." After introducing himself, he said, "You know, you wrote a lot of bad copy this summer but I would bet that this whole class [there were about nine of us] could never write as much collectively in the same time period." Brian and I became very good friends, and after the *Chronicle* and *Star* folded the next year, he took a job as news editor with CFRA in Ottawa. I was flattered when he wrote after my graduation and offered me a job as a reporter. He was an inspiring teacher, for he loved to romanticize about the news business and he was an enthusiastic booster. After class I would walk up Windsor Street with him to his house on North Street, then take the streetcar back to the ferry, and home to Dartmouth. He returned to St. Francis Xavier some years later and served as the university's public relations chief until his retirement. He died some years ago, but I remember him as one of the best newspapermen whom I have known, and this covers the many hot shots I would come to know over many years.

During my time at Saint Mary's I also wrote a sports column for the *Dartmouth Patriot*, my hometown weekly paper. It wasn't a great newspaper, or a rich one, but it served the town well and for many years. The editor was a very genial fellow by the name of Arnold Logan, who had years earlier worked on the Halifax dailies. Arnold was not the most energetic of men, but he was an experienced hand and played a relatively active role in community affairs. He paid me $5 a week to write the sports column, and while it may have lacked the grace and style of the *New York Times*, it was totally local and a heavyweight name drop. Editor Logan had a much-restricted budget for staff, so he not only allowed me but encouraged me to write longish columns, and there were times when I almost filled up a full page with my outpourings. He was a very decent and dear fellow; he later became the manager of the old Casino Theatre on Barrington Street. One of the benefits of my previous indenture with Arnold was that I got free movie tickets on a number of occasions.

December 31, 1948 was a sad day. It marked the closure and sale of the *Chronicle* and *Daily Star* to the Halifax Herald Limited. The old Liberal-oriented papers were merged with the *Evening Mail* and *Morning Herald* to become, as they are today, the *Chronicle-Herald* and the *Mail-Star*. I was at college at that time, and I worked weekends in the Dartmouth bureau; while the loss of income was secondary, the death of the two old papers was an unhappy event. Although I was only a part-timer, I got one of the infamous notes: “Due to circumstances with which you are familiar, your services are no longer required.” The sale of the papers came as a shock as there had been no prevailing rumours. Most of the staff, including myself, learned of the sale in reading a front-page story in the *Daily Star* on that date. I went with Allan Barry, the bureau chief, to a hastily-called meeting held in the newsroom in Halifax that afternoon. Pearson McCurdy, the son of the publisher and owner, F. B. McCurdy—a legendary Halifax financier—made a few remarks of regret that the papers had to be sold and briefly outlined a tale of financial woe. It was little consolation for the more than one hundred or so people who had jammed into the big room. Many of these people had spent a lifetime in the papers' employ, and now they were losing their jobs. Hank How, the fiery shipping reporter, said to poor Pearson, “I hope that when your father gets to hell the devil gives him the biggest shovel he got.” While I never knew the details, some of the older employees were given a modest separation severance, and some of the more able people, particularly in the news area, were given jobs on the newly-merged papers. My two Dartmouth friends, Allan Barry and Jack Regan, both moved to the *Mail-Star*, as did news editor Lou Zwerling of the *Daily Star*, night editor Jimmy Gowen of the *Chronicle*, sports editor Wilfred (Ace) Foley, photographer Pete Sullivan, and a handful from the composing room, including Guy Ross, another Dartmouth man. Most of the others moved elsewhere for journalistic jobs or left the business altogether. Brian O'Connell, the talented city editor, moved with his young and large family to Ottawa and CFRA. It was a traumatic time. I was shortly to receive another unfavourable blow. Edmund Morris, later a member of Parliament and mayor of Halifax, and Bruce Cochran, a cabinet minister in the Buchanan provincial government of a later date, bought the *Dartmouth Patriot* with plans to expand its coverage. I did not know either one of them at the time of the purchase, although they were later to be friends.

One day, returning from Saint Mary's with copy for my weekly sports column in hand, I dropped into the paper. Standing behind the counter was the new publisher and editor, Edmund Morris. Without too much ceremony he said, "Young Mr. Patterson I hate to inform you but your services will be no longer required." He added, " I don't want you to feel bad because, while you are being let go, you are being replaced by a well-known journalist, Russell Lownds." An army veteran, Russ had been a casualty in the closing of the *Chronicle* papers. I knew Russ quite well as he had been a would-be singles sculler at the Jubilee Club and a member of the *Chronicle*'s sports department. Ironically just that winter, Graham Allen, a *Herald* editorial writer lecturing at the journalism school, had drilled into us the dangers of what he called "elegant variation." This, among other things, included the overuse of adjectives and a constant changing of them, and Allen had cited Russ Lownds of the *Chronicle* as one of the major offenders. Russell was surely given to scintillation. Anyway a few weeks passed, and one day I got a call at home from Edmund Morris, asking to see me at the *Patriot* office on Commercial Street, now Alderney Drive. I hastened to see him and was quite thrilled with the reception I received. The co-owners, Edmund and Bruce Cochran, were there to greet me. Morris explained that they had had so many calls about my column and that it was so missed that he would like me to resume my duties. There was no mention of Russ, who I found out later had left. They were prepared to pay me $10 a week for my contribution. Not bad. Arnold had paid me only $5, and the extra $5 would be handy for ferry tickets and streetcar fare to Saint Mary's.

An army veteran who had served as a lieutenant in Italy, Bruce was the perfect gentleman, articulate and sophisticated. His father was a doctor in Chester, and a brother later became an archdeacon in the Anglican church. While I was quite a bit younger, I used to go to frat parties at the Cambridge Library with him. Somewhere along the line, he and Edmund became unhitched, and Bruce left the newspaper business for a career in public relations. I suspect that mounting financial woes caused his departure, as there was hardly room aboard the small *Patriot* craft for two relatively senior people.

Edmund battled on alone. There always seemed to be a storm brewing. He was and is a very clever fellow—more than a bit erratic, in those days at least, but quite wonderful overall. He was a gifted conversationalist and had a great sense of fun, despite the hardships of the struggling paper. We became friends and socialized together occasionally since we were both single. He covered meetings, wrote editorials, supervised circulation, and did all the things necessary in weekly newspapering. But it was not enough. Sometime around 1953, after several years of struggle, the *Patriot* went into bankruptcy. One day as I approached the building, I saw four men jockeying the big, old flat-bed press through the front window; doubtless, the sale of it would go to pay a creditor. Edmund deserved a better fate, for he'd worked hard and had all of the right instincts. If he had a failing—and I think this a good one—he was too generous with his thin wallet. By the time this nightmare took place, I was well established as the city hall reporter on the *Mail-Star*, and a hockey broadcaster with CJCH doing the Big Four games, first with Danny Gallivan and later with my long-time sidekick, Pat Connolly. One night while we were drinking a quart of Oland's in Edmund's small office at the paper, I suggested he try radio. At the time CJCH was moving to new facilities on Robie Street. Finlay MacDonald was manager of the station and had offered me a job as the station's first full-time news editor. I had accepted but upon hearing of my resignation at the *Mail-Star* the managing editor R. J. (Bob) Rankin called me into his office and gave me an unheard of $20 raise. Guiltily I wrote Finlay a dear John letter. I suggested to Edmund that he go and talk to Finlay, that with his speaking and writing skills he was a natural for radio. He not only went but he got a job as a newscaster and commentator and became a major local radio star in the mid-1950s. At a time when radio stations were becoming conscious of the importance of news, Finlay also hired Robert J. (Bob) McCleave, who had been the bureau chief of the British United Press and was a Dalhousie Law School graduate.

Bob and Edmund were a highly effective team, although I don't think they ever personally liked one another. Bob was steadier, but Ed was the more dramatic commentator. Radio was growing powerful in those days before television; and while newspapers were the principal source of news, radio was making inroads. Edmund had run as a federal Conservative candidate in 1953. He was partnered with Halifax lawyer Fred J. Bissett, as Halifax was a dual riding. They lost to Liberals Sam Balcom and John H. Dickey by close to eight thousand votes. Edmund came back in 1957, partnered with his radio colleague, McCleave, and they unseated the long-entrenched Liberals who as a party had held the two seats for twenty-two consecutive years. While they had defeated Liberals Dickey and Balcom by only two thousand votes, they came back the next year, and in the Diefenbaker sweep won by a record nineteen thousand votes. They were returned again in 1962 in a squeaker, and then after not heeding to the party line on some forgotten issue Edmund was shunted into limbo and was not nominated in 1963. After a Liberal won that year, McCleave came back with young Mike Forrestall in 1965 and won the seats back. Each went on to a long career in the House of Commons, and McCleave won an impressive seven times. He later was appointed to a judgeship in Nova Scotia, while Forrestall was named to the Canadian Senate. While Morris' federal career was halted, he did later win a Halifax seat in the provincial legislature, became a cabinet minister, and later became a very popular Mayor of Halifax.

My own reporting career at that point was progressing well as I was the city hall reporter for the *Mail-Star*, covering the mayoralty term of Richard A. Donahoe, who may have been the best speaker in the history of city council. He went on to become attorney general in the Stanfield provincial government, and both of his sons, Terry and Arthur, served with distinction in the provincial legislature as well. I had gone over to the *Mail-Star* as a summer news employee in 1949 and as such was another survivor of the old *Daily Star*. The next year I completed my journalism studies and joined the paper on a full-time basis. We had great fun, sporting around town as reporters. There was a cadre of young journalism graduates: Jack Lusher, Jack Wilcox, Kingsley Brown, Ron Ripley, Stan Fitzner, and others. But the reality we were to learn was that classroom lectures are not a total substitute for on-the-job training. It takes time to win your spurs at a daily. You must work your way upward. As a rookie you write obituaries, cover dog shows, do the luncheon circuit, graduate to the police beat and then, after a few years, the bigger prize—city hall or the provincial legislature.

While as a young reporter it is a wonderful thing to see your byline, there are moments when you wish you had become an accountant. One of the most embarrassing moments I had as a young reporter at the *Herald* came in my first months on the paper. The Nova Scotia Teachers' Association, before they unionized, were having their annual meeting at the Nova Scotian Hotel. It was an important event and one of the senior reporters was assigned to cover it. Unfortunately he fell ill just as he was to depart for the meeting. The city editor, Aubrey Kaizer, called me over and told me to cover it and get a story in for the afternoon paper. I had about an hour to get to the hotel, pick up some information, and then call in the story by telephone. When I arrived at the meeting a woman identified as Miss Aileen Burns, principal of St. Patrick's Girls' High School, was speaking: "He may be the best minister of education this province ever had," she said. "I know all in this room from reading his statements believe that the Honourable Mr. Hicks has a big heart and that he loves teachers." She was, of course, speaking about Henry Hicks, the education minister in the Liberal government of Angus L. Macdonald. Knowing I had only minutes to deadline, I found a phone and called in my story with my lead saying how Miss Burns had paid tribute to Henry Hicks. That afternoon when I went back to the meeting, this time without the pressure of a deadline, I was met at the door by Tom Parker, a prominent educator whom I had known through basketball. He told me the paper was going to come in for heavy criticism, suggesting I sit through it without responding. I smile all these years later when I think of this, as it was highly unlikely that I, a cub reporter, was going to start making proclamations on the paper's behalf. Certainly not to such an august group as schoolteachers.

Miss Burns was again at the podium, but there were no more kind word. She railed at the paper, saying that it had always been anti-teacher and that the headline in the paper that day which proclaimed "Henry Hicks Cited Best Minister Ever" was further evidence of the paper's vicious slant against teachers. What I didn't know, and which I was to learn that afternoon, was that when Miss Burns praised Hicks earlier, she was speaking tongue-in-cheek, and that the teachers were in fact solid in their opposition to the education minister. I, by being thrust into the meeting late, had heard only the tail-end of her remarks and not her condemnation. Later that night, as I sat at my typewriter in the newsroom, writing the story for the next day's paper, in trooped Miss Burns and a delegation of teachers. They went straight to the office of R. J. Rankin, the managing editor, with not a word to me. After about a half-hour they emerged and left chattering among themselves, again with not a nod in my direction. "Arnie, come in here!" bellowed an unfriendly Rankin from the door of his office. I wasn't asked to sit, and he immediately started to rant: "I have just made the most abject apology that I have ever made in my life," he said "and I made it on your behalf. If we didn't have enough enemies out there before. And now you have added the schoolteachers," he said. With that he sat at a typewriter himself and wrote a lead for my new story, which started: "The Nova Scotia Teachers' Association forcibly deny claims made by this newspaper that they were in any way supportive of policies enunciated by the Honourable Henry Hicks." I marked it up to experience.

Writing skills are always important, but establishing contacts and gaining background on issues are probably even more essential. Halifax was a manageable town in the early '50s—under eighty thousand in population—and given the training process of covering Kiwanis clubs, funeral homes, hotels, and police, you wind up knowing a lot of people. When I think of that heady era, when I was a boy reporter, I smile at the fact that as a 22-year-old or thereabouts, I knew the premier, the mayors of both Halifax and Dartmouth, the police chiefs and fire chiefs, the judges, both the Crown and defence attorneys, the rink managers, the school principals, and just about everyone else who made the news. It was great fun. Including the summer of 1949, I spent five years on the *Mail-Star* before leaving for the *Toronto Telegram* in 1954.

While the papers of the Halifax Herald Limited—the *Chronicle-Herald* and the *Mail-Star*—have been severely criticized over the years by politicians, journalists working in other media, and to a degree the general public, it was for me a wonderful place to grow up and work. At this point in my life, after 53 years in various aspects of journalism and business, I think the Halifax Herald papers have been unfairly maligned, certainly in part. The papers have not been wild-eyed crusaders; and perhaps, like our communities, they ignored many of the more unpleasant local issues. Yet in most respects their community involvement has been far-reaching. There are a number of things you have to understand about the papers' philosophies, or certainly the philosophies that prevailed for many years. The papers operated on the editorial premise that we lived in a small province and that, given our intimacy with one another, rabble-rousing was imprudent. Further you should recognize the fact that the Herald papers were for the larger part of their existence, partisan supporters of the Conservative party. One of its early owners, William H. Dennis, was a Tory senator and a key player for close to half a century in the party's stratagems in Nova Scotia. If you read issues of the old *Chronicle* and *Daily Star* papers from as early as the 1920s the partisanship is as pronounced as the *Herald*'s red banner. But that practice was in vogue everywhere years ago; in Nova Scotia the Herald papers were Tory, the Chronicle papers Liberal. At election time they became cheerleaders for their respective political pals. So it was only natural that the Herald papers would have critics, and that Liberals of an earlier era would be prominent among them.

In fairness, however, the Halifax Herald Limited has greatly modified its approach in recent years, and while its claim to be independent was questionable a few years back, I think it is largely true today. Its changing stance was caused in part by the emergence of the *Daily News* as a new force. The Herald papers no longer had a monopoly and saw that balanced coverage was necessitated. From my own knowledge the publisher and owner of the Herald papers, Graham W. Dennis (son of the senator and now a man in his early seventies), is essentially a fair and honourable man, who always has had the best interests of the province at heart. The fact that the papers enjoyed a monopoly position for so long also helped it gain detractors. After the demise of the *Chronicle*, there was no serious alternate voice. Radio news was not a major factor, nor was its opinion, until the sixties when it seemed to mature as a news medium. Television, the Johnny-come-lately, is of course a major competitor in today's news business, and the stations here have active news operations. Sadly radio news has been sapped in recent years with massive cuts to newsrooms staffs at all five local, private stations. They have become simply music boxes.

The Halifax papers are perhaps not great newspapers in the context of say the *Globe and Mail*, the *Toronto Sta*r or the heavily financed *National Post*, but they are good, solid local papers that still serve their communities well and faithfully. When I hear people knock the Herald papers, as many of my Liberal friends have been wont to do, I become a touch defensive because I think of the many talented and dedicated people that have served these papers. R. J. Rankin, the managing editor in my day, is prime among them; the acerbic Frank W. defense, who watched city hall activities like a hawk; Edgar E. Kelley; the very decent Harold A. Shea; and so many others. Most of these people have passed on to their greater reward, but in their day they were all talented and experienced hands who knew the city and province intimately. While I am not conversant with the current Herald crowd, I suspect there is still a lot of talent on the paper. In fact I think the paper may be better than it ever was.

One of the best things to happen both to the province and journalism in Nova Scotia has been the emergence of the *Daily News* as an alternative to the Herald papers. I write with a degree of prejudice; I have been writing a column for the *Daily News* for fourtèen years, starting shortly after I sold my radio stations. Aside from giving readers a choice in its journalistic fare, it also has made the Herald papers hustle more, and this has made them better newspapers. My involvement with the *Daily News* actually predates my joining them as a columnist. Started as a tri-weekly for Bedford–Sackville, the paper was owned by three Brits: David Bentley, who had worked on the *Morning Herald* earlier; and Joyce and Dave Simms. They had moved the paper into the daily field, and were relatively successful in extending both coverage and circulation throughout metro. The addition of Lyndon Watkins as managing editor gave the paper increased credibility. Furthermore his presence allowed Bentley, also an experienced journalist, to spend more time on the business side, which is always an essential ingredient in any operation. Lyndon's reign as editorial boss was short-lived, as in late 1985 or early 1986, Newfoundland Capital, under the irrepressible Harry Steele, bought the newspaper. Harry, a retired naval commander and an avowed capitalist, was uncomfortable with Lyndon's left-wing stance on issues. Watkins was out, and Winnipeg native Doug McKay arrived to assume the role of managing editor. A former *Winnipeg Free Press* editor and son of a former editor of the Toronto *Globe and Mail*, McKay used a substantial increase in the editorial budget to bring in several new and experienced hands. With quiet efficiency, he transformed the paper in a period of months, making it competitive in what had been a monopoly market for more than 35 years. A handsome man, then in his mid-thirties, he slowly and carefully built up a cadre of columnists, adding both spice and varying opinions to the paper. I had retired in June of 1987, after selling the radio stations CFDR and Q104, but I had stayed on as a director of the *Daily News*. Sometime around Christmas in 1987, I lunched with the new editor and agreed to write a thrice-weekly column. It was great fun to return to my first love, the newspaper game.

I carried on with the three-times-a-week offering for a couple of years, but I was wintering in Florida and found it a bit difficult to stay on top of the local issues—and that is what I think local newspapers should be all about. I did, however, retain my column in the Sunday edition, which when introduced became immediately popular, and the newspaper was selling ten thousand more copies on Sunday than any other day of the week. I could never understand why the Herald management didn't respond sooner with a Sunday edition of its own, but for at least ten years the *Sunday News* had the market to itself. It has been only in the last three years or so that the Herald introduced its own Sunday paper. There has been a slight erosion in the *Sunday News*'s circulation figures but nothing dramatic. Both have established fairly solid audiences, and the Nova Scotia newspaper reader is the winner.

I mentioned that there was a time in the newspaper business when papers showed a decided prejudice and bias in their editorial coverage of events. While there are markets in North America where the sides are clearly drawn on political issues, a more independent and less partisan stance is evident in most dailies, particularly in the single paper markets. That is one advantage gained by the reader of the *Daily News*; while the paper in its editorial pages does take a stand on many issues, the paper in its entirety could never be accused of bias, which is largely due to the freedom given its many columnists. At election time you will find support for just about every political idea being expressed, and by different writers. If you are a regular reader, and somewhat discerning, it will take only a short period of time before you recognize the ingrained stances of the various columnists: Steve Kimber and Parker Barss-Donham, both decidedly to the left, both NDP supporters; Ernest Cadogan, very much to the right and subscriber to the principals being enunciated by the Canadian Alliance, as is the talented Harry Flemming which I find mind-boggling; Pat Connolly, Brain Flemming, and myself, all Grits and long-time advocates of Liberalism. Strangely I can't tell you what our gals are doing. I don't know if Susan Porteous or Stephanie Domet have strong political convictions; if they do, they don't share them with their readers very often.

One of the great things about writing for the *Daily News* is that columnists are given total liberty. I suppose I have written more than twelve hundred columns over the years, and I have never been seriously questioned or edited. This is much to the credit of managing editor Doug McKay and, his successor, the current incumbent Bill Turpin as well as the Sunday major domo Shane Ross. This is not to suggest that they or others on the paper share your opinions totally, but it does say a lot about the democratic nature of this young and hustling newspaper.

Chapter Three: Toronto the Good

In 1954 after close to five years on the *Mail-Star* I considered moving on to a bigger market. In my final year at Saint Mary's I had written the *Boston Post* to inquire about possible employment and had an encouraging letter back, suggesting that I formally apply at the end of the school year. In the meantime, I was offered a full-time job on the *Mail-Star*, and I also picked up part-time employment as a sportscaster at CJCH. In the summer months I was CKCL's harness race broadcaster at the Truro Raceway. Given these involvements, I gave up thoughts of Boston. In the interim there was a bigger happening in my life. I got married.

Rockingham native Glorena Hoadley married Arnie Patterson, having met him while she worked in public relations with the CNR.

I believe that being a reporter is a great vocation, for it was in the course of my reporting career that I met my wife, now of 48 years, Glorena Meta Hoadley. She was a Rockingham girl, employed in the public relations department of the Canadian National Railway. In calling on her boss, Doug Lacombe, I encountered this lovely young woman. A romance flowered and we were married on September 5, 1953. I was attracted by her good looks, and we shared an interest in books, reading, the movies, hockey, and the theatre in general. I introduced her to golf, which for her became a defining moment. It is a passion we have shared down through the years, and now with retirement, and the lure of Florida, it is a year-round vocational activity. Given her modest nature, I will not dwell further on our romance but will simply say that marrying her was the most important thing I have done in my life.

Meanwhile my friend Jack Wilcox left the *Mail-Star* in 1953 to join MacLaren Advertising in Toronto in a public relations position. Jack was a Dartmouth boy whom I had known from childhood. He suggested I move to Toronto and go into public relations, which while a somewhat newer but related field was more highly paid than journalism. But my desire to stay in the news business was stronger, and I opted to apply for a job on the *Toronto Telegram*, a very lively and strong paper in the big-city market. I wrote letters to the managing editors of the *Telegram*, the *Vancouver Sun*, and the *Windsor Star*. In Paul St. Pierre, a Dartmouth native, I had an advocate at the *Sun*, for he was one of their top writers. The response from paper's managing editor, Hal Straight, was encouraging; he suggested I write him a note in September when they might have an opening. W. H. Vaughan of the *Windsor Star* said he would put my application on file. Douglas McFarlane of the *Telegram* suggested I call for an interview should I ever get to Toronto. Through the kindness of my friend Paul Emerson of Air Canada, I got a ticket and departed for Toronto on a fine June day. I was able to pay back this favour many times over; when Paul became the airline's public relations director in Halifax any important Air Canada messages got full play on CFDR and Q104.

The weather in Toronto was sizzling hot and, coming from the cool Maritimes, I sweltered in what was my best and only suit. I can remember standing outside of Eaton's, at the corner of Queen and Yonge, with the sweat soaking through my shirt. Up to that time I never knew there was such a thing as a summer suit. My brother Laurie and our friend Gerald Curran, who grew up next to us on Sinclair Street, shared a nice apartment on St. George Street, not too far from downtown Toronto. I was to bunk with them for a few days. Laurie was working as an accountant for Duplate, while Gerald, also a Saint Mary's graduate, was an engineer with John Inglis. We had a good time in the four days I stayed with them.

I arranged an interview with McFarlane at the *Telegram*, and a luncheon date on another day with Jack Wilcox. Strangely, when I went to the *Telegram* the first person I encountered in the elevator was Arnold Agnew, who had worked on the Halifax *Daily Star* in the late forties. He was a desk man at the "Tely" and gave me a warm greeting. He later became one of the paper's top editorial executives. The Tely newsroom was an immense space cluttered with battered desks, ringing telephones, and clacking typewriters. A Miss MacDonald, an Ontario Mac, led me to the managing editor's office, which was in an alcove off the main newsroom floor. Unlike the camaraderie shown me by Leonard Tilley at the old *Daily Star* a few years before, the dour McFarlane—seated in shirtsleeves, a tie dangling below the open neck of his shirt—pointed to a chair.

He was polite enough and asked me about my background. He had never heard of Saint Mary's University, although today with the school's national athletic successes have made it a name known throughout Canada. He was impressed, however, with the fact that I worked with Danny Gallivan on hockey broadcasts. At that time Gallivan was making a name for himself as the broadcaster for the Montreal Canadians. MacFarlane suggested I stay in touch and send him my stories from the *Mail-Star*. "I don't want press clippings," he said, "but the unedited copy." Through July and August I was to inundate him.

The day following I had lunch with Jack Wilcox. I went to the MacLaren Advertising offices on Bay Street to pick him up, and while there he suggested I meet his boss Ken MacGillivary, the public relations manager and a legend in corporate communications. A tall, bald man, in what I would guess was his early fifties, MacGillivary looked at me quickly and said, "How tall are you?" I told him I was six foot two. "How would you like a job?" he asked. He asked nothing else about my qualifications. He then told me that General Motors, MacLaren's top advertising account, was looking for an editor for its company magazine. He arranged for me to go to the company's plant and head office in Oshawa, and the next day I drove down with Hugh Lefoli, a former Vancouver newspaperman and MacLaren's PR man on the account. (He was later a senior editor at Maclean's magazine and a CBC television producer.) At GM I met with Tom Elliott, a quietly dressed, pipe-smoking man in his early sixties. It struck a chord when I told him I had been a fan of the Oshawa Generals hockey club when I was growing up. Led by the brilliant Billy Taylor, later a Toronto Maple Leaf, they won two straight Memorial Cups. I also said I thought General Motors had made a mistake when they gave up radio sponsorship of the NHL hockey broadcasts, allowing Imperial Oil to take over this prime advertising property. He agreed, allowing that he had opposed the cancellation at the time. Anyway our joint enthusiasm for hockey seemed to cement a relationship, and he offered me the job at $110 a week with full benefits. Today that sounds like the minimum wage but in 1954 it was a pretty good salary, particularly for a newspaper kid. I was flattered but I really wanted to work on a Toronto newspaper, and while I didn't have the courage to say no to an executive of General Motors, and a nice man to boot, I simply said that I would talk to my wife about the move and get back to him. I wrote him when I got home, politely turning down the offer.

I returned home and assumed my real life. It was becoming more real in that Glo was pregnant and due in September. It wasn't a fun summer for her as nausea had her hospitalized three or four times. On a Sunday night in August, only a week or two before our daughter Carol was born, I went into the Herald newsroom to check my mail. Waiting was a letter embossed with the words: The Toronto Telegram. I was thrilled to learn that Doug McFarlane was offering me a job on the news staff, although with certain conditions: because the newsroom was unionized, I would be subjected to a three-month trial period before receiving final confirmation; and the pay was $95 a week, which was the Tely minimum-maximum at the time, although overtime was paid. I was making $85 a week at the *Mail-Star*, and had additional income from hockey and baseball broadcasts at CJCH and a stipend from CKCL in Truro for the broadcast of harness racing events at the Truro Raceway. All told, my income was in the area of

Arnie Patterson (left) during his days as a City Hall reporter for the Toronto Telegram, with Mayor Nathan Phillips and Ralph (Kelly) Morton, editor and publisher of the Dartmouth Free Press.

$140. Nevertheless with the agreement of my brave wife, I sent a letter back agreeing to his offer. The baby was born September 6, a year and one day after we married. I left for Toronto in late October, with Glo and baby to join me a month or so later. My early days at the Tely were not totally easy. I knew little about the city, and I was a bit overwhelmed as most of the reporters seemed so bright and quick. Add to this my homesickness. I can remember walking the streets of downtown Toronto, thinking of home and of going back. I hated the thought of admitting failure, though, and there were other complications. Bob Rankin, managing editor of the Herald papers, had personally hosted a farewell party for me. Would I have to give back the gift?

The big blow to my confidence came when I was assigned to cover a metro council executive session. I went with little background but quickly realized it was an important story: metro chairman Fred Gardiner announced that financing had been arranged for an east-west extension of the budding Toronto Transit subway system. Up until then construction had been completed for the north-south line only, but Toronto was in a period of rapid growth. Thousands of immigrants poured in each month, and the city's boundaries kept pushing out further and further away from the downtown core of Bay and Yonge streets. I diligently scribbled away, conscious that the competition had three reporters on hand. I went back to the newsroom and wrote what I thought was a good story, its lead centring on the subway extension. Just as I was putting the finishing touches on the copy the city editor—a towering, very serious man by the name of Arthur Col—beckoned me: "Arn." (He was always to call me Arn.) When I arrived at his desk he was obviously upset, and was in conversation with assistant city editor Jack Cranford and rewrite chief George Brimmell. He showed me the *Star*'s headline. It blared: "Metro Approves TTC Subway Extension To Etobicoke." Their reporters had phoned in the story, catching the final edition. In those days the paper had four separate editions throughout the day. I was shattered—scooped on my first major outing. I could feel the eyes of the whole newsroom on me. "What am I doing here?" I said to myself. "I should be home where I had some weight."

As I grieved, the paper's star reporter came to my desk and gave me a pat. Alan Kent was also from Halifax. His father had been dean of the Pine Hill Divinity College, so I guess the virtues of Christian charity were well-known to him. He consoled me and later went to talk to Art Cole, suggesting that I be given a little time to get oriented with the city. The next day Cole posted me to the rewrite desk for a spell. This five-man team under Brimmell, a speedy and highly efficient reporter, took the phoned-in stories from other reporters, rewrote stories missed in the other papers, made calls to ascertain and extend facts in submitted copy, and handled obituaries and reporting of that nature. There was a downside to the job in that I had to report for work at 6:30 a.m. That meant I was out of bed at 5:00 or so, which seemed like the middle of the night.

While the arrival of Glo and Carol brightened my outlook immeasurably, I remained with reservations about my bold move to Toronto. I had sold my car in Halifax to help pay for our move, so I was busing to work each morning in dominant darkness. I had about a half-mile walk to the nearest bus stop, and one cold winter morning as I walked the last few hundred yards to the stop I spotted the bus approaching, so I started to run. I slipped and went down in a heap, spilling my little cache of sandwiches that Glo had made for my lunch. They scattered in the snow. As the bus passed me by I started to weep softly. What was I doing in Toronto? The pull to go back home was never stronger.

When I think back on it the move to Toronto was a brave one, and probably more so for Glo with a brand new baby; I had lugged her off to a strange new city more than a thousand miles from home. I was, however, caught up with ambition and with thoughts of becoming a great reporter, and somehow this could be an ambition realized only if I were to test myself in a major market. As a Canadian, that came down to but one choice: Toronto.

As I mentioned earlier I had an ambition to follow the journalistic trail from as early as perhaps twelve, and when I was running on the CNR dining cars as a summer

Richard (Dick) O'Hagan, second from left, at a reception in Dartmouth in 1984. He attended college with Arnie, and was also a city hall reporter for the Toronto Telegram in the mid-fifties.

employee at the age of sixteen, one of our trips took us to Toronto. I remember walking its downtown streets with its massive buildings, including the Canadian Bank of Commerce tower, then regarded as the tallest building in Canada. In my two-day stay there, I sought out the shrine of my youth, the Maple Leaf Gardens, my imagination alive with images of Syl Apps, Charlie Conacher, and other my boyhood heroes. Would I encounter a real live Maple Leaf on Yonge Street? I had my eye open to this possibility. I vividly recall walking along King Street and seeing the *Toronto Star* building, then brand new and massive, and further along the *Globe and Mail*, again impressively housed in what was another new building—two of Canada's great newspapers. Did the seeds of my desire to work on a Toronto newspaper one day take root in those early days? I don't remember, though I can recall the almost romantic feeling I experienced in seeking out those buildings. King Street, Queen Street, Wellington, Adelaide, Lansdowne, Danforth—all visible evidence that Toronto, the "Queen City," as it called itself, was a proud outpost of the Empire.

Now, ten or so years later in real life, I had embarked on that career as a Toronto newspaper reporter. It was exciting, but my enthusiasm was tempered by the reality that I was no longer a boy but a young man with a wife and child to support. My most pressing responsibility in the early days of my arrival was to find an apartment for us that would fit my $95-a-week salary. Conveniently I was able to stay with my brother Laurie and our friend Gerald for a few weeks while I searched. In this I was aided by another old golfing friend from Halifax. Bruce Hyland had moved to Toronto the year before and was pioneering the sale of fish sticks and related products for a Newfoundland company. He had the luxury of owning a car and was kind enough to escort me to various places in pursuit of an apartment. After some exploration, I had set my sights on the east end of the city, and I visited three or four apartment buildings on Kingston Road, no more than twenty-five minutes by streetcar from the *Telegram*'s location at Bay and Melinda streets. But these "in close" locations, which in smaller Halifax would have been considered living in the suburbs, were too costly at $110-$125 a month.

While Bruce was kind in escorting me about, I began a regular, independent apartment search upon finishing my shift on rewrite at 3:30 p.m. each day. My means of transportation was Toronto's efficient streetcar and bus system, and sometimes when I explored the immediate north end I would take the new subway. One day Tommy Williams, who was working with me on rewrite, suggested I look in Scarborough where a number of *Telegram* reporters lived. Rental prices were somewhat lower than they were closer to the city, but getting there was not a simple matter. First I had to walk from the *Telegram* up Bay Street to Queen Street, about four blocks away, not an undue trek; from there I would take the streetcar out Queen and up Kingston Road to a stop just short of Scarborough. There I transferred to the bus that took me to my destination, although again there was a short walk from the bus stop to Gleneverest Road, where I was to inspect an apartment. It was about a forty-minute trek.

It was a relatively new building, only three stories in height, with lots of lawn space both in front and on the side of the building. The apartment was on the first floor above ground level with a good-sized living room, two bedrooms, a bath, and a nicely furnished kitchen with space for a breakfast table that was also to serve as our dining room table. Not fancy but nice and clean, and I am pleased to report the monthly rental was $90, with a month paid in advance. The back of the building offered a spectacular view of Lake Ontario and as the building was situated on the famous Scarborough Bluffs, we did on a few occasions make our way carefully down the Bluffs for a swim in the lake. The climb back up was hazardous. I must say that the lake, and others we were to subsequently visit on Sunday outings, were not then inviting to us, who had spent considerable time at the wonderful beaches at Lawrencetown and Hubbards. There were a few other drawbacks to the location. Because of telephone demands in fast-growing Toronto, we were going to have to wait a few months before we got our own phone. In the meantime we would have to use the public phones down the street. Nevertheless we had a nice modern shopping centre (this before they were introduced to Halifax) about a quarter-mile away. My forty-minute daily excursion to and from work was a little painful, given the fact that when first married I could walk to the Herald building from our apartment on South Street. But we were now experiencing big-city life with all of its challenges, and I must add, inconveniences.

When Glo arrived with Carol she was quite pleased with our new apartment and if she felt isolated because of our distance from the city, and other things, she never mentioned it. Being without a phone was, of course, difficult but that was to be remedied within a few months. It took a little longer for us to get a car.

As I had said it was a small apartment building, only eleven units in all, and there were four on our floor. Our next-door neighbours Doug and Dorothy McColm became good friends and we socialized with them quite a bit. Doug was from Oshawa while Dorothy was a Truro girl. Shortly after we had moved there, Stewart and Joyce Anderson took the apartment across the hall from us and joined our "social enclave." Joyce was from London, Ontario; Stew, a reporter with Canadian Press, was from Halifax and had in fact been at St. Mary's in my time. Other couples in nearby apartment buildings made up a warm circle of friends. We had limited pocketbooks and spent most of our money on home entertainment with the exception of one luxury. About every second Saturday night we would go downtown to dinner at a different restaurant. I think one of them was called the Buckingham Hotel.

It seemed as if we had been on a tight budget ever since moving to Toronto. We were just scraping by on $95 a week, and rather than taking the Tely by storm, I'd been relegated to a "learning role" on the rewrite desk. Our financial position had not been helped by a $3500 down payment I had made to a developer in Halifax for a new home; this at the time was the larger part of my life's earnings. As the housing development had been subject to a delay in construction, the developer promised to return my money when his banking arrangements were complete. While somewhat beside the point, I never did get the refund, although I retained ownership of a lot that I sold many years later on my return to Halifax. $3500 was a lot of money at that time, especially for a newly married young couple. But we survived.

I had to pay for my own transport to Toronto and the subsequent family move. The furniture move, if I remember correctly, cost in the area of $400. It probably would have been wiser for us to buy new furnishings, but most of the stuff we had was basically new so we moved it. I had been at the Tely only about two weeks when I got notice that our furniture was to arrive within days and I was going to need money to pay for it. I have since said many prayers for a certain Mr. Hack at the Bank of Nova Scotia. The bank was just up the street from the newspaper and I boldly went up and introduced myself to Mr. Hack, who for some reason lent me the $400. When I hear people criticize banks and bankers, I think of this long-ago kindness—a business transaction certainly, but a kindness extended me by this Toronto banker. I kept my account at this bank until I moved back to Halifax a few years later.

One morning, arriving in the newsroom at 6 a.m. for my rewrite shift, the night editor, with no other reporter in sight, sent me out to cover a reported murder in Regent Park, the city's new low-rental housing project. I was to relieve Don Collins, the night police reporter. I was told the police were not giving out any details. When I arrived the body was covered by a blanket and lying some distance behind a car that had been parked on Danforth Avenue. It was a Studebaker and, given the location of the body, I assumed it was the vehicle of the victim. I caught Collins just as he entered a taxi to return to the office and I asked the cab driver to call the office, and have them check out a license number. Shortly we got the call. The man to whom the car was registered was also the victim: a Polish immigrant named Zdzaislaw Szafran. This 25-year-old salesman, had been in Canada just a few years and had married only the year before. He and his 23-year-old bride, Angela, had just moved into their new home about a month before his death.

Chief Detective Archie McCathie, in his broad Scottish brogue, directed his remarks to our small group of reporters: "I am not giving you fellows any details until we find out what happened." *Star* reporters Ben Rose and Ted Honderick were also on the scene. I slipped away, went down to the next block, and caught a cab to the victim's address at Glen Davis Drive, where I met up with Tely photographer Jack Judges. I knocked and a pretty young woman answered. I explained that we had been told that her husband had been reported missing the night before and that we thought a photo in the paper might help to locate him. Angela Szafran was most cooperative. The living room was modestly but neatly furnished. I noticed a bookshelf laden with self-help books, among the titles: *How to Use Your Selling Power*, *Open Your Mind and Close the Sale*, *Managing Your Money*, and a slim volume entitled *America's Top Twelve Salesmen*—the marks of an ambitious new Canadian. I nodded to Judges and he shot a photo. With Angela's blessing, I borrowed their photo album, which included wedding pictures. One thing you learn on a photo hunt is to leave nothing for the competition. As we were leaving the house, Chief Detective McCathie arrived with two other policemen. McCathie asked snappily, "Who are you guys?" I lied and told him we were with the *Star*. We left in a hurry.

The *Telegram*, with exclusive access to the photos and sole knowledge of the victim's identity, went with a front-page spread. It was my first byline. Playing on page three in a page-wide photo layout was the wedding picture of the young couple, their new home, the shelf of books, the chair on which Angela sat while awaiting her late husband's arrival, and the dining room table on which she had carefully prepared two place settings the night before. The police had not yet announced the cause of death, so at the insistence of the aggressive managing editor, Doug McFarlane, we went with the phrase "Murder is suspected." As it turned out poor Szalran was the victim of a hit and run driver, and this fact was inserted in the second edition. Nevertheless I became an instant, if temporary, hero. The menacing McFarlane came from his executive lair and patted me on the back. Alan Kent, my earlier protector, gave me thumbs up. I went to the washroom and was at the sink washing my hands when Art Cole arrived next to me. "Arn," he said in his deep voice, "how would you like to cover city hall?" I felt as if I had died and gone to heaven.

Strangely, on my way back to the newsroom Bobby Hewittson, the *Telegram*'s veteran sports editor and a Toronto sports legend, signalled me. "Arn, how would you like to join the sports department? We're looking for someone to cover the OHA and I know you follow hockey." Was it possible to find redemption twice in one day? I knew I had made an impression earlier on Bob Frewin, and the veteran Ted Reeve, when handling their phone-ins on the Argo games. On Saturdays there were only three of us on rewrite, and the other two were Brits: Ron Collister, later a CBC newscaster; and Gordie Donaldson, a Scot. Neither knew or cared about Canadian football, so I became the catcher for these rewrites. It was a tempting offer. As much as I loved sport, however, city hall would offer the better and bigger challenge.

Covering city hall in the mid 1950s in Toronto was akin to attending a circus. There was fun and excitement every day. Nathan Phillips was the new mayor. In addition to covering the Toronto political scene, we covered the metropolitan government, which included Toronto and twelve surrounding townships. Fred G. Gardiner was the metro government chairman, and he was one of the ablest men I have ever encountered in either private or public life. His role in running metro in the early years made Toronto and its environs the mega municipality that it is today. Today there is a cross-city expressway named for Gardiner, and Toronto's city hall rests on Nathan Phillips Square. When I visit all these years later I feel like a ghost.

As a city hall reporter I worked out of the hall's small pressroom with two other *Telegram* reporters, Bill Bragg: our chief; and my old friend from college days, Dick O'Hagan. The *Star* and the *Globe and Mail*, each with three reporters, also worked from here although with separate desks if not partitions. Years ago Senator Finlay MacDonald asked me what I thought was the most important element in my career development, and without hesitation I said being a reporter on the *Toronto Telegram*. Also I don't think I ever had more fun in my life. While it was a very competitive environment, with all of us reporters trying to scoop each other, we enjoyed great camaraderie and no bitterness. I think we were, in terms of friendliness, much closer to the *Star* team of Lee Belland, Bob McDonald, and Gordie Bleasdale than to the *Globe* trio of Alden Baker, Wilfred List, and Jon Hall. McDonald had worked on the Halifax papers when I did; he was a native of Stellarton and a graduate of Acadia University. He became a good friend. This beat was, next to the Ottawa bureau, the best posting on the paper. It was responsible for more front-page stories than any other news source, and I had a feeling while working on the Tely that the world really began and ended at the Ontario boundaries, with the City of Toronto as its centrepiece.

Chapter Four: Out of Print

The two years I spent on the *Telegram* were two of the best years of my working career. I learned a lot and gained more confidence. During that time I saw a lot of my Dartmouth boyhood friend Jack Wilcox, who was strongly ensconced in the PR department at MacLaren Advertising. When I was picking him up for lunch one day, I again encountered his boss Ken MacGillivary—and another job offer. This time it was a more attractive proposition: PR account man for MacLaren's at General Motors. Hugh Lefoli had just resigned. With union problems, the Tely had been keeping the lid on salary increases. The MacLaren offer was for $7,000, which was $1,000 or more than I was making at the paper. Further there was a ten-cent a mile allowance for my travel, which would involve four days a week to and from Oshawa, forty miles away. I accepted, although not without some regret. Ironically, the next day, a Saturday, I was taking a turn in the news pool at the Tely office which, even for city hall types, was required on alternate Saturdays when the staff was slimmed down. Jack Cranford, manning the city desk, asked me to go down to the motor city and interview the union bosses. The *Telegram* had just run a series of articles by George Brimmel, highlighting the supposed communist background of several of its union's executive members. The union in response had threatened to boycott the sale of the *Telegram* in Oshawa and turn over the circulation trucks. Jack warned me to keep my wits about me "because they sounded pretty angry on the phone." He gave me a list of names and comments that the RCMP had prepared about the individuals concerned. The comments included details of trips to Russia, membership in Tim Buck's Labour Progressive Party, the Canadian Communist wing, and such related information.

On arrival in Oshawa I went directly to the union hall. I was escorted to a back office where four or five men, all in working clothes, were sitting around a desk. They collectively gaped when I told them I was a *Telegram* reporter. "They sent a bigger guy this time," one man commented. George was about five foot seven and I was six foot two. They suggested that I had a lot of nerve to walk into the union hall. One guy said, "You obviously don't fear for your safety." I assured them that I was not there to add to the criticism that the paper had directed towards them but, in the best traditions of newspaper fairness, to give them a chance to respond. I also told them that George's story was based on official data received from the RCMP. When I pulled out the Mounties' reports from my pocket, they showed a new interest, and one not so hostile. I think they thought that, in showing them the documents, I was committing myself to their side of the story. I don't think I got much of a story out of the encounter, but it was an interesting experience. Within weeks I would be driving to Oshawa in the service of their purported enemy, General Motors of Canada.

I spent only a year on the GM job. After the dash and fun of the newspapers I found work in the corporate field a bit confining and less challenging. In the newspaper business every day is a new day. Yesterday's news is old news, and the race begins anew. As well I didn't really like the public relations manager of General Motors, Bill Austin. While I never had any unpleasant experiences with him, he always made you feel that he was the client and you were there simply to serve him. It was a "man in the grey suit" environment, and everyone in the company's head office was conscious of rank; most were taking either Dale Carnegie courses or other self-improvement lessons. It was a long way from the carefree days of the Tely. The PR department included seven people, four male PR staffers and three secretaries. I was there as "a writer." Austin as the boss did no writing himself but played editor with my copy. Two of the men, both very nice guys, had won promotion into the department from the plant floor. They busied themselves helping stage manage the company's various promotions. The deputy in the department, an engaging fellow by the name of Larry Gough, had been a magazine writer but had opted for the softer life of public relations. In that his sole occupation seemed to be looking over my shoulder while I wrote, I can't say that I thought him an effective operator. I don't want to sound too critical for, overall, it was an interesting and helpful experience. GM in those days was the lord of all it surveyed, and its reach was almost unending. The car business was, of course, its main thrust, but it was also into the manufacture of fridges, airplanes, buses, locomotives, and just about everything else you could name. They dominated the auto industry. The foreign car market at that time was dismissed as irrelevant, as it had less than five percent of the North American market. Japan had not yet checked it, nor had the other latter-day challengers.

My job consisted of writing press releases, new car announcements, financial stories relating to GM's importance to the Canadian economy, copy for several booklets, and the occasional speech for W. A. Wecker, the president. He was an automotive engineer from the United States and a halting speaker; the first time I heard him speak, using my words, I was ready to crawl under the rug, any rug. I also wrote a booklet dealing with the life of R. S. (Sam) McLaughlin, the founder of GM Canada who, although eighty-five years of age, maintained an office at corporate headquarters. He was also the fourth largest shareholder in GM, ranking just behind the DuPont family,

Alfred Sloan, and Charles Kettering. They held an eighty-fifth birthday bash for Sam McLaughlin at the Royal York Hotel, and the automotive world's royalty from near and abroad attended. I had the responsibility of going to the airport to pick up Charles Kettering, the famous automotive inventor. He was a lovely, somewhat older man, who sat in the front seat of my Buick (I would have been shot driving anything else) and chatted all the way in from the airport to the hotel. He told me that the Duco paint drying process, which he had invented, had allowed GM to overcome Ford's large sales lead in the 1920s. Up until the early twenties Ford had close to 65 percent of the market. Because of limitations in paint drying, automotive manufacturers were compelled to stay with one colour for their cars, and this was black. The Duco process allowed GM to produce cars in six different colours, and within five years their models had a big lead on Ford. A lead they were never to give up. Dr. Kettering also told me that the style change in automobiles was the dynamic in the North American economy.

In contrast to William Wecker's retiring personality, G. J. (Jeff) Umphrey was a legend in the Canadian automotive business and, when required, a charmer. As vice president of sales for GM, he ruled his own fiefdom—the sprawling series of GM dealerships throughout Canada—and he ruled with an iron hand. Targets were imposed arbitrarily, and sales were expected to go upwards and onwards. I saw both sides of his quixotic nature. I happened to come up in the elevator with him one day while the young girl attendant was reading a magazine. As soon as he got to his office he asked his secretary to call the office manager and have the girl fired. But sometimes, he was all molasses. The annual GM Motorama was a major sales promotion affair. It was held in the Automotive Building at the CN Exhibition, and the invitation list included not only people in the auto industry but community leaders as well. He placed himself in the midst of the small reception line. At the outset of the evening he signalled to me, saying he wanted me as his point man. My job was to spot the nametags as people approached, and then send the word up the line to him. When Mr. and Mrs. Smith arrived at centre station, a smiling Jeff would throw out a welcoming hand and say something like "It is always great to see the Smiths." He was the epitome of the professional oilcan.

About six years after we had started up CFDR radio in 1956-57, I called on an old friend Phil Carr-Harris, who had just been appointed the new Pontiac–Buick dealer in Dartmouth. I had worked with Phil years before in Dosco, and I went to talk to him about an advertising campaign. A gregarious, outgoing fellow, and a former footballer, Phil told me he was experiencing a few temporary problems with General Motors. As a dealer for General Motors Holding, the finance arm of GM, he was subject to certain adherences. GMHC had decided, he said, that he should build a new showroom in a more traffic-centred area of town. As a trained accountant he had gone through the figures and determined that it was not a good deal for him or his new dealership, so he had refused them. He didn't foresee any difficulties as he had a call into Jeff Umphrey, who had befriended him at a recent dealers' council meeting. Jeff, he said, would understand. I called back a few days later to confirm the advertising plan, and found him greatly disturbed. His new buddy was not taking his phone calls. A week or two later he was forced to resign the agency. It was hardball at its hardest.

In 1957 my former boss R. J. Rankin of the Herald in Halifax was elected president of the Atlantic Provinces Economic Council, and he invited me to return home as APEC's first public relations officer. I was quite comfortable at the time and was making $7500 at MacLaren's. I got to spend only a day or two a week in the Toronto office, but MacLaren's provided a creative atmosphere with a lot of bright people. My old friend Dick O'Hagan had moved over to the PR department as well, working the Dominion Store account. At Mr. Rankin's request I flew to Halifax on a Saturday to be interviewed by O. Nelson Mann, the executive director and vice president of APEC. We chatted at the Lord Nelson Hotel. APEC, with a mandate to promote and increase business and business opportunity in Atlantic Canada, was in its first year of operation. Nelson, a very nice and hard-working man, told me that their hope and aim was to increase private membership in the council. This is where I was to come in—the prime promoter. At that time the council had less than 250 members and was largely supported by government grants. I was intrigued both by the idea and with the opportunity for Glo and me and baby Carol, then just over three years old, to return to Halifax.

APEC's offices were located in Halifax, although I spent a good measure of my times travelling the Maritimes. Newfoundland was technically a member of the council, and the government supported it financially, but Premier Joey Smallwood did not want invasion of his kingdom by this new mainland force. The other three provinces were more involved. My first task was to organize a master mailing list. This encompassed thousands of businesses, large and small, throughout the three provinces. Once this was set in motion I visited towns throughout, promoting membership drives. While not a cash-rich organization APEC, through Nelson Mann, had built up a fairly broad group of directors throughout the region. I was able to call on them to assist in the membership campaign. I spoke to public groups in Saint John, Moncton, Newcastle, Bathurst, Edmundston, Campbellton, Summerside, Charlottetown, Truro, New Glasgow, Sydney, Yarmouth, Dartmouth, and other smaller centres. Normally, the local director and I would arrange for me to speak at an evening meeting of business people or to a Lion's or Kiwanis club. I would arrive the day before and also call on the local newspaper editors, one of the best parts of the job, and arrange for publicity. In this regard I made a lot of new friends, including Harry Sutherland, editor of the *New Glasgow News*; John Murphy, the *Truro News*; Roy Duchemin of the *Cape Breton Post*; Rod Raymond, the *Campbellton Tribune*; and many others. One of my notable calls, which was to cement a long-time and continuing friendship, was with Brigadier Michael Wardell, owner of the *Fredericton Gleaner*. More about him later. Usually I also would line up a radio interview the day of my meeting with the prospective members. While we had no money to buy advertising, I got a wonderful reception from media people who saw the economic council as a worthwhile organization and one deserving of support. I was basically selling the flag.

As I remember it was a wonderful summer for weather and I travelled the three provinces by car. In my days as a hockey broadcaster I had been to Saint John, Moncton, Charlottetown, and most of the Nova Scotian towns, but my visits to the smaller towns offered a new experience. We had rather remarkable success in recruiting new members. Most were small firms whose dues were in the range of only $25-$100, but they added new muscle to the council. By late summer our numbers exceeded thirteen hundred. Nelson was elated. We were staying with Glo's parents in Rockingham. With a score of cousins dropping by, Carol was having a wonderful time. It was nice for Glo too, as she and her mother were close; and after three years away, the return home was welcomed by her family as well as us. Our return also gave me a chance to reacquaint myself with harness racing, which I had enjoyed so much in my youth and in the four years as the radio broadcaster at the Truro Raceway. Glo's sister June had married Jack Cruickshank a year or two before. Jack and his father, Captain Jack, were co-owners with the B. C. Cruikshank family (no relation) in the Halifax area racetrack Sackville Downs which had opened in 1955. Jack was the vice president and general manager. I became the track announcer and also gave him a hand with general publicity and promotions. There was racing twice a week, Wednesday and Saturday, and as such it did not impose on my job with the economic council, which had priority. This side job was great fun; we socialized together with our wives, and Jack and I were in constant contact.

The racetrack was located at Lower Sackville, just outside Halifax. It was an excellent facility, a lighted half-mile track with wide turns. Halifax had not had regular racing cards before the outbreak of the Second World War, when the old Provincial Exhibition track at Almon and Windsor streets was taken over by the army for barracks. There had been winter racing on the Halifax Commons over the years, but it was on an abbreviated track without any supporting facilities. A track had been built on the Walker property at Lower Sackville, just above the Downs, in the early fifties, but it closed after staging only about three race meets. In the thirties and forties there were a number of small tracks operating at Bridgewater, Truro, New Glasgow (which had two facilities), North Sydney, Sydney, Inverness, Amherst, Springhill, and I think Middleton. All had disappeared by the mid-fifties, with the exception of the Truro Raceway and the Sydney track. Truro had introduced night racing in 1949. The track was quite successful as a racing facility and as the site for the Central Nova Scotia Exhibition, which was a major summer event in Colchester–Cumberland. The newly-refurbished Sydney operation, under the aegis of Jimmy Ferguson, also had made a comeback. Sackville Downs, however, with its population base and newer facilities, became the big track in the province with the largest crowds and biggest mutual bets.

My love of harness racing, goes back to my boyhood when winter racing on the Dartmouth Lakes was a big attraction. It seems that we had colder winters in that era, and the lakes were almost certain to be safe in January, February, and March. I can recall events with great clarity. While racing occasionally took place on Lake Banook, Dartmouth's first lake, most events were centred on Lake Mic Mac, the second lake. The track (a cleared ice path) was about a quarter-mile in length, and the racecourse itself was defined by rows of cars lining either side. Hundreds of spectators would congregate at the finish line. The races were staged under the auspices of the Eastern Driving Club, of which my latter-day mentor and friend Fred M. Lahey was president. Horsemen, mostly farmers, would truck their horses in for the event, which offered but small purses. Jack Scott, a big, bluff man with a resonating voice, ran a pari-mutuel from a small trailer. It may not have been Yonkers Raceway or Roosevelt but, in the then small town, weekend racing on the lakes took on a carnival air. I can remember most of the horses to this day, sixty or so years later. Guy Britain, owned by George Turner; Vesta Bars, owned by Wilfred Baker; Brian Yorke, owned by Guy Dauphinee; Walter Brown, owned and driven by Scott Weeks; Sparkle, owned by George Kuhn. One tragic event I recall was the drowning of a horse named Witty Guy. His driver had fallen out of the sulky at the finish line and Witty Guy kept racing. Several other drivers took off in an effort to stop the horse but I think they only frightened him. Otto's Ice Company had done a harvest about a quarter-mile down the lake, and the open water waited for Witty Guy. He splashed in and drowned.

Sackville Downs operated for 31 years. It was a major operation for a local undertaking as on race nights it gave employment to several hundred people. Jack Cruickshank acquired total ownership from his father and the Cruikshank partners, and he became the driving force in its operations. A sharp businessman who knew the value of a dollar and hard work, he was in my mind always the key to the track's success. While he often battled horsemen and others about purses, wagering, and other things, he was the main reason why the track survived for so long. Sackville Downs was the most successfully sustained sporting operation of any kind in Nova Scotia from 1955 until 1986. When Jack sold in 1985, the track became vulnerable to real estate hawks eyeing the valuable property. Its new owners, Dafyd Williams and John Hampson, sold it for real estate development. Today it is a massive shopping complex with a Wal-Mart as its anchor. Its loss was a blow to harness racing, not only in Halifax but also in the Maritimes, for it was the big track. Over the years it sponsored and featured some of the best racing in the history of the sport in the Maritimes; and the B. C. Cruikshank Memorial, the Maritime Pace and its richly endowed stake races for young horses attracted thousands.

Chapter Five: Dosco Days

For young readers and those from away who are unfamiliar with this bitter industrial fight, the A. V. Roe Limited takeover of the giant Dominion Steel and Coal Corporation, Limited in 1957 was a monumental event that won widespread attention from the Canadian business community. This battle, waged throughout the summer and early fall months, was of particular significance in Nova Scotia because Dosco was the province's largest industrial employer, with close to twenty thousand employees. It had been a bellwether for the provincial economy for more than fifty years, operating plants and mines in many parts of the province. While the battle for control of Newfoundland's Fishery Products International was at centre stage early in 2001, with Nova Scotia interests led by John Risley of Clearwater Fine Foods, taking control, it was a minor-league tussle compared to the Dosco–Roe standoff. Interestingly, one of the principal Clearwater players in the recent Fishery Products takeover was Frank Sobey, grandson of Frank H. Sobey who along with Roy A. Jodrey fought the Dosco acquisition by the Toronto-based Roe company. While 44 years has intervened, there is evidence that some things change little in Nova Scotia.

While many saw the profitable and modern A. V. Roe as a saviour for Dosco, others were vehemently opposed to its sale to these Central Canadian, albeit English, marauders. Two of its principal opponents, as mentioned, were Jodrey and Sobey, prominent Nova Scotia businessmen. Both were long-time directors of Dosco, and both were major shareholders in the corporation. Jodrey was the owner of Minas Basin Pulp and Paper, a Nova Scotia conglomerate, and Sobey, president of a large grocery chain. Both were native Nova Scotians. Jodrey resided in Hantsport and Sobey in Stellarton. They fought the takeover on the basis that it would be bad for Nova Scotia, which had over the years witnessed many of its old companies in various fields leave the province after being acquired by companies located in other parts of Canada—or, as these two old-fashioned Nova Scotians phrased it, "Upper Canada." For most, the translation means Bay Street and Toronto.

In his biography *The Story of R. A. Jodrey* author Harry Bruce says that Jodrey saw the takeover as financial intrigue to exploit Maritimers. While most of the big players in the Canadian business elite were prepared to accept Roe's purchase of the older, tired Dosco, Jodrey was a conspicuous holdout. In his book Bruce writes: "He was the man who said 'No' to the inevitable. A man who was normally reticent outside his own kingdom. A man who apologized for his flaws as a speechifier and ducked invitations to sound off in public, he nevertheless hurled himself into a campaign that transformed him overnight into a national figure." And according to Bruce, he was "a limelight spokesman, a leader, even the reluctant darling of certain business journalists." I would question neither Jodrey's nor Sobey's dedication to Nova Scotia and its interests, but I would suggest that their motives were not totally altruistic. Jodrey had $2 million in Dominion Steel stock, and Sobey too was a major shareholder. That amount today would be twentyfold at least.

I remember the fight vividly, and ultimately got to play in it. Jodrey and Sobey spent considerable money in waging both a newspaper advertising campaign and a personal mailing campaign to block the sale to Roe. The Roe forces were not idle, and their spokesman A. R. (Ron) Williams, assistant to the president, made a series of statements contending that the Roe takeover would be great for all concerned and especially for Dosco's steel operations. Dosco's vulnerability to outside buyers had been sparked earlier that year by the death of its highly regarded president, L. A. (Laddy) Forsyth. Forsyth, a Nova Scotian, had led Dosco to two profitable years—more than $7 million in earnings both in 1956 and 1957. Its sales in that period were more than $200 million, making it one of the largest industrial concerns in the country. Roe's profits and sales, mostly in government contracts, were about the same. Under Forsyth's presidency the company had modernized the steel plant, mechanized its big iron ore operations in Newfoundland, and introduced the Dosco Miner, a massive machine to strip coal from the underground seams. The company, which had faced bankruptcy in the early 1930s and had struggled for most of its more recent existence, was on a good roll. As well, Forsyth was popular in Cape Breton, the heart of the company's operations. As a young reporter on the *Mail-Star* I had covered his speech to the Canadian Club in Halifax in which he was buoyant about the prospects of the Nova Scotia coal industry. He was a masterful speaker, one of the best I have ever heard. I was hardly knowledgeable about the coal industry, but I didn't share his enthusiasm or beliefs that better days lay ahead for Old King Coal.

Meanwhile Roe was looking for a big stake in the steel industry, which was one of the prime industrial sectors in North America in that era. Just the year before they had bought a ten percent interest in Algoma Steel of Sault St. Marie. With Forsyth's death they saw an opportunity to acquire Dosco, and while not as successful as Algoma, it would come at a much better price. At the Atlantic Provinces Economic Council offices we were keen spectators to the battle taking place in our backyard. A native of Sydney, Nelson Mann was particularly interested. From my days living in Toronto, I was familiar with the Roe organization and its importance as an industry in Ontario.

They were one of Canada's leading firms relative to high-tech, and its fifteen thousand employees encompassed some of the best engineering minds in the country. My personal leaning as a Nova Scotian was in their direction. This was capped during a phone call from my friend Dick O'Hagan in Toronto, who seemed to intervene in my life with regularity. He had been following the fight in the Toronto papers. We discussed Ron Williams (only a name to me then), and Dick said he had been a high-powered newspaperman, and a former city editor of the *Toronto Star*. He said I should meet him. Williams was staying at the Nova Scotian Hotel from which location he was volleying on a daily basis with the Jodrey–Sobey combo. I called him and invited him to come and speak to us at the economic council. He accepted the invitation, and we met in our small boardroom in the United Services Building overlooking the famed Citadel. Four or five of us gathered to hear his pitch. He made a strong presentation, telling us that Roe, with its own strong finances, would be in a position to greatly strengthen the Dosco operations. He said with certainty that Roe's extensive business contacts throughout the country could boost steel sales. I took an immediate liking to Williams. He was a big man, smiley, with a good sense of humour.

APEC's annual meeting was slated for about three weeks after our meeting with Williams. Given the interest in the Dosco–Roe battle and its significance to our own economy, I suggested we invite him to be the main speaker at the annual dinner at the Charlottetown Hotel. Nelson agreed, but said that I would have to go down to the Herald Limited and sell Bob Rankin, the APEC president, on the idea. Surprisingly, Rankin was receptive, remarking that the resulting publicity would be a good thing for the council. So he gave me the go ahead and, with Nelson's blessing, I called Williams in Toronto, and extended the invite. He accepted. I can't recall the numbers now, but the 1957 annual meeting in Charlottetown was well-attended. The Honourable George Hees, then minister of transport in the federal government, was the key speaker one night, as was Ron Williams on the second and final night. There was an overflow crowd for the A. V. Roe executive's speech, as interest in the battle over Dosco had heightened. Williams again emphasized that his company had the highest hopes for a strengthening of Dosco and that the Maritimes and Maritimers would be the main beneficiaries. He was a good solid speaker although not an oratorical star. Following the meeting, a number of the guests, most involved in some aspect of business in Atlantic Canada, approached Williams and congratulated him. A. Murray MacKay, for whom the second Halifax Harbour bridge is named, was one of them. Then president of Maritime Tel and Tel, MacKay said that he planned to mail in his shares the following day with support for the Roe takeover.

In his remarks that night Williams had suggested that, judging by the support his company was getting countrywide (this based on the shares already tendered), effective control of Dosco was now in the hands of the aircraft company. Within a week or two Roe had control of 73.6 percent of the shares and was the new owner of the

Maritimes' biggest industry. Within weeks the parade of Roe brass began: Sir Roy Dobson, the chairman of Hawker Siddeley, England; Sir Frank Spriggs, a Hawker Siddeley senior director; Crawford Gordon, the president of A. V. Roe Canada, who would later become involved in a high-profile fight with Canada's prime minister; Ron Williams; and a handful of others. They made a swing through Nova Scotia, stopping at Halifax, Trenton, Sydney, and several Cape Breton coal towns. They held receptions in the coal towns and assured the local business people, "We are builders not financiers," said Sir Roy, who was famous in England for being the prime force behind the building of the RAF Lancaster bomber during the Second World War. I had a private meeting with both Crawford Gordon and Ron Williams, who suggested that one of the company's most pressing needs was for a better public image, not simply in Nova Scotia but throughout Canada. While Dosco had some local PR input, there were no public relations advisers at head office in Montreal and no coordinated program for the company as a whole. I was offered the job. The money was substantially better than I was receiving at the economic council, and other side benefits were included. It meant moving to Montreal and away from home a second time.

Glo agreed, and when we moved to Montreal in 1958 the city was far more amenable to anglophones than it was after 1963, when the separatist movement started to flower. Even today, Glo favours Montreal over Toronto as a place to live, even though we lived in the Ontario metropolis three times. At first we rented a duplex in Notre-Dame-de-Grace; then after about a year we bought a nice house in Montreal West, an anglo enclave, with Jewish families dominant in our sector of the town. It was only a small township of about seven thousand people, about twenty-five minutes from the heart of downtown Montreal. We loved the neighbourhood; most of the people were about our age, so there was a lot of socialization. Many of the friends we made at that time, forty and more years ago, remain our friends today. Montreal was a spectacular city, far more glittering and interesting than Toronto. Certainly, I can't recall experiencing in that time one unpleasant moment because I was a unilingual anglo. For the most part though it was a case of two solitudes. The English-speakers largely were separate, living in selected communities. Cote-Saint-Luc, Westmount, Beaconsfield, Laval, Point Clare, Outremont, Rosemere and other such townships were more English than French, despite the ten to one ratio that existed provincewide. Our children went to English-speaking schools; and Dorval's Summerlea golf club, to which I belonged, was largely English although there was a mixture of both languages. Today, many years later, I am told the club is dominantly French.

When I first joined Dosco in Montreal, the head offices were located in the Canada Cement Building at Phillip's Square. The more visible office areas were what one would expect for a major blue-blooded corporation. The reception area was finished in dark oak, the walls were decorated with Jack Gray paintings, which were massive and included depictions of the shipyards in Halifax, the steel works in Sydney, and a number of seascapes for which he was famous. It was very impressive. The company had several floors throughout the building, and mine was located on the top floor, which housed most of the executives. My immediate boss was Allan C. MacDonald, executive vice president of A. V. Roe. He had been the president of the Canadian Car Company (CanCar), the old railway equipment company also owned by Roe. His job was to cement the marriage between these two companies—not an easy task in that they were miles apart in terms of not only product manufacture but also temperament. His presence was to be temporary until such time as they found a top steel executive, and for this there was a talent hunt underway in the steel towns of the United States. Tough and a perfectionist, MacDonald had come up through the illustrious ranks of the Canadian Pacific Railway. He wasn't a particularly warm man, and he was not liked by the old Dosco executives whom he had inherited. They saw him as a "hatchet man," though he personally did very little blood-spilling. He did bring in a few people of his own—a vice president of finance from Canadian Car and a corporate lawyer from CanCar—but there was no carnage at the head office. Out in the field, however, the story was different. Most of the senior people in the corporation were men in their sixties, some older. Harvey Smith, a former vice president of production for Avro Aircraft who had been imported from Roe, had very fixed ideas about how things should be run. One of his key principles was that his managers should be relatively young. Smith was an American, a product of the Henry J. Kaizer organization in whose many business endeavours he had been involved. These included shipbuilding, dam building (the famed Marshall Ford Dam), and the aborted Kaizer automotive exercise. Roe had brought him to Toronto to deal with production problems in the building of the CF-100 for the RCAF. Smith won a reputation as a wizard, although his relationship with the Roe executives was contentious.

In February, 1958, A. V. Roe dispatched Harvey Smith to Dosco to assume the vice presidency with responsibility for a manufacturing sector that included such companies as Halifax Shipyards; Canadian Bridge in Windsor, Ontario; Trenton Works in Pictou County, Nova Scotia; the Truscon Steel fabricating plant in Montreal; a steel fabricating plant in Toronto; the Pender Nail plant in Saint John; and other smaller operations. He had no responsibility for the steel plant in Sydney, nor for coal, nor for the big iron ore operation at Bell Island, Newfoundland. He was quick off the mark, causing the timbers to rattle as he carried out wholesale management changes in the subsidiaries. His nickname, which he brought with him from Roe, was "Hard Rock," and he certainly lived up to it. R. J. R. (Bob) Nelson, a legend in Halifax business circles and Canadian shipbuilding, had reached his seventies and therefore was retired as general manager of the two company yards in the area. He was replaced by John Lezie, an American in his early forties who had worked with Smith at Kaizer. Lou Fulton, an old steel hand, also close to seventy if not past it, was replaced as general manager at Canadian Steel in Montreal by Harold Young, in his early forties. Harold,

A ship launching at the Halifax Shipyards, a Dosco subsidiary. (left to right) Mrs. Fairley, A. L. Fairley, Jr., Arnie Patterson. J. Earl Clubb, C.A., vice president of finance for Dosco, is behind Arnie in the fedora. (1961)

another American, had come over from Avro with Smith. Clair Riley, another septuagenarian, was retired as general manager of Canadian Bridge in Windsor and replaced by Dan Scouler, Jr., a young engineer in his mid-thirties. Dan had come out of the ranks at Halifax Shipyards, where his father was the long-time assistant general manager to Bob Nelson. William Knoll, Sr., general manager at the huge Trenton Works in Pictou County, was replaced by a much younger Howard Bezanson. There also were major changes in the management ranks at Truscon Steel in Montreal and the Toronto fabricating plant. With these sweeping changes the old guard in the company got nervous; most were in their sixties, and they felt threatened.

Dosco was an amazing company, and one filled with autocratic oligarchs. Clem Anson, who was in his sixties, ruled the steel plant operation with an iron fist. Harold M. C. Gordon, the vice president of coal operations, was also czar-like in his reign. One of the most physically fit men that I have ever known, Harold too was in his early sixties. Harry McAvoy, vice president of steel sales at head office, was in his sixties and another strong man. Charles W. Appleton, vice president of coal sales, was also in his early or mid-sixties. He, however, was a very gentle man and a graduate of the pit. Clifford Broadbent, vice president of administration, was another long-time veteran, and he was in his sixties. Although he had been a military medal winner in the First World War, he was somewhat meek in most ways. He was very efficient, however, and had served a number of presidents and others through the years. Rand Matheson, manager of transportation, was another senior executive. Rand had been manager of the Maritime Freight Rates organization and an expert on railway subsidies as they applied to the movement of steel and coal. He had been a sprint champion while at Dalhousie University in Halifax and was a charming, thoughtful man. He was not of the same mould as some of the tough old rhinos who had ruled for so long.

Talk about "man in the gray suit" intrigue! We had two separate camps and both busy watching the other. On one side, tough, grizzled steel and coal veterans; on the other the buoyant, more confident Roe forces. The enmity was real but never evidenced publicly. I was aware that, initially, I had been looked upon as one of the Roe people, although I had never worked for Roe. The fact that I was a Nova Scotian eased matters as time went along, and I never really had any difficulty with the strong-minded men who were on average more than 35 years older than me. I really liked most of them and became friends with many. The quest for a president and chief operating officer was settled in the summer of 1958 with the arrival of Albert L. Fairley, Jr. A tall, angular man with a deep sonorous voice, Fairley was an immediate hit with the Dosco crowd and the Roe brass who had spearheaded the hunt. He was born in Jackson, Mississippi, and grew up in Birmingham, Alabama; his charming accent was distinctly deep South. He had worked as a mining geologist for the United States Steel Corporation's subsidiary, Tennessee Coal, Iron and Railroad. He came to Dosco from Pittsburgh, where he had served as vice president for the Shenango Furnace Company and its subsidiaries. He was 45 when he moved to Montreal. We were to develop a very close working relationship and a warm friendship. He was a complete gentleman, with a sense of fun and an infectious friendliness that people liked. He was an easy boss to work for, and considering Dosco's many public relations problems and my knowledge of the Maritimes, my services became important to him.

I spent five years of my life, 1958–63, as the public relations director for the company. There were days when I thought I was the chief purser on the *Titanic*. There was always trouble on at least one front: coal mine closures, problems in iron ore, ships burning, mine explosions, government attacks, labour unrest, internal executive battles, and more. Dosco was a company built on a foundation of tough times, but for all that, it was an abiding presence on the Canadian scene and weathered almost as many storms as the Royal Navy. In Nova Scotia today there are remnants of this once-proud industrial power. The Halifax Shipyards and Dartmouth Marine Slips, old Dosco properties, are now owned by the Irving Company of Saint John. The yards continue to

After a tour of Number Four colliery in Glace Bay. (left to right) Frank Doxey, General Manager of Dominion Coal; Angus MacDonald, manager of Number Four; Albert L. Fairley, president of Dominion Steel and Coal Corporation, Limited; Rainnie H. MacDonald, Glace Bay superintendent; T. J. (Ted) Emmert, president of Hawker Siddeley Limited; H. M.C. Gordon, vice president of Dominion Coal Company; Arnie Patterson. (1962)

operate, and given the peak and valley existence of Canadian shipyards, they have been relatively successful. The Trenton Works, now in private hands, remains a major factor in the life of Pictou County. The immense plant there encompasses a million square feet under roof. The steel plant at Sydney is greatly diminished, and under new ownership, will employ only two hundred to three hundred men. As I write, its continuing future is in doubt. In its heyday it employed more than three thousand. Old King Coal died on May 20, 2001, when the federal government announced the closing of Cape Breton's last mine, the Prince. Given the massive losses, some $1.8 billion since the Cape Breton Development Corporation took over the pits in 1967, the closure, sad as it is, came as no surprise. That once-great industry, which gave employment to more than ten thousand miners, finally succumbed after years of the government propping it up. The old iron ore mines in Newfoundland were closed many years ago. At one time fifty companies operated under the Dosco umbrella. All have since been dispersed or dispensed to other owners.

Dosco's roots can be traced back to the early part of the nineteenth century, but the dig for coal precedes it by a century. Early French explorers sailing past Cape Breton had noticed blackened seams on the hills and coastline of this new land. Around 1720 they put their soldiers to work, mining coal as a source of heat for the huge fortress and buildings at Louisbourg. In 1824, long after the British had wrested Louisbourg from French control, King George IV granted his brother the Duke of York the lease to all mineral wealth in Nova Scotia. The spendthrift duke assigned his rights to creditors, mostly jewellers, who in 1826 formed the General Mining Association to exploit Cape Breton's rich coal deposits. In 1872, just five years after Confederation, two Scotsmen built a big forging plant at New Glasgow and called it the Hope Iron Works. The first molten steel in Canada was poured there, using the coal that was also so abundant in Pictou County.

In 1899 a group of investors, mostly Montreal tycoons allied with British investment, grouped these disparate iron and coal companies together under the name Dominion Iron and Steel Corporation. Essential to their plans was the construction of a new steel mill at Sydney, which was then a small, dusty town ideally situated on tidewater. With additional investment from Americans, the plant was opened in 1900. There was an abundance of good coking coal in Cape Breton, and iron ore in neighbouring Newfoundland. Its birth was heralded. In his exceedingly well-written series of portraits of Canadian business leaders entitled *Flame of Power* (1959), author Peter Newman relates that many Canadian titans of the early twentieth century were involved with Dominion Iron and Steel and its successor companies. The richest man in Canada, Sir Herbert Holt, a long-time president of the Royal Bank of Canada, was a director for many years. Newman wrote that in 1929 Holt had ambitiously endeavoured to weld all of the major steel producers in Canada into one mighty force. As a start he paid $50 million for the Dosco holdings, then known as the British Empire Steel Corporation (Besco). While he was able to add about thirty companies to this base, he failed in his bid to enlist either Stelco or Algoma to his steel cartel. Under Holt, the Besco name was changed to the Dominion Steel and Coal Corporation, Limited. Many other Canadian business monarchs were directors of the conglomerate over the years, including Lord Strathcona and Sir William Cornelius Van Horne of the CPR. Sir James Dunn, later the owner of the Algoma Steel complex, was a lawyer for Dominion Iron and Steel in his early career.

Despite all of the power and wealth associated with the company, it had a troubled history. There were financiers and stock promoters who made a fortune from its many gyrations, but it was never easy sailing. Many of the richest families in Montreal and Toronto profited from coal in its early days. J. K. L. Ross, whose horses won two Kentucky Derbies, was president of the corporation. Part of his wealth created the Ross Pavilion at Montreal's Royal Victoria Hospital. The Webster family of Montreal and the Gundys of Toronto were also major shareholders.

I have always loved the slogan that fueled the union's 1925 fight against British Empire Steel. It was "Learn to hate Besco with all the honesty in your heart." Besco

Greeting Quebec Premier Jean Lesage as new steel fabricating facilities were added to Dosco's Montreal steel works. (left to right) Arnie Patterson; A.C. MacDonald, executive vice president of A.V. Roe Limited; Quebec premier Jean Lesage; Albert L. Fairley, Jr., president of Dosco. (1963)

was in a pitched battle with union forces led by Jim McLaughlin, president of the United Mine Workers, who was known as "Red Jim" because of his supposed communist leanings. There was total breakdown in the coal towns, and the army had to be brought in to quell rioting in Glace Bay. Those bitter days were never forgotten in the coal towns. By the time I joined the company 35 years later, much of the suspicion and lack of trust remained, although relative prosperity during the forties and fifties had improved feelings immeasurably, as did the presence of Laddy Forsyth as president.

When Forsyth died in 1957, he was succeeded by Charles B. Lang. A tough, taciturn steel man, Lang was leader of the group that sought to sell the company to A. V. Roe. He was in his seventies and so stepped in as caretaker until the company could recruit a younger man. A. C. MacDonald, the Roe senior vice president, was also a temporary leader. When the experienced and charming Albert Fairley assumed the presidency in the summer of 1958, he had little trouble winning support throughout the company and so immediately set out to win public support for Roe. He travelled to every plant location in Atlantic Canada and made several key speeches in Sydney and Glace Bay, Dosco's major home towns. The highly articulate Fairley won further converts. He was featured on a series of business interviews on the CBC, and was sought out for feature articles in many business publications, including *Business Week*, the *Financial Post*, and the *Financial Times*. Moving to affluent Westmount, he and his wife Claire won immediate entry into Montreal's social swirl. As president of one of the city's oldest industrial companies, he was quickly embraced by the Royal Montreal Club and other leading social institutions. And, while the company made headway in the early months of his arrival, a major tragedy awaited at the Springhill mine.

Chapter Six: The Springhill Mine Disaster

One of the most traumatic happenings in my life occurred on October 23, 1958 at the coal-mining town of Springhill, Nova Scotia, when the lives of 75 men were lost following a massive underground "bump." I can recall the sight of three separate hearses driving by the offices of the Cumberland Railway and Coal Company, en route to the graveyards. It was a sad, pitiful sight, and worse when you knew that this would be repeated so many times in this small community in the space of a few days. It was as if the whole town was draped in black, and I suppose this somewhat appropriate in that the men who had worked these mines for more than one hundred years were in quest of the black seams of coal that lay so deep underground. The building in which I stood was one of the biggest in the town of seven thousand people, and one of the handful made of brick. Normally, it was the head office of the coal company and the usual haunt of bookkeepers, engineers, and others who administered to the needs of the company's fortunes. That day and for the next few weeks it would serve as press quarters for the more than two hundred reporters, cameramen, and other journalists, who came to tell the tragic tale that had engrossed readers and viewers throughout the world. I remember too walking the less than a quarter-mile distance from the office building to the pithead and its towering head frame, with thoughts that men were trapped somewhere under the ground on which I walked. There were fading hopes that any would be found alive.

The two weeks following my arrival at Springhill were among the saddest and happiest that I have ever experienced. The day before the mine disaster our company, the Dominion Steel and Coal Corporation, Limited, had held its annual meeting at the Nova Scotian Hotel in Halifax—the first time in the industrial giants more than 58-year history that its directors and shareholders had assembled there for the annual meeting. As the company's public relations director, I believed this choice of location was long overdue as more than fifteen thousand Nova Scotians worked for the company at its shipyards, railway car works, steel plant, and coal mines. A galaxy of company brass, including that of A. V. Roe Canada and the parent company, Hawker Siddeley of

England, was present, including our three belted lords: Sir Frank Dobson, Sir Thomas Sopwith, and Sir Frank Spriggs. There was a full brigade of striped suits from the banking and financial communities along with a large number of shareholders. The Halifax Herald papers, not traditionally kind to the company, saluted the move and suggested that the meeting here was evidence of the company's renewed interest in the province and the company's roots, which went back well into the nineteenth century.

The meeting was co-chaired by Sir Roy Dobson and Albert L. Fairley, Jr., the company's new president, and they left the shareholders happy with the news that a solid profit was recorded and that the promise for the future was rosy. The Halifax stop was the first in a grand tour that included visits to company operations and a dinner and reception both in New Glasgow and Sydney. Our first stop was New Glasgow. We were hosting community leaders and local company officials at the Norfolk Hotel, and an enormous lobster had just been placed before me when the hotel manager, Walter MacPherson, told me that I had an urgent phone call. I excused myself from my seatmates, Harry and Bill Sutherland of the *New Glasgow News*, Jim Cameron of the town's CKEC radio, and W. J. (Bill) Flemming, superintendent of the railcar plant at Trenton. I took the call in the manger's office.

Harry Calnek of the Canadian Press was on the line. He told me in an excited voice that there had been another explosion at the Springhill coal mine. Two years earlier an explosion there had claimed the lives of 39 men. While his information was sketchy, his news had the portents of a similar disaster. Before returning to the dining room, I made several quick calls to Springhill. With the help of the operator I managed to reach Dave Morse, the industrial relations officer at the mines. The news he told me was calamitous. There had been a major underground upheaval no more than thirty minutes before, and hundreds of men had been working underground at the Number Two colliery, the deepest coal mine in the world. They were working the 4:00 p.m. to midnight shift, and thus far no word had been received from underground. All of the phone lines had been knocked out, as was the underground rail system.

As I talked to the soft-spoken Morse, he paused to tell me that he had just heard that the first men to reach the pithead said, "It's hell down there and a lot of men have been killed." He added, "It could be worse than in 1956." I had never met Dave Morse but I knew he was a senior employee there. I instructed him to call every hotel and motel, in both Springhill and nearby Amherst, and reserve all available rooms in my name; as well, to call the phone company and have additional phones and a teletype machine installed. Judging from the previous disaster, I knew that shortly we would be inundated with media people from all over North America. I told him that I would be en route shortly and that he should prepare for a media avalanche.

Sir Roy was giving his welcoming remarks to the town leaders when I re-entered the dining room and as quietly as possible, went to the head table to whisper the bad news to Albert Fairley. Sir Roy scowled in my direction, resenting the intrusion, and I walked back to my seat. Fairley whispered to Roy, retrieved the microphone, and told the gathering that the meeting would be shortened as there had been a reported mine explosion at Springhill and a number of those present would have to depart. Bill Flemming volunteered to drive us; it was about eighty miles to the coal-mining town. Harry Sutherland, Al Fairley, and A. C. MacDonald, the executive vice president of A. V. Roe, joined us. Before leaving, Fairley had called Harold Gordon, the coal-mining boss in Sydney, to tell him the bad news. Gordon had already left Cape Breton with a crew of draegermen, miners trained for rescue operations.

When we arrived in the mining town we went straight to the company office where we were met by Dave Morse, and the office manager, Norm MacNeil. We left Harry with Norm, and the three of us went to the small office at the pithead with Dave Morse. As we entered the office there was a coal-blackened miner pouring out a story of terror to another man, obviously an official. We didn't interrupt. Introductions could wait. The official, a slim, dark-haired man in his early forties, gave us a frown but continued to take notes. The miner told him that there had been a resounding "crack" underground, and immediately the walls and ceiling of sections of the pit had begun to erupt and cave in. Now, two hours after the explosion, he estimated that there were close to 150 men still underground. Hundreds, he said, had made their way to the surface by walking up the deep and darkened slope.

Grimly, we introduced ourselves to the two men in question: Randolph Carter, the assistant mine manager; and Art (Noisy) Noiles, a senior underground official. Carter updated us on the situation, which he said was not promising. This had to be a special nightmare for the soft-spoken Carter, who had been the manager of the Number One colliery when it had exploded two years before, killing 39 men. The three of us left and walked to the staff house, just up the street from the mine property. We were greeted by Margaret Philpott, the housekeeper, and her assistant and daughter, Jean, who was in her early forties. Both were long-time employees of the coal company. Before heading back to the office to help set up the pressroom, I went to my room to put on a clean shirt. Alas, all I had left there were formal shirts for cocktail parties and dinners. I decided to leave on the one I was wearing, and it would stay put for another 24 hours.

When I arrived at the office it had taken on all the trappings of a newspaper city room. Desks were neatly set in rows, a typewriter sitting on each one, and teletype machines were being installed in a corner of the office. Norm MacNeil and Dave Morse had moved quickly and efficiently. The avalanche was about to begin. Fifteen minutes after I got to the office, the first of the media crowd arrived. It was my old friend Bob MacDonald of the Toronto *Telegram*, who had been in neighbouring Moncton on another story when he heard about the disaster. Coal towns were not new to him, as he had grown up in Stellarton in Pictou County. Shortly after, Doug Harkness, then a nineteen-year-old cub with CKCW, Moncton, checked in, followed by Joan Watson of CKDH, Amherst. Within the hour dozens of media people were milling around.

Our staff was reinforced as well. Lawrence Doucet, the company's public relations officer in Sydney, arrived in early morning; and Jim Loveys, the PR manager of our cousins, the Canadian Car Company, flew in from Montreal to help. Harry Sutherland had stayed on and was giving some of the local reporters assignments as "stringers" for some of the big American papers and radio stations looking for reports. It proved a busy and hectic night and day. There had been 178 men underground when the explosion, later termed a "bump," occurred the night before, but when I left the pressroom at midnight, Friday, there were 94 men unaccounted for. Those who had scrambled up the darkened shafts, through and over the rubble, had got out within hours of the bump. There had been no new developments for hours, though the rescue crews were underground seeking more survivors. The reporters spent the day interviewing family members and survivors on what they had experienced, and delivering backgrounders on the town and the history of coal mining in the area.

When I arrived back at the staff house there was a note from Mrs. Philpott telling me that there were sandwiches and milk in the fridge. As I opened the fridge door I heard a voice saying, "Don't take all the sandwiches, laddie." It was Harold M. C. Gordon, the vice president and general manager of Dosco's extensive coal holdings. I had not seen him since his arrival in Springhill as he had gone underground immediately, along with his draegermen. He had obviously been to the washhouse at the pithead, as he was dressed in casual clothes and was clean-faced. In a sarcastic tone, he said, "Who is this Mr. Patterson who seems to have taken command of things here in Springhill?" Obviously angry he continued, "To get rooms for the draegermen I had to get permission from a C. A. Patterson. He seems to have taken charge of everything." Then he added, "I am the boss here and I don't take orders from some young kid [I was 29] who seems to want to coddle the press. To me they're just ghouls. If I had my way I would surround the property with fifty policemen and beat the hell out of them if they crossed the line."

Even in his sixties, Harold was a menacing man in some respects. He was big—over six feet—and superbly conditioned after a life underground. He was one of the last oligarchs, and in the coal towns he was Lord on Highest. I wasn't intimidated as I knew him quite well, had travelled with him occasionally, and had been underground with him several times in Cape Breton. So I stood my ground. "Yes, Harold," I said, "and your way of doing things has made us bloody unpopular in the province. We're seen as a bunch of bullies." He said nothing but gave me a cold stare. I said, "We couldn't get a reporter here if we paid them unless there was something of significance happening, and the fact that we have a hundred or so men killed has attracted not only their attention but that of the general public."

"Put away the damn milk," he said, "and sit down with me and have a real drink." With that he pulled out a bottle of Bells 20-Year Reserve. It was his favourite Scotch, and whenever a senior official checked into the Dosco suite at the Isle Royale Hotel in Sydney, a bottle of Bell's awaited with a short note from the coal czar.

He was a handsome man with pale blue eyes set in an angular face and the trim build of an athlete. He was also a man who knew no fear as he had worked at this perilous trade of coal mining all of his adult life and had battled underground fires, cave-ins, and other assorted dangers that go with the business. He pushed a glass towards me, reached over a poured a hefty dram. "Drink that and you'll be able to push over a bus," he said, smiling for the first time. I took it as a peace offering. He added, "Arnie,"—I was no longer "laddie"—"you have more patience than I have, and I must admit from what I have heard and seen that you're doing a good job. You'll have no trouble from me or my people." A complete and surprising concession, as Harold Gordon was a man who never knew how to back up, or not often at least. We sat at the table for at least an hour and we had a few drinks and he told me of developments underground and about the shocking, frightening situation that prevailed. Just about everything had been uprooted and destroyed; there were major blockages in the tunnels, which prevented speedy advances by the rescue crews. While 88 men had made it to the surface, he had little hope for the 94 who were missing.

I was to have many involvements with Harold Gordon in my five years at Dosco. While the circumstances were often difficult—mine closures, layoffs, coal commission hearings, and related bad news—our personal relationship was always pleasant. When I think back through my life, Harold Gordon stands out as one of the most remarkable men I have known, faults and all. He was a hard-nosed, stubborn, arbitrary man, but a man of great nobility nonetheless. That night in the kitchen at Springhill he told me things that I have never forgotten. "Your know, laddie,—this time a friendly "laddie"—"I have, and have had almost all of my adult life, a terrible responsibility. Lives to protect and save. There is nothing in life as painful for me, devastating a better word, than to lose the life of a miner." He continued, pouring a little more Scotch in both glasses, "You have your job to do and I respect that, but public opinion has never been a major concern of mine. I have to live with my conscience, and if it is comfortable with my actions, I do not seek the blessings of others." Wow! Never in my life have I met anyone so sure of his convictions and his decisions. I have always been happy when I thought right a little better than fifty percent of the time.

Our chat produced another benefit for me, and for the company. The following day, he agreed to appear for a press conference after coming up from underground. It was an exercise that was to be repeated at least five times in the days ahead. The strange thing about this press-shy, reluctant dragon was that he was a natural for television. Despite his reserved nature, and supposed disdain for public recognition, he was a spectacular success with the media. He would stand in front of the assembled, his face blackened with coal dust and his imposing frame clad in pit clothes, and he would give a Shakespearian performance. Although he had moved to Cape Breton from his native Scotland when he was six, he still at times had the Scots' accent. It was exaggerated, and I thought not unkindly, for theatrical effect. The media, certainly the Americans and out-of-towners, saw him as a heroic figure. Of course, he always spoke not only with authority and knowledge, but also with absolute certainty. He told of the horrible conditions that existed underground, and of the slow progress that was being made to explore the deeps as solid rock and accumulated debris blocked their way. There was no optimism. He said no one could be left alive, given the violence of the bump.

Springhill was a town dominated by coal. Coal was first mined there as early as 1833, and it was the town's only industry. Its people were not unfamiliar with tragedy; in the heart of its downtown stood a stone and marble monument topped by the figure of a miner—a tribute to the 125 men who had died in Springhill's first major disaster in 1891. And, of course, there had been the explosion that killed 39 miners in 1956, and a fire that had devastated the downtown only a year later. It was a community totally mindful of the peril that it constantly faced. At the time of the 1958 bump, Number Two mine was the only operating colliery in the town. Numbers One, Three, and Four had been closed. Number Two was the deepest mine in North America; its highest level was 4,400 feet underground, and the deepest working face was 13,800 feet deep. No electrical tools or explosives were used in this mine for fear that sparks would set off an underground blast. The men used compressed air-picks to chip out the coal. The mine had experienced a few minor bumps that summer, and as a result the company, under chief engineer Louis Frost, relined the faces of the working galleries. (Another Brit, Louie was known as "the long wall man.") With this system the men worked the entire thickness of the seam, and in Number Two this meant carving out a tunnel 400 feet long. While certain leaders in the United Mine workers Union were unhappy with this action, Frost had just inspected the colliery on October 22, and said the mine was never in better condition. Harold Gordon, who met with Monson Harrison, president of the UMW local, argued strongly in favour of the realignment. During the two weeks after the Springhill disaster rumours kept reaching me at the pressroom that widows of the slain miners were going to descend on the staff house and kill Gordon, whom they blamed for the tragedy. Nothing ever came of this threat, and I treated it as what I thought it was—just a rumour.

There were no new developments at the mine. The rescue work, now focused on the retrievals of bodies, continued. The mood was pessimistic. At one point there were more than two hundred media people at the scene. With hope diminishing, many had already left town.

At 1:45 p.m. on Tuesday, October 29—almost seven full days after the bump—there was a startling development. Blair Phillips, the chief mine surveyor, went into the tunnel near the 13,000 foot level to do a routine check for gas. He attached a bottle of water to an exposed air pipe. If the air was contaminated with gas the colour of the water in the bottle would change, indicating that breathing conditions would not allow anyone to survive at that level. Phillips bent over the pipe so that his helmet light would shine on the opening. Little did he know that at the other end of the pipe, trapped miners Harold Brine and Gourley Kempt, two of the twelve men sealed off in a pocket of the mine, were checking for sounds they thought they heard coming from above. Brine saw the light shining through the pipe opening and alerted Kempt, who immediately started to holler, "There are twelve of us in here! Come and get us out!"

Needless to say there was great relief and happiness on both ends of the pipe. The nearly-starved, unshaven, battered twelve had received an answer to their prayers. With solid rock and coal in their way, the "barefaced" rescue crew chipped away, and at 4:30 p.m. they were just forty feet away. By 6:30, however, they had been able to advance only five feet in two hours of hectic digging. Fresh crews were sent down on a continuing basis. The men smashed at the wall, and at 9:30 p.m. they were only twenty-five feet from breakthrough.

Back up top, Dr. Arnold Burden, who had worked in the mines during college days, approached the mine manager, George Calder and suggested sending water down through a copper tubing inserted in the air pipe. Calder immediately agreed and they sent out for pipe, which was quickly inserted. Dr. Burden went down to the 13,000-foot level, worked his way up through the line and, when he got to the air pipe, shouted that were going to try and send water down. Gourley Kempt on the other end said they could sure use it as they had been without water for days. The doctor gave strict instructions: "Take only one mouthful at a time. Swallow slowly," he said, "then count to five hundred and take another swallow."

"Did you say to count to five hundred?" Kempt asked. The answer was in the affirmative. "Doctor," came back the reply, "some of these guys can't count to five hundred." The experiment worked and the men captured the water in their water cans.

News that men had been found alive was sent to the surface along with the names of the twelve survivors. Jubilation reigned in the downtown streets. It seemed that every car in Springhill swung into the main street, their horns blaring in one big celebratory traffic jam. Hundreds of people ran to the pithead, although it was not until 12:30 a.m. that the rescuers made the final breakthrough. And it was not until 3:30 a.m. that Gourley Kempt, the first man to surface, emerged on a stretcher. Despite the early hour, hundreds were lined up outside the shaft terminal. By 5:00 p.m. on that Wednesday morning, all twelve were out of the pit and hospitalized at All Saints. There were two badly injured men, one with a broken hip, the other a broken shoulder. The others, while ten pounds thinner and suffering bruises and minor cuts, were said to be in good shape.

In the face of the great tragedy, rejoicing in Springhill was short-lived. The day after the twelve were rescued, Harold Gordon stated with some certainty that there was little chance that men would be found alive, although recovery activities would continue. At this news a pall settled over all. Little more than a week had expired, but it had been a hectic time for the media people. By and large the reportage from the scene had been fair and of a high standard. Despite the competition a camaraderie had developed among the reporters and many new friendships were established. With the drama now played out, many made plans to return home on Friday. I thought it might be a nice gesture on the company's part (for we had been treated fairly) to hold a small reception. Given the sadness that prevailed in Springhill, it would not have been appropriate to hold any gathering there. So I called the Fort Cumberland Hotel in Amherst on Thursday and booked the ballroom for that night. I also booked a room for myself as I planned to stay over. I alerted the office as to my planned whereabouts, and suggested that I be called should anything out of the ordinary occur.

The party was a great success. After a hard-driving week, one in which most of the reporters had worked eighteen- or twenty-hour days, the crew was ready for relaxation. Everyone was in an upbeat mood because of the rescue of the twelve miners, and this gave them something to celebrate. I think we had about a hundred people turn up. Although no entertainment had been planned, Ray Timson of the *Toronto Star* proved himself an accomplished party pianist. Tom Toner of Moncton's CKCW radio stepped in as an able songleader, and the party whirled on until shortly after midnight. I was awakened by a ringing phone just after 5:00 a.m. A voice on the other end said, "More men have been found alive." I called downstairs and directed a bellhop to make the rounds and awaken all journalists.

Springhill is only about a half-hour's drive from Amherst, and when I arrived on Main Street, people were already streaming towards the pithead in an atmosphere of elation and excitement. It was hallelujah time again. Before long the media troops arrived, most unshaven and a some a bit shaky from their night of celebration. In a second miraculous recovery, seven men were brought to the surface alive. The recovery process was much quicker in this instance, and by 9:15 that morning all seven were in All Saints Hospital, and all were in relatively good condition despite their ordeal.

When I got back to the staff house early in the afternoon I was told there was an important call for me from Ed Sullivan in New York. At that time the Ed Sullivan Show on CBS Sunday nights was the biggest show on television. I called back and the host himself came on the line. He wanted me to bring two of the miners to New York the next day for that night's show. He suggested it would be helpful to the Springhill Disaster Fund which Mayor Ralph Gilroy had announced a few days before. I told him I didn't know what shape the miners were in but that I would check and call him back. I went to the armouries, which had been turned into a temporary hospital for those not seriously injured. I talked to Caleb Rushton and Gourley Kempt, both of the team of twelve, who said they were well enough to make the proposed trip to New York. I had also talked to Dr. Burden who said he would be pleased to come with us. Wives were invited, of course. Before I left, Gourley expressed concern that his wife really might not have the right clothes for the big city. I told both him and Rushton to send their wives shopping and to forward the bill to me at Dosco. They took me at my word for they each spent more than $400, a pretty good sum in 1958.

(left to right) Unnamed President of the Public Relations Society; Roy Guest, editor of the Imperial Oil Review which was cited as an outstanding company publication; Arnie Patterson, named Public Relations Man of the Year in Canada for his work in connection with the Springhill mine disaster in 1958.

I called Glo, who often visited with her parents in Halifax while I was on the road, and though she was pregnant she readily agreed to come. We had seen one another for only an hour or two in the previous two weeks. Before leaving, Al Fairley warned me to keep a low profile on the trip. He was fearful that people would interpret my participation in the Sullivan show as an effort by Dosco to promote the disaster fund, and thus evade some of its own financial responsibilities. We stopped at Boston en route to New York. There we were met by Norman Knight, president of the CBS's Yankee Broadcasting System, who came as an emissary for Ed Sullivan. Norman was to become a good friend of mine, and he helped me with CFDR radio some years later. Coincidentally, Ambassador Joseph Kennedy, the father of the future president, was at the same airport to meet Lord Beaverbrook, the Canadian who became a highly successful British news baron. Beaverbrook spoke warmly to the two miners. After checking in at the New York Sheraton we went directly to CBC Studio 50 for a late afternoon rehearsal. Sullivan's son- in-law, Bob Prechtm, met us at the door and escorted Gourley and Rushton to the stage. I walked out front and took an audience seat some distance from the stage. When Sullivan, in the midst of organizing his rehearsal learned who the two men were, he immediately went to them and embraced them. He talked to them for a few minutes, then went to the front of the stage and, overlooking the orchestra lights, cupped his hands over his eyes and yelled, "Arnie, are you out there?" Beckoned, I went to meet him. He confided that the men seemed a bit nervous, and suggested that I join the interview. I demurred, mentioning Al Fairley's concern. He agreed and then proposed that rather than do an interview, he would introduce Gourley and Rushton and their wives from the audience and make appropriate remarks.

The next day, upon returning from a bus tour of New York City, I had a phone call from Ed Sullivan asking what we had planned for that night. Nothing had been finalized, so he suggested that we see the hottest musical in town, *My Fair Lady*. He had six tickets. The problem was that there were now nine of us; Phyllis Griffin, an old friend from the Tely in Toronto, was there covering the event. Rather magnanimously Glo suggested that the Springhillers use the tickets (even though she loved the music from *My Fair Lady*) and that the three of us take in another show. We opted for *The Bells Are Ringing* with Judy Holiday, and that was very funny and enjoyable. At breakfast the next morning Gourley said their show was just so-so; they would have rather heard some "cowboy music." Glo and I did see *My Fair Lady*, the road version, when it came to Montreal a year or two later.

Shortly after, we returned to our normal life in Montreal, but the episode in Springhill was not forgotten. In fact that year I was named Public Relations Man of the Year by the Canadian Public Relations Society for my work at Springhill. The next Summer Al Fairley and I attended ceremonies on the old mine site as the Town of Springhill was awarded the esteemed Carnegie Medal for the courage and bravery shown under difficult circumstances. I had gone to Springhill about a month after the whole affair with Al Fairley, Harold Gordon, and company lawyer Rufus Cromwell to formally announce the permanent closure of the mine and the end of Dosco's long involvement in the town itself. This caused a bitter, if short-lived, reaction with the mayor, the UMW, and others assailing the company for its planned departure. But internally there was never any question as to what decision should be taken; 114 men had been killed in mines there over a two-year period, and it would have been criminal for the company to carry on. Most of Dosco's properties were turned over to the town. The company owned a few nice houses on MacDougall Street, just up from the mine. One was the staff house occupied by the Philpotts. I am pleased to report that I was able to get them the purchase of this well-conditioned, five-bedroom house for $1,000.

One other sidebar was that with the need to feed the draegermen and other officials, I had a tent erected on the mining property to house what I jokingly referred to as the

"Dosco Cafe." Benny Dyson, a well-known Truro restaurateur, volunteered his services and ran the operation in concert with a number of Canadian army cooks. Most of the food was supplied by the Red Cross. It was a huge tent; if I remember correctly it could seat up to seventy people at one time. Mayor Gilroy suggested that it might be a nice gesture if we could extend the food services to the families of the miners, who were gathered at the pithead waiting for news. I consented, and we substantially increased our services. As I had no budget for this operation, and had observed a packed house on a few occasions, I thought it might soften the blow if I let Al Fairley know now that I had an unauthorized activity going on. One night I invited Fairley and Allan MacDonald to the "Dosco Cafe" and, intrigued, they accepted the invitation. They were impressed to find the large tent, sawdust on the floor, and a beehive of activity. A month or so later when I got a $1,300 bill for the odds and ends involved, no one raised an eyebrow in giving approval. In the meantime we had served over three thousand meals—nothing fancy, for the most part a good stew.

For a number of years, I visited Springhill periodically and looked up old friends, especially the Philpotts. Just last Summer I went to Springhill and appeared as a guest on a television documentary about the disaster produced by the History channel. Happily the town itself has survived, and with the location of a correctional centre and several small industries there it looks as prosperous and as busy now as it was in its coal-mining heyday. It is a place that has a warm spot in my heart even 42 years later.

Chapter Seven: The Bull and Dief the Chief

The early days of A. V. Roe's takeover of Dosco were promising, despite the anxiety existing within the executive ranks of the steel and coal company. Fairley's arrival allayed a lot of their doubt and fear. The scalping that had taken place in the manufacturing sector preceded his arrival, and it was clear to all that Harvey Smith had been the assassin. And yet even Smith's harsh critics, of which there were many, would have to agree that his retirement of the four key managers in the manufacturing sector—at the shipyards, the railcar plant, the bridge company, and the steel fabricating plant—was logical. All four had been past the normal retirement age: three in their late sixties and one in his seventies. Their replacements were men in their thirties and forties. One of the most remarkable things he did in the early days of the takeover was to have painted all of the plants under his jurisdiction. The paint companies had to love Harvey Smith, for these plants encompassed acres and acres of space plus buildings under roof. The buildings were painted white, the stationary parts yellow, and the moving parts green. It was quite a staggering transition, especially when you consider that the Trenton Works alone had a million square feet of space under roofs and more than a hundred cranes. Psychologically it signalled to local communities that there was new life in the old outfit.

Compared to the highly energized and opinionated Smith, new president Al Fairley was neither demanding nor arbitrary. In fact I would say that he demonstrated some of his strongest management skills as a conciliator. He was a long way from being a ruthless, hard-nosed buccaneer and much more a Southern gentleman of refinement, great manners, and attractive accent bespeaking his Southern roots. From the outset he sided with the "old crowd": Harry McAvoy, the steel sales vice president; Clem Anson, vice president of steel at Sydney; Cliff Broadbent, vice president, secretary; Harold Gordon, vice president of mining; and the other long-time Dosco veterans. This cadre was joined by J. E. (Earl) Clubb, vice president of finance, who, although recruited from CanCar, comfortably joined these ranks and in turn sycophantically echoed his laments against Roe and against Harvey Smith in particular. If this group was joined at the hip on any question, it was that they all were opposed to Smith. He was their target, usually behind closed doors. Now that I am older, and have had many years to reflect on the situation, I think that their reaction was in part rebellion, or at least rejection, of the new boys at Roe.

In 1958, my first year at Dosco, we seemed to be on the high road. Most of the varied operations were relatively successful and employment remained high. And given A. V. Roe's added financial muscle, with company goods and services worth $200 million, multiply that twenty times over in today's market, pressure was being applied to steel buyers in Ontario to expand their purchases with Dosco. While the two giants were worlds apart, there were promising advantages to the marriage: Dosco, with its head office long established in Montreal, was a strong presence in that city, which was at that time the equal of burgeoning Toronto; Roe's base, like those of most of its key players, was in Toronto and elsewhere in Ontario. We sort of had the best of both worlds.

Though resident in Montreal, much of my work was centred in Nova Scotia where the company had for so long played a prominent role. The relationship between company and province was not an easy one, and there were few days when there was not a problem on one of the fronts. I spent considerable time travelling from Montreal to Sydney, Halifax, and New Glasgow. As a Nova Scotian boy it was wonderful, even though the problems at times were perplexing. Not many nights passed that I didn't receive a phone call from Ian MacNeil, the managing editor of the *Cape Breton Post*, looking for a response to problems relating either to steel or coal. He was a diligent journalist, and he and his boss, Roy Duchemin, the publisher, became good friends of mine and remained so until their deaths a few years ago.

Coal was a much greater public-relations headache for the company (and for me) than steel which was at that time profitable. While there were operating mines in Sydney Mines, New Waterford, Glace Bay, Thorburn in Pictou County, and Springhill in Cumberland County, which employed a total of ten thousand miners, they were barely profitable. The only factor that allowed their continuance on a major scale was government railway subsidies, or, as they were more politely termed, "subventions." This program, which helped the Dominion Coal Company to move its coal, came as a provision in the Maritime Freight Rates Act enacted in the early 1930s. In Dosco, industrial and public relations were two separate functions although I worked closely with Percy Pattee, the corporation's overall industrial relations boss. I also developed a close relationship with most of the United Mine Workers' executive, including William H. (Bull) Marsh, president of District 26; Jack H. Delaney, the international member; Steve Dolhanty, the vice president; and others. In time we became friends, although we were on the opposite sides of the fence.

We had a good breakthrough in the summer of 1958 when Ontario Hydro announced the purchase of $2 million worth of Nova Scotia coal. That had been a market denied to Nova Scotia, as it was cheaper for Ontario users to buy coal shipped from the nearby

United States. I beat the PR drum heavily, and Toronto newspaper friends helped in getting us good play in the media there. Trumpets sounded in Nova Scotia as well, as this was seen as a major boost to the long-ailing industry. Arrangements were made to have Harold M. C. Gordon, the vice president of mining, speak to the Canadian Mining Society, which was meeting in Toronto early that fall. The speech was well-reported and it gave Nova Scotia coal further attention. In a meeting with Gordon and Al Fairley prior to the event, I suggested that it would be a good show of unity if we were to invite the newly installed UMW president, Bull Marsh, to the dinner and arrange for him to sit at the head table. This, I said, would also give company officials an opportunity to better know the new union boss. Harold almost snarled at me. He said, pressing the base of his thumb forcibly on the table, "I'll put him under there as I have done to the others and I squeeze and squeeze until I have them shaped up." Bull didn't come to Toronto with us.

For me, it was as if I were a dual personality, each with its own set of responsibilities. My greatest responsibility, of course, was to the company that employed me; and the second was to my home province of Nova Scotia. I did, however, develop a genuine liking for the UMW fellows and usually visited with them at their offices when I was in Glace Bay. Occasionally they would visit Montreal, often on returning from visits to Pittsburgh and UMW headquarters. I would often take them to hockey games or other sporting events. We were all at ringside the night that Yvon Durelle, the fighting fisherman from New Brunswick, fought world light heavyweight champion Archie Moore for the world title at the Montreal Forum. In addition to Marsh, Delaney, and Dolhanty, Brigadier Michael Wardell, the eccentric publisher of the *Fredericton Gleaner* and *Atlantic Advocate* was with us. It was a different social setting for the Brigadier, who in his younger days was an intimate friend of the Prince of Wales, later King Edward VIII.

It was a spectacular fight. Durelle came within a whisker of winning the world championship, knocking the wily Moore down twice in the early going. From the fifth round on though, it became a blood fest as Moore systematically, if carefully, pummelled the New Brunswicker with jabs and hooks, severely cutting him. By the end of the battle Durelle was a bleeding hulk. The decision went to the champion and this without dispute. The veteran Archie was, however, lucky to have escaped from an early knockout. The usually sedate Brigadier, wearing his black eyepatch and dressed in semi-formal, dark attire, was a standout in this sporting crowd, and on one occasion he stood atop his chair shouting, "Clout him, Yvon! Clout him!" The mining men watched in amazement. The only thing missing was a black umbrella for the Brig to wave.

On another occasion we, the three union leaders and I, were gathered in my room in the Nova Scotian Hotel in Halifax. There had been production cutbacks in Cape Breton and the UMW had been beating us up in the media. I remember that I had a copy of the Dominion Coal Company's annual report with me; I opened it and started to quote significant figures to my audience. The profit was minimal, and for about the tenth year in a row no dividends were paid to the preferred shareholders. I remember heatedly saying that if their objective was to bring the company to its knees, they had succeeded. I said that without dividends and profits no one was really concerned and that the only benefits being gained at the time was employment for the miners themselves. I added that the men in the pits were getting far more out of the company than the poor abandoned shareholders. I am not sure that they accepted my arguments fully, but we did establish some common ground, which served both them and me well in the future. I always thought that they knew I was supportive of their general aims, if not certain of their specific actions.

A year or so later my friendship with Marsh and company was to prove beneficial to both them and the company. Given the distances that had to be travelled underground—several of the mining operations were more than five or six miles from the pithead, and under the ocean—costs continued to escalate and sales were not buoyant. Many of the traditional coal markets of even 25 years before had been lost. Home use, once a major sale factor, had been almost totally lost to oil. The railways, once major users, had gone to diesel locomotives, and industrial uses also were being lost on a daily basis. The only major coal users left were the hydro power plants, and even here many were gearing up for the use of oil and gas. So it seemed that we were in a losing battle.

Coal company officials had concluded that Number Sixteen colliery in New Waterford should be closed. It had been a mainstay in the coal-mining town of about eight thousand people, and was the mine in which Bull Marsh himself had worked. When the decision to close was officially announced in late 1961, the union responded with an immediate and fighting response in the press. It clearly annoyed coal boss Harold Gordon that the union went over his head in this way, and he demanded a meeting with the company president, Al Fairley. Fairley, an old hand himself in coal and steel, was sympathetic but nonetheless firmly supported the decision for closure. The bleeding, he said, had to stop. Working closely with him, I knew his feelings intimately and I knew that there would be no compromise. The mine would be closed. While a gentle man, he had a strong, American point of view when it came to closing down losing operations; and when trouble occurred, he was both baffled and angered at intervention from governments, at any and all levels. He said to me on many occasions, "If this was in the States those operations would be closed without any real debate." He preached the dictate that things that don't make money are of little use to anyone in the long-term, you can't give a raise and jobs cannot be guaranteed.

When the UMW delegation arrived at our head offices for the meeting with the president, they were shown to my office. We were in fancy new digs on the extensive CanCar property in the west end of Montreal, where we had moved the year before. Marsh, Delaney, and Dolhanty comprised the delegation. They were to meet with

Fairley; Earl Clubb, the vice president of finance; and Harold Gordon. Marsh was in a particularly combative mood. He said closure would be a deathblow to New Waterford. After giving them coffee and suggesting they cool off a bit, I said, "Do you want an idea as to how you can save the mine?" Startled, they agreed almost in one voice. Then I told them what I thought they should do. I said that Fairley was going to turn them down flat because of the losses, but rather than push him hard and directly, they should suggest that the company, with the UMW support, ask the federal government to assist with the losses for a period of time. If the government failed to respond favourably the mine would have to be closed.

I didn't attend the meeting in the president's office, but the UMW trio came out all smiles, telling me that Fairley had agreed to their proposal to seek government help to keep the mine open. After they departed I went in to see the president and he too was all smiles. He said, "You won't believe what happened. Bull actually said he didn't want the company to lose any more money and that, unless the government agreed to support a new plan, he would agree to closure." Even the granite-willed Harold Gordon was surprised at Marsh's mellow stand. I offered little in the way of comment. A meeting with Prime Minister Diefenbaker and senior members of his government was scheduled for the next day in Ottawa. I drove over with Fairley, Gordon, and our lawyer, Rufus Cromwell. The prospect of a pleasant time was unlikely. Diefenbaker was annoyed with the company for its closure announcement, and our affiliation with A. V. Roe had caused him so much discomfort. We met in one of the large committee rooms in the East Block. The Honourable Paul Comptois, mines minister, was joined in attendance by the Honourable George Hees, the Nova Scotian in the cabinet. There was no smile on the prime minister's face when we entered the room, and no handshake, simply a shrug of the shoulders and a shake of the head as he took his seat at the head of the table. All portents seemed unpromising.

The first words of the meeting were chilling. The prime minister, with almost religious zeal, reminded the company officials of its obligations to the communities in which it worked, and he went on at length about the hardship the mine closure in New Waterford would inflict on its residents. His lament evidenced his strong bias against the company, and his rhetoric was reminiscent of the small-town lawyer trying to impress a jury. Encouraged by the prime minister's obvious disdain for the company and its proposed closure, Bill Marsh jumped in and joined the attack, expressing gratitude for Mr. Diefenbaker's understanding of the grave situation and his "grave concern for the plight of the miners." But the agitated prime minister was apparently not going to award apples to the union for he snapped, "You seem to have had a change of tune, Mr. Marsh, for your comments in the *Cape Breton Post* about me and my government were hardly favourable. "Nothing was really determined at that meeting, although the prime minister later told the press that the matter was being studied. Some weeks later the company made a submission to the government, indicating that the mine could remain open if the government was prepared to assist with the losses. Shortly thereafter an agreement was reached. The mine was able to operate for a few more years, but ultimately it was closed.

As I reflect on these times so many years later I have nothing but warm feelings for the union bosses. While they caused me anguish on occasion, they were faithful to their cause and support to the men they represented. However, the problem was that, in the coal industry, there were no winners—only losers. The union bosses were good men trying to do an impossible job, as were we on the company side. I also had a special feeling for the coal towns: Springhill, Glace Bay, New Waterford, Sydney Mines. These were in some respects tired towns, reflective of a less prosperous industry, yet the people were open and generous. A few years ago my golf partner Dr. Gavin McInnes and I played in a tournament at Pugwash. I had asked a friend, Eddie Harper of Halifax, to book us reservations at a motel. He suggested we try the Farmer's Market. When we got to Pugwash we found that the market really was a market, situated behind a big white house which we assumed was a bed and breakfast operation. We went into the market and met a young woman, Ellen Macauley, who operated the facility with her husband. She took us into the house and showed us the bedrooms, asking what we would like for breakfast, and welcoming us to the beer and pie in the fridge should we need a snack.

That night when we returned from golf we sat around with the Macauleys, Ellen and Brian, and talked. I asked how business was, and if American visitors were key to the operation. She smiled and somewhat surprised said, "No, our business mostly comes from the campers." I asked her how many rooms they operated, thinking bed and breakfast. She again smiled, "This is not a bed and breakfast. You're our guests." Eddie Harper, unable to find any available accommodations for us, had sent us to the home of his sister-in-law, Ellen Macauley, and she and Brian had taken us in. Then I found out she was from Springhill. That figured. Who more generous than someone from a coal town? Who but someone from the Bay, Springhill, Waterford, or the like would take in two strangers and accommodate them? That's the coal town for you. One time when I was en route to Toronto, this long after Dosco, I encountered Bill Marsh on an Air Canada flight. I was travelling executive class, and he, the good union boss, was in economy. The seat next to me was unoccupied, so the Bull joined me and we talked over old and good times. The stewardess was not pleased with this development, however, and kneeling down, politely informed Mr. Marsh that he would have to return to the economy section of the aircraft. He smiled and told her he was comfortable where he was. As she was about to reinforce her arguments, I put up my hand and said, "Miss, forget it. This is one battle you'll lose. He's a union boss. He has spent his life winning arguments."

Chapter Eight: The Arrow Dream Ends

It may have been the greatest Canadian creation of all time. Certainly supporters of the Avro Arrow thought so as Canada and Canadians designed and built the fastest supersonic jet fighter plane of its era. But on Friday, February 20, 1959, a dream was shattered when the federal government under Prime Minister John Diefenbaker cancelled A. V. Roe's contract to produce the aircraft. That day was to become known in the Toronto region as "Black Friday," as the cancellation meant the loss of fifteen thousand jobs at the Malton plants of Avro Aircraft and Orenda Engines. Forty-two years has elapsed since that tragic time; one would expect the Arrow to be little more than a faded remembrance. But in recent years CBC television produced a major, full-length documentary entitled *The Arrow*, which has greatly revived interest. Canadian actor Dan Akroyd played the lead role of Crawford Gordon, president of A. V. Roe Canada Limited, producer of the aircraft. Gordon proved as ill-fated as the plane itself. The film took its inspiration from a biography on Gordon entitled *Arrow Through the Heart*, a brilliant work authored by Greig Stewart, whose earlier work was *Shutting Down The National Dream*, a detailed story of the final days of the Arrow. While gloom settled over Toronto with its heavy payroll loss, the dark clouds also descended on Dosco bastions in Montreal and Nova Scotia, for our white knight had been shot down. Rather than becoming a saviour for Dosco and its troubled parts, the crumbling Roe empire rested on them like a heavy burden.

I had little to do with the Arrow (both Avro and Orenda had strong public relations forces), but I had visited the plants on several occasions and travelled the country with the top executives, including chairman Sir Roy Dobson and president Crawford Gordon. They were undoubtedly the driving forces behind Roe's growth and ambition. In the late summer of 1958 the company brass, including Dobson and Gordon, toured Roe's Canadian installations. I had the responsibility for the eastern part of the tour and travelled with the entourage. Unbeknownst to me and others at Dosco, Roe's multimillion-dollar contract with the government for the Arrow was in jeopardy. One night in a suite in the old Newfoundland Hotel in St. John's, we drank a jubilant toast to Avro test pilot John

Maritimers inspect the Avro Arrow at Malton. (left to right) Brigadier J. Michael Wardell, publisher of the Fredericton Gleaner; Frank MacKinnon, president of Prince of Wales University in Charlottetown; O. Nelson Mann, executive vice president of the Atlantic Provinces Economic Council in Halifax; Jan Zurkowski, test pilot; John Plant, president of Avro Aircraft Limited; Arnie Patterson; Frank H. Sobey, president of Sobey's Limited, Stellarton; and R.D. Hurst, president of Simpson-Hurst Limited in Halifax.

Woodman who had flown the Arrow at a speed of 1400 miles an hour earlier that day. Surely, Sir Roy told the small gathering, the government would have to be impressed.

A few months later Crawford Gordon, in an acrimonious meeting with Prime Minister Diefenbaker, was told the contract would be cancelled. This news was not confirmed nor the edict enforced for six months, but the die had been cast. News reports said the exchange between the prime minister and the industrialist was heated. Further, it was rumoured that Gordon had been drinking prior to the meeting and that the teetotalling prime minister took great offence. Given my own exposure to Gordon, his quick temper, and his sometimes acerbic tongue, I know the meeting would have been a disaster. He was an enigmatic fellow, one of the young lions who had worked in Ottawa under the Honourable Clarence Decataur Howe during the Second World War. As minister of munitions and supply, it was Howe's job to ensure the Allied war machine was well provided for. Canadian factories all over the country were recruited to turn out essential goods, and young men like Gordon were assigned the task of making sure production targets were met. In peacetime he returned to Toronto with a reputation as one of Howe's celebrated "whiz kids." Gordon, who was only 27 when he joined the Howe organization in 1941, ultimately became the director general of organization for the department and was credited with strong management.

Crawford Gordon was the son of a banker. Though he was born in Winnipeg, both of his parents were Torontonians, and he received his early education in Ontario private schools, later graduating from McGill University with a commerce degree. Following college he worked for a number of years in administrative jobs with Canadian General Electric. Following the war and his return to the private sector, Gordon became president of English Electric Limited and executive vice president of Toronto's then massive John Inglis company. However, after a few years he returned to the government as co-coordinator of defence production, leaving this to become president of A. V. Roe Canada Limited in 1951. Under his leadership the company grew rapidly in the 1950s, although most of its revenues were from government contracts. He became like a son to Sir Roy Dobson, chairman of the London-based parent company Hawker Siddeley, and the two of them teamed up to give the young Canadian aircraft company strong leadership. After the collapse of the Arrow program, their affection and admiration for one another was replaced by bitterness and disillusionment. Sir Roy blamed Gordon, and his battles with the prime minister and others in government, for the final cancellation of the program. He said the enmity that developed between the egocentric Diefenbaker and the proud and combative Gordon had as much to do with the contract loss as financial matters.

I met with Sir Roy in Toronto a year after the debacle and he told me, emphatically, that revenge on the part of Diefenbaker was a key factor in the cancellation. He said that the quick and arbitrary decision by Gordon to lay off the fifteen thousand employees also riled the prime minister, and that this only escalated the bad feeling that existed between Gordon and the prime minister. Roe, however, was ultimately the big loser, and Gordon, sadly, was forced to follow the other fifteen thousand workers in quest of a new job. The golden days of the Roe empire were over. When I met Crawford Gordon for the first time in late 1957 he was a true titan of Canadian industry. A good-looking man—about five foot eleven, two hundred pounds and largely bald, he wore his self-confidence and sense of command on his London-tailored sleeve. Heavy drinking had obviously taken a toll, however, as his face often showed red patches, and he was further beset by an asthmatic condition, which would not have been helped by his constant cigarette smoking. Nevertheless he was at the pinnacle of power, and the dramatic downward slide that was only a year and a half away was then wholly unforeseen.

Along with other Maritimers, Brigadier J. Michael Wardell, publisher of the Fredericton Gleaner and the Atlantic Advocate, is briefed on the famous Orenda engine later scrapped by the government. Arnie Patterson is on the immediate left.

A. R. (Ron) Williams, who was a much more important player than his title of assistant to the president implied, was terribly distressed by Gordon's drinking and behaviour. Williams, as principal publicist and strategist, had quietly and successfully cultivated Gordon's image as a major player on the Canadian business scene, but he was becoming disenchanted with his boss as events led up to the cancellation of the Arrow contract. Ron himself was my mentor in the organization; I spent a lot of time with him, shared in his thoughts about the company, its people, and its prospects. In addition to other problems, shortly following the collapse of the Arrow program, Gordon divorced after fourteen years of marriage and three children, two daughters, and a son. His ex-wife, Mary, a gracious and attractive woman, continued to live in Toronto, while Crawford and his new bride, Billie Raphael, moved to Montreal in late 1959 or early 1960. The English-born Billie was the daughter of an Italian contessa and had met Crawford during his visits to London and the parent company.

Crawford's move to Westmount, a rich and privileged enclave situated on the hills of the great city, meant giving up certain aspects of his former life, such as membership in some of Toronto's most prestigious clubs—including the Toronto Golf Club, the Granite Club, the Badminton and Racquet Club, and the York Club. As he had attended university in Montreal and had business associates there, he was not unfamiliar with the city but he did not have the weight of major corporate power behind him. Before too much time elapsed Crawford called me at home, looking for hockey tickets to the Montreal Canadians game. I was custodian to four reds situated directly behind the visiting players bench; the wife of Boom Boom Geoffrion and a daughter of the legendary Howie Morenz sat in front of me. These were seats acquired by the Canadian Car Company in the thirties when there was little demand, and I was fortunate enough in that hockey-mad city to be the latter-day inheritor. I was always able to accommodate him although at times I had to scramble for extra tickets, as in that era the Canadians won five Stanley Cups in a row.

Crawford called me one Sunday morning at about ten and invited Glo and I to join him and Billie for "brunch." We were able to secure a babysitter for both Carol and Lori, our second daughter, were small. Our home in Montreal West was only about fifteen minutes from Westmount, so we arrived at the new Gordon mansion before noon. We congregated in the den, which had been an organ loft built by the late president of RCA Victor and which Crawford had turned into a bar. Crawford ranted on about Dosco, forecasting that one day it would be dismantled and sold off for its most valuable parts. There was a sense of betrayal in every comment he made about Roe–Dosco and a particular disappointment in Sir Roy. He dismissed my boss, Al Fairley, as a "Southern gentleman but a weak sister." Anyway it was after 3:30 p.m. when we left, and Glo contends to this day that we never got "brunch."

Some time later the Gordons hosted a glittering party at their new home. It was, I suspect, an announcement of their entry into Montreal society. Most of Montreal's rich and famous were there—the Anglo side anyway—including Donald Gordon, president of the Canadian National Railway; Earl McLaughlin, president of the Royal Bank; Noah Timmins, the mining tycoon; one of the Molsons; and other luminaries of the day. Glo and I were invited, and I am sure that we as thirty-year-olds were at least twenty years younger than any other guests. There was a small string orchestra in attendance, bars set up everywhere, and enough food to feed a small army. It was a rather mystical night. Crawford kept introducing me to his moneyed guests as "a brilliant public relations man." In self-protection Glo and I stayed close together. However, the night did not end quickly. As the guests were starting to leave, Crawford signalled to me to stay behind. Reluctantly Glo agreed and, after the final departures, he told me we were joining Larry Hart and his wife for a nightcap at the Ritz Grill at the Ritz Carlton Hotel on Sherbrooke Street. Brian Mulroney would not have discovered the Ritz by then, as he would have been a student at St. F.X.

I was to drive. We had a little difficulty squeezing Crawford and the elegantly-dressed Contessa in the back seat of my Pontiac, as it was equipped with a baby seat that stubbornly refused to be moved. But somehow the problem was solved. As we joined the others, dancing was in full swing. Larry Hart, a rather dashing figure in his early fifties, ushered Glo to the floor and she later told me he was the best dancer she had ever danced with. Larry and I had known each other in the company days; his office was close to mine. Just months before, he had left his position as a CanCar senior vice president. A scion of an old Montreal industrial family and one of city's Beau Brummells, Larry was shortly to be involved with Crawford in what turned out to be a series of business disasters that seriously diminished Crawford's resources. Despite his charm and good manners, Larry was a bit of an ineffectual fellow whose social cachet and family name won him more good jobs then he probably deserved. He and Crawford, with a newly created company, got into the transportation and transportation trailer business. The companies foundered after a year or two and, aside from an occasional trip to the company's offices, I doubt whether Crawford had really involved himself.

Some time in mid-1958 after the arrival of Albert Fairley, I suggested it might be good public relations, particularly in Nova Scotia, if the deposed Roy Jodrey and Frank Sobey were asked to re-join the Dosco board. Both were directors of Canadian banks and influential in their own circles. Fairley agreed, and I suspect with the agreement of the Roe people, the two were welcomed back.

I had the responsibility of looking after Frank when he came to Montreal for board meetings. He always liked to go out for dinner and a few drinks. Jodrey kept farmer's hours and was to bed early. On one of these outings with Frank, I suggested we visit Crawford at his home in Westmount. Billie graciously greeted us and ushered us into the organ loft where Crawford awaited. Crawford, a bit in the juice, predicted a dire future for Dosco, saying the company was building all the wrong things in the wrong places. I remember a heated discussion on Dosco's plans to build a steel rolling mill at Contrecoeur, just outside Montreal. Sobey thought the mill should be located in Sydney, but Crawford contended that the company had to have a stronger position in central Canada where the major markets were located. It was on the overall an interesting night but no one won the debate. The mill was later to be located at the Quebec site.

When I left Dosco in 1963 to join Falconbridge Nickel Mines Limited in Toronto I lost contact with Crawford. I had been back in Nova Scotia a few years when, in 1967, I was shocked to read his obituary in the Halifax papers. It was a short, insignificant notice, which told of his passing in New York at age 52. I knew that he had gone through hard times in the intervening years. He had taken a job as president of Shakespeare Company, an American firm renowned for its recreational products, including fishing and golf equipment. According to sources he lasted only six months, as he "drank himself out of the job." I never learned the details of his tragic death until I read Greig Stewart's *Arrow Through the Heart*, which described Crawford's drink-ridden final years in a small New

York apartment. At 52 he was broke, alcoholic, and unemployable. Stewart wrote, "Alcoholism has often been referred to as the disease of denial. Alcoholics rarely admit to themselves they have the disease, or they minimize it, just as heavy drinking." Crawford, Stewart wrote, "faced an additional problem because of his powerful personality and high intelligence. Alcoholics who are former senior executives, especially those with high intelligence, pose a special dilemma for those trying to treat them." And he added, "These people create a more elaborate system of alibis than the guys on skid row. They can't accept a situation that they can't control."

Even in my early encounters with Crawford his drinking problem, which was to drown both his great talent and his judgement, was evident. Earlier in this tale, I mentioned a trip to Newfoundland with the A. V. Roe brass which was for the primary purpose of visiting the big Dosco iron ore operation at Bell Island, though a fishing expedition had also been planned for the group. I had arranged this through Newfoundland's tourism minister Oliver Vardy, who was to provide us with guides and equipment. I purchased suitable clothing for the group. Just before departing the Newfoundland Hotel for our trek to somewhere beyond Bay Bulls, Crawford informed me that he would not be going; he had some work to do. Sir Roy, Fred Smye (the president of Avro Aircraft), and the others suited up and we spent the day fishing—alas with little luck. When we got back to the hotel sometime around seven, I found that my room had been searched and that several bottles of Scotch alone were missing. I was the booze custodian on the trip, and several cases had been stacked in my closet, the remnants from a cocktail party we had staged the night before for the local media and others. I went down to the master suite where Sir Roy held court and all were gathered—Crawford, bleary-eyed and slumping in a chair. I knew where the Scotch had gone.

But like most people, Crawford Gordon had another side to him, and I recall one story in particular which depicts that other self—the decisive man-in-charge. The night before our fishing trip, Crawford summoned me to his room to tell me that one of the co-pilots and the steward of the Roe company plane had been arrested. Apparently they had met two girls at a restaurant and decided to take them to the airport to show off the plane (and I suspect to avail themselves of the contents of the well-stocked bar). In a moment of showing off, the co-pilot started the engines. Unfortunately the plane was parked near the terminal's parking lot, and the end result was that the windshields of about six cars were damaged. Gordon, holding me by the shoulder, said, "Arnie, I want you to go fix this. Go down to the police and get them out and promise whatever you have to promise." I went down to the RCMP quarters where our men were detained. Luck was with me, for when I entered the offices I encountered Sergeant Charlie Daley of the RCMP, whom I had known in Halifax years earlier; in fact, he had been the subject of a feature on safe driving that I had written for the paper. Through his good offices I had a generous introduction to the sergeant-in-charge, who agreed to release my cohorts, provided I would call all six car owners and tell them the company would pay for damages incurred. I spent the night on the phone, and the episode was forgotten. But that in many ways reflected the real side of Crawford, a side admired by those who knew him.

In his book *Arrow Through the Heart*, Greig Stewart gives us a tragic, almost pathetic portrayal of this man who once touched on greatness. Billie had persevered, staying with Crawford and loving him despite his pursuit of self-destruction. They lived in a small apartment in New York—no big estate in Montreal, no chateau in the south of France, no money. The dream had evaporated. Stewart presents a particularly heart-tearing account of a phone conversation between Crawford and CBC journalist Dave Reynolds. After agreeing to accept a call from New York, Reynolds was greeted:

> "Dave, this is Crawford Gordon."
>
> "Crawford. I can't believe it, everyone thinks you're dead."
>
> "Yeah, well Dave (cough!) I'm not dead. And if you think I've forgotten about those bastards in Ottawa and what they did to A. V. Roe and my Arrow, well I haven't. Now listen."
>
> "Where are you Crawford...what are you doing now?"
>
> "I'm living (cough!) off Park Avenue, new wife and on my way back. (cough!)"
>
> "Well, what do you want from me?"
>
> "You know lots of press guys (cough!) and you were always good to me and A. V. Roe, so I wanted you to have the scoop on my new company. If you're still living in Weston, I think I have your address around here somewhere, I'll send you the details in a couple of days."
>
> "And Dave? (cough!)"
>
> "Yeah, Crawford?"
>
> "You know I'm still gonna get that sonovabitch (cough!) Diefenbaker someday."
>
> "Yeah, I believe you will," whispered Reynolds into the phone "I believe you will..."

The next day, January 26, 1967, Crawford Gordon died in New York. As mentioned, he was just 52. Stewart reported that the funeral was held in New York City over the weekend of January 28, 1967. Only twenty people—mostly friends of Billie; his son, Crawford, and his wife; his daughter, Diana; and his old friend Len Lumbers from Toronto—were there to say goodbye. Gordon was cremated, and to this day no one knows the final resting place of his ashes, not his friends, his family, no one.

All these years I feel sad later just writing these words, for the Crawford I remember was a tall, proud man so much in command of himself and whatever ship he sought to steer.

Chapter Nine: Falconbridge

My move from Dosco to public relations and advertising manager of Falconbridge Nickel Mines Limited meant relocating to Toronto, and Glo and I pulled up stakes with a degree of sadness and some regret. We loved Montreal, the neighbourhood in which we'd lived, and the friends we'd made. In fact now, more than forty years later, we maintain contact with several former neighbours. Furthermore, although it was one in which I'd lost as much as I'd won, my job at Dosco had been enjoyable, and it had allowed me to continue my connection with Nova Scotia. Al Fairley was an exceedingly good boss, and over the years I had developed a close rapport with him. I can't ever remember us having angry words although we had lots of disagreements, particularly concerning company operations in Nova Scotia. He was though a reason why I left the coal and steel company. But not because I didn't like him or enjoy working for him.

Fairley enjoyed a high profile in Canadian business circles, and apparently the publicity accorded him created a backlash and, I suspect, jealousy at the A. V. Roe office. Crawford Gordon was long gone, and the company (renamed Hawker Siddeley Canada Limited) had a new president in T. J. (Ted) Emmert. Ron Williams had also departed and was then the publisher of the Vancouver *Province*. His replacement was J. N. (Pat) Kelly, a small, tidy fellow in his late fifties who had a long association with Roe in his role as manager of public relations for Cockfield Brown, then one of Canada's leading advertising agencies. I knew Pat well and, while we were friendly enough, I thought him a bit of a popinjay; he would sit around and theorize about public relations and related topics but when the work or writing had to be done he simply became an adviser. As a player, his approach never appealed to me.

Pat never liked Al Fairley, who in turn dismissed Kelly as inconsequential. For some reason, however, Pat had a good relationship with Sir Roy, who I think played a role in inserting him at Hawker as Ted Emmert's PR adviser. I had a call from Pat, asking me to come to Toronto for a meeting. Struggling then with only the remnants of its aircraft empire, and a few other industrial holdings, Hawker Siddeley had offices on the top floor of the National Trust building at 7 King Street East, a prime Toronto business address. We met at the King Edward Hotel, located next door, and while sipping a martini over lunch Pat suggested I move to Toronto and assume the role of public relations director for Hawker Siddeley. He said that he thought I had accomplished all I was going to accomplish in Montreal and suggested that the challenge in Toronto was greater since that was where the real power in the company was going to reside. He would generously give up his title as public relations director and become the assistant to the president. I would be reporting to him directly. I recognized the power play for what it was and I declined on the spot, and as graciously as I knew how. My real instinct was to tell him to go to blazes.

I had travelled with Ted Emmert on several occasions and I never liked him. I found him to be a cold, humourless, condescending man, who seemed to hold little regard for the Maritimes. One night when we were in the Dosco suite in the Isle Royale Hotel in Sydney he made a smart-alecky remark about a sports jacket I was wearing. It had a split in the tail and Emmert, commenting to one of the guests, probably another Central Canadian, said, "That's a fancy jacket for a Maritimer to be wearing." I replied, "Yes, this is the jacket that Prince Phillip gave me when I covered the Royal tour." This ended any further comment about my sartorial splendour although the real truth was that I had bought the jacket at Holt Renfrew in Montreal a few years before. Anyway I didn't like him and I had no intention of working for him.

Illinois-born Ted Emmert, then 48, had come to the presidency of Hawker Siddeley from the farm equipment giant Massey Ferguson, where he had served as vice president of North American operations. He had an impressive business background, having worked at Boeing Aircraft in Seattle, and came to Canada in 1947 as an assistant to the president of Canadair in Montreal. In 1948 he joined the Ford Motor Company in Toronto as a director of organization, and left to join Massey Ferguson in 1950. By 1959 he was a senior vice president. He took over the presidency of A. V. Roe, later Hawker Siddeley, in 1961. At both Ford and Massey he'd had the reputation of being a "hatchet man." When I returned to Montreal after my meeting with Pat, I said nothing to the people at Dosco about this turn of events. I told Glo that I was determined to seek another job, however, and she fished two ads out of the *Financial Post*: the first for MacMillan Bloedel, the big pulp and paper company in Vancouver; the other, Falconbridge Nickel Company in Toronto. Both were seeking public relations directors, and in the instance of MacMillan, an assistant to the president.

The first to respond was MacMillan, so I went to Toronto and met with the management consultant who was doing the screening. The interview went well, and the job on offer was as an assistant to Judge J. V. Cline, the president of MacMillan. I was interested. The money was good and so was the challenge, but British Columbia was a long way from home and I thought that if I took it I would never get back to Nova Scotia. Glo too had reservations about the distance it would take us from relatives so I wrote a letter declining. A few days later I had a call from Gordon H. Garbutt, who was serving as a public relations consultant to Falconbridge. He was a well-known figure in Canadian public relations, had been the public relations director at Ford Motor and, while I didn't know him personally, I knew of his reputation. Then in his sixties, he was operating a small consulting business with only four clients. He invited me to Toronto for a series of interviews.

Falconbridge in those days was located on the twentieth and twenty-first floors of the National Trust Building on King Street. Hawker Siddeley was one floor up, in the penthouse. I was fearful of running into Hawker people, so I walked to the third floor and took the elevator; in turn I walked the whole 21 floors on my way out. My first meeting was with Gordon Garbutt. It was a short, pleasant talk. He remembered my work at Springhill and was highly complimentary. Then we went to the office of Reg Campbell, the vice president of finance, and with him were R. C. (Shorty) Mott, the vice president of mining; and George Jewett, the vice president of sales. They were pleasant men, and we talked about a wide range of subjects. Mott was especially interested in my experiences in coal mining. It seemed to me that they were as intent on selling me on the job as I was in getting it. While Falconbridge's main nickel operations were in Sudbury, through its ownership of McIntyre Porcupine it had mining operations throughout Canada in addition to the storied Kilembe copper mines in Africa. A polite, gentlemanly man, Reg Campbell told me that the major role for a public relations and advertising manager would be to help the company expand its commercial sales in the United States. The company was highly profitable and had just that year made $20 million on $75 million worth of sales, while Dosco had a profit of just $3 million on more than $200 million in sales.

Much of Falconbridge's success came through what were captive sales to the United States strategic metals stockpiling program. For ten successive years the company had sold the bulk of its nickel and copper to the United States government. The program had just been curtailed, and Falconbridge was faced with the prospect of developing commercial markets. It also meant a heads-on battle with the industry giant International Nickel, which had a dominant sales position in the States. It sounded like a fascinating challenge, and Toronto was a lot closer to Halifax than Vancouver. While nothing was concluded that day, they asked me to come back a week later to meet the company president, Dr. H. J. Fraser, who was then in Japan. I agreed. While she didn't jump up and down at the prospect, Glo agreed that I should take the job if offered, although it meant leaving our nice neighbourhood and many close friends. We had enjoyed five years in Montreal.

Horace Fraser was a big man, weighing well over three hundred pounds. At that time, he would have been in his early sixties. He had a full head of white hair and a generous mustache. Prior to his election as president of the company, he had served as the general manager of the mining operations in the Sudbury Basin. He had the reputation of being an outstanding geologist and, although a Canadian, had been a professor at the prestigious Cal Tech in California. We talked easily for at least an hour, and he too mentioned Springhill and the disaster with which he was somewhat familiar. He didn't know Harold Gordon but knew of his reputation in the coal-mining industry. He mentioned a salary figure somewhat higher than I was making at Dosco, and also agreed to a golf club membership (I always had my priorities right). We shook hands and I agreed to join the company as soon as I cleared things up in Montreal, which included, among other things, selling my house.

When I made the move to Falconbridge in 1963 my most recent venture, CFDR, was brand new and in operation. In its infancy, it was not in a position to support the kind of salary that I was getting elsewhere. As well, I needed monies simply to pay the interest on my loans. Our losses in the early going were such that we exhausted our bank line of credit, and there was a need to inject more cash into the radio business. With the monies from the sale of my house and my pension contributions from Dosco, I was able to give additional support. My years at Dosco were at an end, and the year ahead proved to be an interesting one.

Falconbridge was an entirely different challenge than Dosco. There were few calls from reporters demanding to know what the company was going to do about its latest problem. The focus of my work was more on advertising and sales promotion and, in this, attention to the big American market, I had little difficulty fitting into the new company, although my role was a new one in their corporate life. Dr. Fraser was receptive to my efforts and interests, and I found him to be one of the smartest men I had encountered in business or, I should say, anywhere. And while I was involved in such normal activities as speech writing, preparation of annual reports, and liaison work with the United States Steel Institute, most of my time was spent on the marketing side.

The challenge was to find new markets for Falconbridge's massive nickel surpluses, and the small sales department enthusiastically sought my help in this. As a highly profitable organization with a need for new markets, the company could provide a sizable budget for advertising and promotion. One program initiated before my arrival was the daily placement of a full-page ad in an American steel publication. It was a publication that I had known from my Dosco days, and while it had a circulation of only fifteen thousand, it went to the desk of every senior steel executive in the United States every day. Our ad was on the publication's back cover, and in the corner of the full-page ad was a box inviting inquiries from prospective customers. Every day there was a response.

The thrust of the sales effort was carried by Marr Henderson, the general sales manager, and a big, engaging fellow by the name of Bruce Connolly. They were constantly on the road in the United States, trying to fill the void that had been created by the stockpiling contract. I was busy preparing sales brochures and other supplementary materials to support their cause and, at the same time, we made our forays into the

American metalworking trade shows. Our booth attracted a lot of attention, and one of our minor ploys was to pass out maple-leaf lapel pins made of nickel.

While my entry into the sales activity was energizing and fun as we were having much success, my work on the corporate side continued as well. Dr. Fraser had taken on the presidency of the Ontario Mining Association, one of the most significant business associations in Canada. They had been beset by problems since the federal government had initiated tax changes that could, if enacted, adversely affect the essential depletion allowances: tax write-offs that allowed companies to expand spending on exploration work, which is the lifeblood of any successful mining enterprise. In one of our morning sessions, Dr. Fraser asked me to join the public relations committee of the mining association, suggesting that I could be helpful in disseminating to both governments and the general public their message about the importance of exploration. Innocently I asked why he didn't go to Ottawa and talk to Prime Minister Lester Pearson about the problem. I said I thought the prime minister, conscious of the importance of the mining industry and its association, would be receptive. "Do you really think so?" he said, looking at me doubtfully. I said I would make the arrangements.

My old friend Dick O'Hagan was press secretary to the prime minister; and a somewhat newer friend, Jim Coutts, was the principal secretary and executive assistant to Mr. Pearson. I called, and within an hour Coutts called back to confirm an appointment for Dr. Fraser for the following week. Dr. Fraser seemed a bit incredulous when I told him that the appointment was made, and at his request I travelled to Ottawa with him. When we arrived it was a typically scorching summer day. (I always thought our capital remarkable in that respect—terribly hot in the summer, and frigid most of the winter.) We taxied to the Chateau Laurier, where we planned to lunch before our 2:00 p.m. meeting with the prime minister. As I mentioned, Dr. Fraser was an immense man. He could put on a new suit and within an hour it was rumpled. Anyway on this occasion he changed to a nice grey suit and added one of his big bow ties, which he generally wore with every business ensemble.

We were barely seated in the hotel's Grill Room when one of the waiters, an older man, came in our direction carrying a pitcher of ice water, much welcomed on such a hot day. "This," the waiter said, "will refresh you!" And with that he poured the water, missing the glass but generously dousing my table mate. I have to laugh as I write these words so many years later, but poor Dr. Fraser, so proper in his new finery, was not only soaked but also livid. I tried to calm him by saying that we had more than an hour before our meeting and that a walk up Parliament Hill in the sunshine would dry him out. It was a labouring walk for my big companion but we made it. We got a warm greeting from Coutts and, while I didn't attend the meeting between the two, the prime minister in coming out of his office spotted me and said, "Well Patterson, what do you think of Team Canada?" I had met him on the road with O'Hagan a few years back and watched a hockey game on television. Hockey was a passion we both shared. Dr. Fraser's meeting with Mr. Pearson turned out to be a success, and the depletion allowance was left in place. It seemed I had earned my spurs.

Through its Ventures mining affiliation—a fiefdom spawned by explorer–financier Thayer Lindsley, a legend in Canadian mining—Falconbridge owned mining properties in many places. The major component, however, was the nickel–copper mine at the township of Falconbridge in the rich Sudbury Basin. The Canadian Pacific Railway, in building its thread of steel westward in the 1880s, created a town site at Sudbury and brought to light the mineral wealth that resided there. By the turn of the century the new International Nickel Company had several operations under way. The famed inventor of the electric lightbulb, Thomas A. Edison, visited the area in 1901 and staked a property that later became the township of Falconbridge. Edison and succeeding owners had little success, and it was not until 1928 that Falconbridge Nickel Mines Limited was formed to develop these properties. Until not so many years ago the Sudbury Basin produced more than ninety percent of the world's nickel. It remains the number one producer although finds in other parts of the world, including Africa, have reduced its dominance. Although I enjoyed Falconbridge and its people immensely, the call from home and Nova Scotia proved strongest.

Chapter Ten: The Moose Is Loose

Chance ended my days at Falconbridge after about a year. In 1964, Mayor I. W. Akerley led a delegation of Dartmouth businessmen to Toronto on a trade and awareness promotion. I helped with some of the arrangements at the Toronto end, which included a small luncheon tendered by Toronto mayor Phil Givens, whom I knew well in my reporting days. That night I went to a nightclub with a number of the Dartmouth visitors, including Mayor Akerley and Derek Oland, the twenty-five-year-old marketing vice president of his father's Moosehead brewery in Saint John. Moosehead was building a new plant in the Burnside area of Dartmouth, and at one point during the evening Akerley leaned over to Derek and, with both of us in earshot, said, "Here is the guy you should hire as your general manager," and he pointed to me. Derek expressed an interest.

In a follow-up I wrote Derek, telling him that I would be interested in the job. His father, Phillip, came to Toronto shortly after and we met at the Park Plaza Hotel. I had been introduced to him years earlier when I was with the Atlantic Provinces Economic Council. He was a soft-spoken, thoughtful man then in his mid- or late fifties. He was impressed with the idea that I was a homegrown Dartmouth boy with a pretty comprehensive knowledge of Nova Scotia. We didn't cement the tie that day, but he suggested I visit the brewery in Saint John for further talks. Much of my time in this visit to Saint John was spent with Derek who was a most agreeable host; I remember that on the night of my arrival we sat in the brewery's Alpine Room, drinking beer and talking about the market prospects in Nova Scotia. Moosehead was the kingpin in New Brunswick, with more than eighty percent of the market but, without a brewery, in Nova Scotia they had but a seven or eight percent market share and were dominated by their cousins, the Halifax Olands.

The next day, a Sunday, I lunched with Phillip and his wife, Mary, at their lovely home in Rothesay. We strolled down to his father's house, located only a few hundred yards away, where I met his father, George Oland, then in his late seventies, and Phillip's three brothers, Alfred, Paul, and Tony. All were involved in the brewery operation but

Phillip was clearly the boss. It seemed I was there for inspection. It was a casual affair with drinks being poured. I took an immediate liking to George Oland, who too had been born in Dartmouth and who remembered my father's uncles as great skaters. Whenever I would visit Saint John in the future, he insisted on driving me to the airport. It was always a hazardous ride for he just rambled through town in a big Cadillac, talking all the while and periodically punching the air for emphasis. But he was a nice man and I enjoyed him. Sadly he died only a year or so after I joined the company.

I remember that afternoon vividly. George Oland asked me, "Do you think you can sell beer? For that's what it's all about. Because of chemistry you could make beer today out of swamp water, but selling it is the key." I answered in the affirmative, even though at that point I didn't know the difference between ale and lager. It is a wonder I didn't blow my chances when I told the assembled how much I liked their cousin Victor Oland, then the president of S. Oland and Sons brewery in Halifax. Victor had been the president of the Halifax Atlantics hockey team in the days when I was doing hockey broadcasts. Little did I realize that there was enmity between the two families, dating back many years. George Oland, Phillip's father, and Sidney C. Oland, Victor's father and the chairman of the Halifax Oland brewery, were brothers. Sidney was the older of the two and I suspect was the number one inheritor of the Halifax brewery, which had been started by his grandmother in 1867. She was Susannah—the "S" in S. Oland and Sons Limited. I never knew the details of the family dispute. I suspect that as the younger brother George had to strike out on his own and so moved to Saint John in the 1920s where he opened his own brewery, which he named Moosehead. In 1933 he got a listing for his products in Nova Scotia, and I believe he moved back to Halifax at that time. George had been recently divorced and arrived back with a new wife. While I had the word from only one side of the family, I was told that his brother Sidney's wife, Linda, a devout Catholic, refused to have anything to do with the new bridal couple. This added to the developing schism in the family. It would be my thought too that the rivalry between the two brewing companies for the Maritime market had as much to do with the coolness that was later to prevail.

I went back to Toronto with the dual tasks of moving back to Dartmouth and telling the Falconbridge people that I was resigning. Although I had been there only a year I had developed a number of friendships, and I was particularly fond of Dr. Fraser. I had planned to go to Los Angeles with him that week, and I thought this would be a good opportunity for me to break the difficult news. Our purpose there was to explore the possibility of obtaining sales representatives in California for the sale of nickel and copper. One of the prime candidates was Ducommon, a big California-based sales agency dealing with metals and metal products. They were our number one prospect.

We met with the Ducommon people in the office of its president, Charles Ducommon, a major figure in the metals trade. They served us coffee and were especially solicitous. Dr. Fraser told them about Falconbridge and our campaign to establish a stronger commercial sales base in the United States. Were they interested in representing our company? In the most diplomatic terms Mr. Ducommon said that, because of conflicts with other clients, they were unable to accommodate us. He then admitted that they hoped to gain the Inco account, which would be much bigger than that of Falconbridge. After a few pleasantries we prepared to leave. As we stood at the door, he asked if we knew a Canadian by the name of Leo Dolan. Dolan, he said, had played a key role in helping him and other community leaders bring the Brooklyn Dodgers franchise to Los Angeles a few years earlier. Leo was then the Canadian consul general in Los Angeles and, more important to the Los Angeles baseball cause, a close friend of fellow Irishman Walter O'Malley, the president of the Dodgers.

I jumped at the opportunity to tell him that Leo was a friend of mine and that I visited with him whenever I was in Ottawa. A native of Fredericton, Leo was a former newspaperman whom I had gotten to know years before when I interviewed him on a visit to Halifax. In my Dosco days, I had him travel with me and invited him to be an after-dinner speaker at many functions in which I was involved. He was a dandy. I was also able to tell Mr. Ducommon that Leo was now Dr. Leo Dolan, as he had been given an honourary doctorate of laws by the University of New Brunswick. Delighted with this news, a now smiling Mr. Ducommon said, "It would be an awful thing for me to turn down a friend of Leo Dolan's, so why don't you meet with my sales manager in the next week or two and discuss terms and procedures." We left with the knowledge that Falconbridge would shortly have new reps in sunny California.

I was determined to tell Dr. Fraser of my leaving, but he was in such a happy frame of mind during our trip out west that I couldn't get up the courage to do it. On my return to Toronto I had a phone call from Phillip Oland, inquiring as to when I would assume my new duties. I had to tell him I had not yet resigned although I would the next day. Jokingly I said, "Perhaps I should just leave and write them a letter telling them I've gone." He was shocked, not realizing I was having a bit of fun. He was always a pretty serious fellow. The next day I told Dr. Fraser of my decision. He was generous and said that he thought I could have had a good future with his company. I suggested that not being a geologist or a metallurgist I was just a specialist, much like the place kicker on a football team. Further I said I was intrigued by the opportunity to return to Nova Scotia. He smiled, saying he had a lot of Nova Scotia coal miners working for him in Sudbury, adding, "You are like homing pigeons. You always go home."

I arrived back in Dartmouth in May 1964 to assume my new duties. The new brewery was under construction and months away from readiness. It was a modern, low-lying building, only two stories in height, located in the north end of Dartmouth on the edge of the burgeoning industrial park. I rented a temporary two-office suite on Queen Street in downtown Dartmouth. Moosehead was selling some product in Nova Scotia, about eight percent of the provincial market, with its sales predominantly in Amherst and the area bordering New Brunswick. I was not going to wait for the brewery to open before I set a sales plan in motion. My first job was to hire a secretary, and in this regard I was lucky. A young, red-haired, British lady by the name of Joyce Hipgrave answered a newspaper advert. She was pleasant, highly efficient, and unflappable in the more than four years that we worked together. She was in every respect a star.

Also in that early period we started to hire people for the plant. Urban Murphy, the industrial relations manager at Moosehead in Saint John, came over to do the job interviews. While Dartmouth had a fairly buoyant economy, brewery jobs were seen as good ones, and we had a host of candidates. I presented him with a list of my own nominees, a dozen or so, which he accepted but not without a few questioning glances. Among them were Perry Locke, the provincial golf champion and a personable young man; Cobey McCluskey, a former Maritime boxing champion; Carl (Soupy) Kelly, a Saint Mary's hockey star; and a few others. Dartmouth has a fairly large black population—about six thousand people lived in neighbouring Preston—I suggested we also hire from the community. To assist in this I called a few old friends: Spencer Colley, a member of both the Dartmouth Police department and a well-respected Preston area family, and Gerry Tynes, a schoolteacher whom I had known as a youngster. Spencer gave me the name of his brother-in-law, Donald Thompson, who had just returned to the area after serving as a paratrooper in the Canadian army. I made an appointment for him to see Urban but had him drop by my office beforehand. He was a strong, well-built young man with whom I was impressed. Off he went to the interview.

Urban made it a practice to drop in to see me at the end of the working day to review his progress. I said, "Did you see my man Thompson?" Yes, he said rather slowly. "How did he get along?" I inquired, "Well," he said pausing, "he is awfully black." I nearly fell out of the chair laughing, as Donald was indeed very dark. "Well, Urban, I guess then there is no doubt that he is black, and that's what I am looking for." He was hired and proved a solid employee.

Even before leaving Toronto I had been working on a marketing plan for the new brewery. While I had never sold beer, I knew the province well from my various experiences and I knew a lot of people, particularly in the sports world. Derek had supplied me with Nova Scotia sales figures that showed the Halifax peninsula as solid Oland territory. The Halifax Oland family was highly regarded in the city, and they had endowed just about every existing organization and charity. This was going to be the toughest market to crack but it was the biggest in terms of sales. Cape Breton also offered a sizable and strong market, and I knew many people there through my Dosco days, so I singled it out for priority attention. Despite the fact that we had only about an eight percent share of the market, the company had initiated a television ad campaign earlier that year which was causing some talk. It featured two stevedores, "Big John" and "Casey," talking about what a great product Moosehead was. Today these ads would probably be considered amateurish, but I thought at the time (and I had nothing to do with their creation) that they were quite effective. Cost-wise and by today's standards, they were pretty cheap.

I had several other preconceived ideas about selling beer. In reading a broadcast magazine on a flight to Halifax from Toronto I came across a story dealing with how Anheuser-Busch had replaced Schlitz of Milwaukee as the best-selling brewery in America with its Budweiser brand. A few years earlier Anheuser had switched the bulk of its advertising program from the print media to broadcast, primarily television. Schlitz, with its King of Beers reputation, had cut its television budget. Within two years there was a marked turnaround; Budweiser became the king, and Schlitz has never recovered to this day. Though you will find small amounts of their product in American supermarkets, it sells at reduced prices. Derek Oland, as the company's overall marketing manager, had the responsibility for advertising, and I suggested that we buy up every bit of television time in Cape Breton that we could find. Fortunately he was of the same mind and had already made a strong move to saturate that market.

Another preconception was that sports and sports people are the natural market for beer. Maybe that's not a novel idea, but it's one in which I had a firm belief. And while the competition, Oland's, had a long involvement in sport, it was largely centred in Halifax. I don't think I was on the job three days when two big Dartmouth policemen came in to see me about sponsorship of their Class "C" softball team. They became the first of a long line of teams that we embraced. At one point in Cape Breton alone we had more than sixty teams: bowling, softball, darts, hockey, and others. You could hardly pass by Senator's Corner in the coal town of Glace Bay without running into a fellow wearing a Moosehead shirt.

Advertising played a major role in our growth, and yet I think that in many ways our involvement in sport made an equal contribution. In those days, the 1960s, brewers and distillers were not allowed to approach liquor store managers directly. We had to be content to call on officials at the offices of the Nova Scotia Liquor Commission, who did the ordering. I suppose they also influenced sales in that they could fill the shelves with our product, and yet we had to make sure it moved. I am not diminishing the importance of the exposure in the stores, but it was important as well to have people asking for the product. The presence of our sporting teams in Kentville, Bridgewater, Glace Bay, New Waterford, Sydney, Dartmouth, wherever—and we were everywhere—gave us an army of public relations players. While access to the store managers was prohibited we were allowed to sell and call on the clubs, taverns, and other beer outlets without restriction. I don't know how many sporting connections we had at peak, probably over a hundred, and this gave us contact with hundreds of able-bodied young men, and a limited number of women.

Of course there was no end to the numbers of people seeking commercial sponsorship, and we were very careful in whom we selected. For the most part it had to be teams, or people, associated in some way with the beer trade. Waiters, store managers, club operators, or others who had their own bowling or dart teams. In the first years I sought out championship teams that could win us publicity. Our first star aggregation was a Dartmouth women's bowling team led by Betty Hodgson (later a top curler), which won the Maritime ladies ten pin bowling title. I think in our second year of operation, however, we had three softball teams vying for Maritime championships, but not in the same categories. We had the Dartmouth Mooseheads going for the senior crown, which they won; the Glace Bay Alpines seeking the "B" team title, and again a winner; and the Liverpool Ten Pennies in quest of the "C" championship, which they lost in the final. This was great in one respect because it won us publicity, but the cost of sending as many as 18 guys on the road and have them play their way through about four sectionals was a costly enterprise. That year, after bills came in from hotels everywhere in the Maritimes, I changed our strategy. When people came seeking sponsorship I always asked, "How good is your team?" When they said they had a team of championship calibre, I passed. I wanted teams that could finish third or fourth—respectable, but not costly.

Not everything went as planned. Billy Joe McLean, the operator of a tavern in Port Hawkesbury, asked if we would sponsor his hockey team. He was also the mayor of the town and influential in that part of the province. We quickly agreed. Some weeks later on a sales trip to Cape Breton, Don Valardo, the draft sales manager, and I stopped at Billy Joe's tavern on a courtesy call. We were told that he was at the rink at a practice. Good news as we would have an opportunity to see our team in action. When we got to the rink there was an Oland's team on the ice. I spotted Billy Joe leaning over the boards, yelling at one of the players. I approached him and asked him where our team was. He said, "This is your team." Mystified, I said, "What are they doing wearing Oland's team sweaters?" Billy Joe responded with a smile, "Oh, I bought sticks and other gear with your money, and Oland's bought the sweaters."

There were few sporting activities in that period that we did not get involved in. Among the most unique events were the ox pulls. These are popular at the county fairs, and one of our tavern operators, Orland Johnson of Bridgewater, was a participant. I suggested Moosehead get involved as a sponsor, and I went to a meeting in rural Caledonia where we organized what we called the Maritime Ox-Pulling Association. Orland, a colourful and fun figure, was the president. I almost always got personally involved in these activities, heading off to Meteghan, Bridgewater, and Digby to be the master of ceremonies for the pull. We had a set of weights constructed for the events, and these were painted red with the Moose insignia emblazoned in white. We also had one of our big trucks present as a backdrop. This effort not only won us Orland's support at the tavern, but proved to us that these big, strong country sportsmen loved to drink beer. We had more ambassadors.

In our second year of operation (1965) we sponsored the Dartmouth Open. This golfing event was open to golf professionals not only in the Maritimes but elsewhere.

In celebration of success, Arnie points out achievement and expansion at Moosehead Breweries in 1966.

Also top amateurs took part in the play, which was conducted over two days at the old Brightwood course. This was my personal baby, as I had promoted the idea at the club and pursued it with enthusiasm. While I had a pretty free hand in most respects, and no budget in the first year of operation, our bigger promotions were subject to approval by the company's marketing committee under the chair of Derek Oland. Bill Redden, the dean of the business school at the University of New Brunswick, was the committee adviser and a major influence on many of our plans and activities. Bill Robinson, the company vice president of finance, and Alphonsus Ferguson, the New Brunswick sales manager, were also committee members. I was the lone Nova Scotian.

There were times when my own opinions and plans differed from those of the committee as a whole. On one occasion Bill Robinson, who operated out of Saint John, said rather snidely, "Colonel Manuel (the Oland general manager at the Saint John brewery) is very cost-conscious." I interpreted this as an attack on my spending on promotions. I rather snappily replied, "While he may be tough on expenses, but he sure can't sell beer." Although we had been in operation only for one year, our market share in Nova Scotia now exceeded the long-established Oland's share in New Brunswick. This was one of many differences that we had during my four years at the brewery. I had less trouble with the committee after a year or two, and after we had established budgets and sales projection targets. While I sometimes went over budget, we always exceeded sales targets and enjoyed continuing sales increases. Our disagreements never lasted that long for we were meeting with success, and certainly the marketing committee played an important role in that.

Now in my senior years when I reflect on my own stubbornness and cocksureness, I realize that I must have appeared terribly egocentric to my confreres. I regret that. The marketing committee was an asset to the company, and working with it also taught me a lot personally. Derek, who is president of the company today and Phillip's oldest son, was a strong chairman and he remains a highly organized individual. Bill Redden was brilliant, bold, and innovative. In addition to planning strategy, the committee's practices included quarterly meetings, which allowed us to review progress and results of the past three months and to plan for the future three months ahead. Our emphasis was on promotions largely directed towards the more rugged, blue-collar sports. My idea to stage a professional golfing event won little support initially; Derek and Bill Robinson in particular opposed it. However, Professor Redden thought it a worthwhile venture, and after a long and almost unending debate I got the go-ahead for the event. Despite such a challenge from the committee I was confident in all I was doing, and I felt that we were winning our war in Nova Scotia. Further I was not simply a quarterback but ran the ball with enthusiasm.

In that first year after the brewery opening, I must have made more speeches than Prime Minister Lester Pearson. There were sports banquets at New Waterford, Sydney, New Glasgow, Halifax, Dartmouth, Liverpool, and other centres. The Alpine Room, Moosehead's entertainment lounge on the second floor of the brewery, may have been the busiest meeting place in the province. It seats about 150 people, and in that first year we were regularly booking community groups, softball teams, firemen, tavern owners, lounge waiters and waitresses, navy ships' companies, and others of our varied audience. In addition to the free beer, we offered light snacks. When I first returned from Toronto I had an invitation to speak at a banquet for the Halifax-area lounge waiters. After the dinner they had a singsong and this young man, Peter Gaudet, played the piano and sang. He was employed as a waiter at the Lord Nelson Hotel lounge, but I told him that if he was ever looking for a job he should give me a call. He did a week or so later, and I hired him to run the Alpine Room. As part of the nightly routine with groups, everyone would gather around the piano and join the outgoing Peter in a songfest. He played a key role in our sales effort.

In terms of sales recruitment—a key job in a brewery—we were fortunate to have three strong personalities. Don Valardo, the draft sales manager, had come to us from the Saint John brewery where he had run through the ranks of the union and its presidency and then into sales. He was a non-stop worker and one of the physically strongest men whom I ever encountered. Laurie Power, long well-known to me, was another popular choice. Laurie had been a senior hockey referee and before that a hockey player and star oarsman. The third of the trio was Robert O. (Bob) Dauphinee—and what great fun we had with him. A Saint Marys grad and a hockey player, Dauphinee, like Laurie Power, gave us a strong connection in Halifax as they both knew the sporting crowd and were popular. After a few months we added Perry Locke to the sales staff. Perry had started in the "keg room" but was a natural for sales. A Nova Scotia amateur golf champion, Perry complemented what became a very strong sales team.

Giving away free product is an excellent way to increase future sales, but as I discovered very early in the game, it's only "free" to the customers. It all started the day I was invited to lunch by Ken Easton, who was to be our brew master at Moosehead.

At the Moosehead-sponsored ox pull event in Meteghan, Arnie Patterson (right) presents the championship trophy to Orland Johnson of Bridgewater.

Ken was then serving in that position at O'Keefe's Toronto brewery, and I had not yet moved back to Nova Scotia. We were joined by several other key members of the O'Keefe brewing staff, including veteran brew master Jack Watson, who suggested to me that one of the best ways to sell beer was to give away sample cases. He said that when Molson's opened their new brewery in Toronto, they inundated the city with free cases of beer. They left them right on the doorstep, with a nice note. I tucked this thought in the back of my mind—and it was to cause me no end of grief in the months that followed. When I first came home I would go to the Mic Mac Amateur Aquatic Club, Brightwood golf, or some other gathering and, as expected, find most beer drinkers sipping Oland's or their Schooner brand. I would make a mental note, compile a list of names, and send them a case of beer. I had about three different delivery services dropping off free product, not to mention how generous we were in giving beer to softball groups and others who were having banquets or related social functions.

This was not a new practice in Nova Scotia. Oland's also sent beer to various groups and individuals, but we probably gave away more free beer in two months than they had in two years. The last time I had noticed an Oland beer giveaway was on Dartmouth Natal Day. I had our people deliver twenty cases to the Dartmouth fire station for the firemen who were to march in the parade that morning. My cousin George Patterson was the fire chief, and I went down to see him. I spied ten cases of Olands stacked in a corner and suggested to George that he put our beer in the fridge, which he did. Three months to the day, I was in Saint John for George Oland's eightieth birthday party and received a phone call from Don Valardo, who was in Cape Breton doing the tavern rounds. He said that the RCMP had stopped our beer delivery truck and found ten barrels of draft for which there were no order slips. Don had met with Inspector Doug Wright of the Mounties and was told that a charge could be pending under the Nova Scotia Liquor Control Act, which forbade giveaways of alcoholic products. Don said he and the Mountie—a big, forceful man—had had heated words, and this concerned me, as Don could be combative. Anyway, unbeknownst to us the RCMP had been conducting investigations in several parts of the province, seeking out individuals and groups to whom we had given beer. Apparently the Liquor Control Act also specified that charges could be laid only if the act in question was not more than three months old. We later discovered that Oland's had reported us for our giveaways, but had themselves refrained from similar activities for the three-month period. But the practice of giving free beer was an old one and followed by breweries everywhere.

A few days later, RCMP Inspector Wright arrived in my office with Corporal Joe Fraser. He told me in no uncertain terms that there was much evidence of our giving beer away, and that we would face multiple charges. Corporal Fraser, whom I didn't know, seemed a bit sympathetic and warned me that there was evidence that I myself had given the product away. I smiled at them and said, "Well, if you have to summon to a hearing everyone we gave beer to we will have to hold the proceedings at the Halifax Forum. The only thing I didn't do was drive the truck down to Portland Street and give away beer on the street corner." Derek Oland, also in attendance at the meeting, told them that we had given beer to an RCMP softball team. This certainly alerted them. And while it was true, it was my quick instinct to get as few people in trouble as possible. So I said, "No, they were members of the Dartmouth police force." The Mounties accepted that, although I suspect these two wily investigators knew I was not telling the complete truth.

The provincial government was taking matters more seriously that I thought, however, and we were later charged with multiple violations of the Liquor Control Act, mostly in Cape Breton, and fined $37,000. I think we established a Canadian record of some kind. Phillip Oland and I, along with our Cape Breton draft salesman, Ray McChesney of New Waterford, met with Attorney General Richard A. Donahoe to discuss the matter. I knew Dick well from his days as mayor of Halifax when I was a city hall reporter. While he was very pleasant, he explained that there was still a consequential temperance group active in Nova Scotia and the government had no choice but to follow the law, which clearly indicated that we were in serious violation of the Liquor Control Act. The court cases proceeded and our attorney, Reg Cluney, pleaded guilty to all charges. It was all done quietly.

In a funny sidebar to this event: my friend from Dosco days, Ian MacNeil of the *Cape Breton Post*, called to read me the story they planned to run the following day saying that the whole affair was a public relations ploy planned and executed by yours truly, a man "who had been named the Public Relations Man of the Year" in Canada a few years back. We at Moosehead thought we had the problem out of the way, and the fines were paid; I asked him not to run the story, which would undoubtedly anger the government. He laughingly agreed.

Strangely the publicity about the convictions and fines didn't hurt sales; in fact they seemed to help, as we continued to gain ground. One benefit was that the requests for free beer decreased dramatically, and we were able to tell others who called that we were no longer allowed to have the product sampled in that manner. One of the offshoots of this episode was the creation of a Brewers' Institute, a self-policing body which the government encouraged in an effort to extricate itself from the brewery sales wars. John MacInnis, a prominent Halifax lawyer, was named chairman and was given the power to fine and discipline the breweries should they contravene the Liquor Control Act. Similar institutions existed in other provinces. Moosehead had its own investigator, retired RCMP sergeant Don Davis, a pleasant and conscientious man who performed his duties with diligence and fairness. We were caught a few times, and fined for what I considered minor violations. One Christmas we were fined $1,000, unfairly I thought, for giving each employee a case of beer for the holidays. David happened to be on the parking lot at closing time when the men were walking out, each with a case of beer under his arm.

I can recall appearing before John MacInnis on only one occasion. It was an informal hearing held in his office. One of the salesmen had been accused of giving beer to a tavern operator for a staff picnic, and I was asked to appear and explain. John found us guilty as charged and we were given a small fine. He was an all-knowing type of fellow, and I can remember him saying to me smilingly, "Arnie, I know that you have a lot of liberality built into that sports machine of yours," and he warned that they were watching.

As mentioned earlier I had pinpointed Cape Breton as our major battleground; I thought Oland's most vulnerable there. Also I knew a lot of people from my Dosco days, one of which was Angus MacDonald, a legend in the Glace Bay region, a councillor, and a big player in the Canadian Legion. A former miner, "Blue," as he was known universally, asked me if I would come to the bay and be master of ceremonies at a ceilidh to be held at Dominion Park on Canada Day. Their plans involved dancing and piping competitions and a band concert by the bay's popular MacDougall Girls' Pipe Band. I not only readily agreed, I also suggested we expand the day's program to include softball tournaments, for both men and women, and a tug-of-war. Blue was delighted and the program was extended.

I had arrived in the bay the night before and attended a meeting of about one hundred people—the softballers, tug-of-war contestants, and others—at the Legion hall. I had the opportunity to speak and did so briefly, wishing all of the participants luck in their endeavours the next day. Blue, the organizer, rose to thank me. He was an old rabble-rouser, a veteran of union political wars, who with his broad shoulders and thick neck had undoubtedly been a physical force in his younger days. While schoolteachers would have been shocked at his ungrammatical speech, he nevertheless gave his messages with gusto and with a shout more appropriate to the baseball park. After an excessive tribute, he told the gathering, "If you enter a pub or a club where they don't have Moosehead beer, tip over the tables." My thought was that I might get arrested in

Glace Bay for starting a riot. I loved the coal towns, and Glace Bay, in part shoddy and downtrodden after a long-faltering economy, was a particular favourite. The charm, of course, was the people—warm and generous with a sense of fun hardly experienced anywhere that I have been.

The next morning, Canada Day, we were greeted with a brilliant sun. I was a little tired as I had spent the night before at the Social Club in the downtown with my old friend Jack Delaney, the international vice president of the United Mine Workers of America, District 26. And while it had been a longer night than I had wished for, it had been great fun, for Jack was a wonderful host and had such a talent for friendship. I'd felt as if I was running for an election. Jack had me make the rounds of the club, shaking hands and modestly bowing my head as my ebullient friend, in his natural Irish way, told one and all that I had been a great friend of the coal miners in Nova Scotia. After this unstinting praise I bought a round for all assembled. The night wound up with Jack, a great tenor, giving us a rendition of all the old Irish songs.

Fully dressed in kilt and all the trappings, I left the Glace Bay Hotel shortly before noon for a walk to nearby Victoria Park where the Scottish dancing competitions would be held. En route I encountered Soupy Kelly of the brewery staff, who had arrived early in one of the company trucks with a load of beer for distribution at the party we were planning for the softball players and tug-of-war contestants. I asked him what he had done with the beer. "It's safely stowed away," he laughed. Blue had met them and taken them to the jail where, using his authority as a councillor, he'd had it stored in an empty cell. Well I spent the afternoon in the boiling sun, enjoying the piping competition and presiding over a host of young girls performing the various Scottish dances. It was great fun. One of the highlights was the performance by the MacDougall Girls' Pipe Band—all youngsters I would say from ages 13 to 17. I got so carried away with enthusiasm for the band (the pipes and drums do that to me), that I invited them to come to Dartmouth the following month for the opening of the new brewery. They came and paraded on the brewery's big front lawn, and gave a thrill to the large crowd that attended this propitious affair. The Glace Bay ceilidh wound up with a reception for the team-sports participants at the famous Caledonia Hall; the Caledonians, of course, a legendary name in English rugby circles and at one time national champions. The hall was packed with both the softballers and the rope pullers, and the centre of the hall was filled with cases of beer. Everyone was polite enough to allow Mayor Dan "The Baker" MacDonald to make his remarks, and then there was a dive for the beer. I think all got a good share.

The Moosehead years were good years and I made a lot of new friends. I was not a desk-bound executive but travelled the province extensively, taking a very active part in both the public relations and sales programs at the brewery and spending much time in Cape Breton, where eventually we wound up with more than fifty percent of the market. Don Valardo and I often drove the entire loop of the province, going from Halifax down the South Shore to Yarmouth and then up the Digby shore through the

Annapolis Valley. Then we would head out to Truro–New Glasgow, and on to Cape Breton. And we would stop at every tavern en route.

In the early days there had been a strong resistance to the Moosehead product, which had earned a bad reputation during the war years. Phillip Oland told me this was due to the distribution of "green"—improperly brewed—beer during the absence of the company's professional brewers, himself included, who went overseas with the Canadian forces. We had initial success with the lager Alpine, but Moose was very slow to catch on. I can remember at one marketing meeting when Bill Robinson suggested we eliminate the brand in Nova Scotia. I loved the name, and thought it a good product. So we stayed with it and ultimately met with pretty good success, particularly in Cape Breton where it became a favourite.

My departure from the brewery was in part provoked by the demand that I give up the presidency of the Canada Summer Games, slated for Halifax in the summer of 1969. By 1967 I had already put together a pretty good organization, spending considerable time and energies in what I believed would be good exposure for the brewery and an opportunity to strengthen our reach into the Halifax market, which was still somewhat a weak link. It was a major event for Halifax and involved several thousand volunteers. I think that Derek and Bill Robinson convinced Phillip that it would take too much time from my other duties, so I was told that I had to resign. I was disappointed. We'd had fun putting things together, and I had been highly successful (through Allan MacEachen) in getting the Feds to increase the capital budget for facilities. With these monies we were able to upgrade the stadium at St. Mary's; build a running track at Beazley Field in Dartmouth, a softball stadium on the Commons, lawn bowling facilities at the Wanderers Grounds, and tennis courts on the South Commons; upgrade paddling and rowing courses in Dartmouth; and make other improvements to the sporting plant of Halifax. These were major contributions to the athletic infrastructure of the cities, and these facilities remain in place today.

During that period the Dartmouth Liberals were urging me to run as their federal representative in the 1968 summer election. This would mean a big change in my life; if elected, I would be moving the family to Ottawa and giving up my job. The radio station was maturing but it was not in a position to pay me the salary that I could earn elsewhere. I can't say that Glo was jumping up and down waiting for me to throw my hat, or whatever, into the ring, but she agreed. So I decided to resign from the brewery, again not an easy decision, as I enjoyed my time there. Phillip Oland came over that week on other business and, when he and I adjourned to the Alpine Room for a beer, I told him of my decision to leave and consequent to that my plan to seek the Liberal nomination in Dartmouth. He made comments about the insecurity and uncertainties of political life, and said that I should think things over for a few days. I declined that kind offer, as I had my mind made up and I knew there was no turning back. When I left the brewery in May 1968 we had a market share of 36 percent and had in fact reached 38 percent for the month. It had been a successful run, but for me it was over.

Chapter Eleven: The Candidate

Once my mind was made up to run in the 1968 election I gave it my full attention. I had the blessing of the majority of the riding executive and many old Liberal friends. I was, however, not without opposition, and the crowning was not totally unanimous. There were two other contestants: a man with the improbable name of Dr. John Doe, a marine scientist; and a lawyer by the name of Ace Furlong. (Ace was a name he acquired when boxing at Dalhousie.) The doctor, with the support of latter-day Dartmouth mayor Eileen Stubbs, was the only real opposition.

There is always an up side to most things, and one of the benefits of this preliminary was getting to know the grass roots of the Liberal Party and its adherents better by campaigning for the delegate vote throughout the whole riding. This included visits and speeches to groups in both large centres and small villages: Dartmouth, Bedford, Jeddore, Musquodoboit Harbour, Eastern Passage, and other localities. The finale came with the nomination meeting at the Dartmouth high school. The preliminary scuffles helped generate a capacity crowd and while I was nervous (you can't take part in any election without moments of doubt), I was at the same time confident. As it turned out I won handily on the first ballot. Dr. Doe was a distant second; poor Ace registered a "knock out," with himself as victim.

All these years later I regret one minor incident. My opponent was J. Michael Forrestall, the sitting Tory member of Parliament. I had known Mike since we were boys. In fact we grew up on the same street, and while I was a few years older we were friendly and I certainly had no personal animus towards him. Someone on the campaign committee suggested that I attack him, so I included a line in my nomination speech about him being "a do-nothing member." That night as I stood on the podium, I scratched out those words and made no reference at all to my opponent. Unfortunately I had only one copy of the remarks, and I gave them to the reporter for the Halifax *Mail-Star*. The next day my remarks about the "do-nothing member" were featured high up in the copy. I always regretted that because while I was to run two elections against Mike (I was unsuccessful in both), I never dealt in the negatives, nor did I attack him publicly at any time. It just wasn't in my nature and isn't today, so long after the fact.

Before I dwell on the ensuing contest, I should explain why I would make the irrational decision to run as a candidate in the first place. Many times over the years I have suggested to younger friends contemplating political office that, for most people anyway, it is a decision made in the midst of the night, and it is not ever a rational decision. My nod to seek the job was irrational: it involved quitting a good job and embracing the possibility of moving my family to a far distant city. But at the heart of my quest was Pierre Elliott Trudeau, the newly minted prime minister, and his call for a "just society." This appealed to every idealistic bone in my body. Further, the seat in question, Dartmouth–Halifax East, was newly created, and this would be the first time that Dartmouthians and their closer neighbours would elect a member on their own. Historically it had been a dual riding simply known as Halifax. As a Dartmouth boy, a son of a Dartmouth boy, a grandson of a Dartmouth boy, and a great-grandson of a Dartmouth boy, I thought it fitting that I endeavour to represent my home town in the House of Commons.

I had become enchanted with Pierre Trudeau the previous year at the 1967 Liberal leadership convention. I went to Ottawa as a supporter of native son the Honourable Allan MacEachen, and on his behalf I took part in a television broadcast directed at the voting delegates. I was a great admirer of Allan, and remain so today. I had been with him in Moscow that year for the Russian home Olympics, and we'd had great fun. He was not seen as a major contender for the leadership though those close to him, knowing of his oratorical abilities, believed that he could gain momentum with a great convention speech. Also he had strong credentials as a Liberal. He had been first elected to the House in 1953, had stayed on to work with Lester Pearson during the years in which the party was out of power, and had come back as a cabinet minister in the Pearson fold when they were returned. As labour minister, and then again as health minister, he played a lead role in important legislation and had been minister of health when medicare was finally approved. So he was a worthy candidate for the leadership of the Liberal Party, even with the media contending that he was not a threat.

It was obvious during the first few days of the convention that Allan was indeed a long shot. Even our small Nova Scotian delegation was split; Robert Winters of Lunenburg and Cape Breton's MacEachen both were in quest of the leadership. There was little question that Winters was better-known. He had considerably more pull with delegates from central and western Canada, as he had been the president of the major Canadian mining company Rio Tinto; and he had been a member of earlier Liberal cabinets. My own allegiance remained firm but given the mood that prevailed it would have been foolhardy not to have a second, albeit private, choice. My hope was that, should his bid founder, Allan would throw his support behind Pierre Trudeau, even then a somewhat new face and figure on the Liberal front. John Turner and Winters seemed to be the only other serious contenders.

On nomination day our hopes were dashed when MacEachen, fighting a cold, gave what was for him a mediocre speech. The content was strong, left of centre, which was to be expected, but it lacked the lilting oratorical flourish that on occasion made MacEachen one of the all time-great speechifiers in the country. Knocked out in the early going, his intentions unannounced, MacEachen delighted those of us who had been intrigued by Trudeau when he walked over and shook hands with the Quebec minister. And although he was to win and to succeed Lester Pearson, not only as the leader of the Liberal Party but also as prime minister, Pierre Trudeau was not without a serious challenge. Robert L. Stanfield, the premier of Nova Scotia, had been elected leader of the Progressive Conservative Party in an acrimonious battle, which included among the fallen warriors John Diefenbaker. Canadians were slowly getting to know Stanfield, and what they saw they liked. As a Nova Scotian I had known Stanfield for quite a long time, and I knew that he was not only a formidable opponent, but a man who would make a solid prime minister. Timing, of course, is important in politics, and the sad thing that happened to Bob Stanfield is that Pierre Trudeau came along at the same time, and he was a much more appealing public figure. I am tired of the word "charismatic," as it has been used far too often when Trudeau's name is mentioned, and yet it is a word that truly fitted this new political personality.

Former mayor of Dartmouth Joe Zatzman agreed to serve as my campaign manager, and there are few in our midst more wise and wily in the ways of politics than this former grocer turned housing magnate. We had another gem in his assistant campaign manager, budding lawyer John A. Young. Today John Young, as a former president of the Nova Scotia Liberal Party, is recognized as one of the brightest political brains in the province. I can say that even as a youngster (and he was in his early twenties when he worked with me in 1968) he was always one of the brightest guys in the room. There were many others—too many to name, and most staunch old Liberals who were there to support you because you were the party standard bearer; had you been running as an independent, or as a Conservative, they would not have been present. It is a wonderful feeling, and one that I have never forgotten, having so many people, many whom you never knew before, out knocking on doors, making phone calls, and doing the dull, dreary work of organizing mailing lists. I have never lost my feeling of obligation to these workers.

For me the duties and responsibilities that come with being an electoral candidate were never a chore. I am a "people person," and the opportunity that elections present for contact with others is of course what the game is all about. I enjoyed the hustle and bustle of meeting nights in various parts of the constituency, but my particular favourite was the door-to-door canvass. I could not do it today, but in those years as a candidate I was more athletic. Walking was easy, and I enjoyed this one-on-one contact with the voter.

When I ran in 1968 there was an expectation by many people that I would win and uproot the sitting member. Certainly we had a strong organization and, while I may

Candidate Arnie Patterson with Prime Minister Pierre Elliot Trudeau at a rally at the Dartmouth K-Mart.

have ultimately lost, it turned out that I was an easy candidate to raise money for. We had a substantial budget, and although money and its expenditure do not win elections, they help. Also I was buoyed up by the conviction that Trudeau would win. I remained enraptured by his performance on the national scene. Under the chairmanship of my brother-in-law Jack Cruickshank, the provincial organization gave us strong support, as did the national party under the chairmanship of my old friend Keith Davey. In fact both of these branches of the organization believed that, outside of Allan MacEachen, I had the best chance of winning. Candidates such as Harry Flemming up in Cumberland–Colchester, Jim Kinley in Lunenburg, and Dr. Greg Tompkins in Halifax were not seen as contenders, and for this reason the Dartmouth seat was given many preferences.

There were three negative factors confronting me in my daily canvasses, and these were not things over which I had any personal control. The most disturbing was anti-French bias. Many times I would meet someone I knew and they would say, "Arnie, I would like to vote for you but I can't support Trudeau, Marchand, Pelletier, Oulette,

Lalonde and those other Frenchmen." This was not widespread, but a prejudice that was out there. My only retort was that, if elected, I would represent Dartmouth and its views. Another concern was the antipathy of the service vote, especially that of naval people and former naval people, who numbered in the thousands. Traditionally the service vote was almost always a Liberal vote. As late as 1965, Halifax Liberal candidates Gerry Regan and Jack Lloyd won the election on the late-arriving service vote. But that changed when the Liberal government moved to integrate the three armed services. It was a terribly unpopular move and particularly resented by members of the Royal Canadian Navy and thus of consequence in the Halifax area. The unification program of minister of defence Paul Hellyer had alienated most people in the service. They were out for revenge, and their way of showing it was to vote Conservative. Regardless of their political stripes, people are normally polite when candidates knock on their door. Yet the only doors slammed in my face were those of two naval officers. One morning while doing a hand-shaking exercise at the gate of the Naval Armament Depot, three naval personnel threw my brochure back at me. One man, a tall, good-looking officer, took my brochure, walked about twenty yards, came back and roughly handed it back to me saying, "Forget the navy boat, Mister, you are dead in the water." Rather appropriate. Clearly unification was not a winning issue for a Liberal in the Halifax area, and while I thought (and still do) that unification was a mistake, I was tarred with the Hellyer brush.

The third concern, and a greater threat, was the desire of Nova Scotians to make Robert L. Stanfield, one of their own, the prime minister of Canada. I confronted this reality on the doorstep every day. Stanfield, who had been premier for ten years (1958-68), was highly respected, and I always had the feeling, in both of my campaigns, that he was the opponent I personally faced; his was the name I encountered. Stanfield was running just across the harbour in the Halifax seat, and his proximity was not very comforting.

The fight in Dartmouth created some interest on the national scene, and I was chosen as a candidate to be featured nationally in both radio and television interviews. Undoubtedly, Keith Davey had much to do with this selection. While the campaign was moving along favourably—we had a good sign-advertising program, lots of helpers at campaign headquarters, and good turnouts at our meetings—there was an obvious danger developing. Our major opposition, the Conservatives, saw us as a threat and started to focus their guns on Dartmouth almost exclusively. Stanfield's victory was pretty much conceded from the beginning, although he had a worthy opponent in Dr. Greg Tompkins, the handsome and popular Halifax medical practitioner. In most elections Greg would have been an easy winner in my opinion, but in facing the national leader of the Conservative party he was at best a sacrificial lamb. Bob McCleave, who had been first elected in 1957, winning again in 1958 and '62, losing a squeaker in 1963, but won again in '65. He was also a shoo-in against little known Liberal Alex

Cregan. Confident of victory in these two seats, Tory strategists diverted almost all advertising and promotion monies from these campaigns to Dartmouth and the Mike Forrestall bid for re-election.

A funny thing happened when I was singled out for a national television feature on *The Most Promising Liberal Newcomers*. A CBC television crew spent two days with me on the campaign trail, and a considerable amount of time filming me in my home and family environment. The show was to be topped off by a face-to-face interview with Peter Herndorf, then one of their hot guns. Herndorf, now a major figure in Ontario television and journalism circles, was a graduate of Dalhousie Law School and a friend of my assistant campaign manager John Young. I had to go to the Lord Nelson Hotel for the final shooting, which was to take place in Herndorf's hotel room. John, for some reason that escapes me, was going to be late for the interview but said he would drop in to say hello to Herndorf.

I found the Toronto broadcaster a bit aggressive and not too friendly in his early questions. As an old reporter I knew the signs, and for some reason he was out to have me make some mistake in judgement. For instance his first question was "Do you want to be prime minister one day?" This was a bit of a staggering start but I came back quickly with the response "I have to get out of Dartmouth first." He followed that up with "Do you think you will go to heaven when you die?" I had to laugh at that but I answered, "I think so but I am not prepared to leave, and hopefully, for some years yet." He had just hit me with a question on unification, one I could not win on, when the door opened and in came John Young. They immediately embraced, and Herndorf asked, "How is my old friend Aggie Kukulowicz? Have you seen him lately?" Before John could answer I said, "Do you know Aggie Kukulowicz? I had dinner with him in Moscow last summer." A look of shock came over John's face. Little did I know that this was a charade that Herndorf had carried out in his years at Dal. He would go to a cocktail party or gathering, and say things like: "Did you read Professor Aggie Kukulowicz's paper on the new revelations in biochemistry?" "Who do you think is the more outstanding poet: Carl Sandburg, or Aggie Kukulowicz?" Many times, to shield their ignorance, victims would simply say, "Professor Kukulowicz, of course." Anyway, the college prankster Herndorf had read Aggie's name on the sporting pages, as he had been an outstanding western junior hockey player. He became intrigued by the name and used it in his ruse. He immediately confronted me asking, "How did you get to know Aggie?" and this too in an aggressive tone. I explained, and innocently, that I had dinner with him when I had visited Moscow the year before with Allan MacEachen, and that Aggie was the Air Canada representative there. That didn't quite stop him, for he looked puzzled. And then I added, "Of course I knew him slightly when he was a hockey player. He was up for a cup of tea with the New York Rangers and played but a handful of games." John looked relieved, and Herndorf shook my hand and said I was the first person he'd

Visiting Moscow in 1967 for the Russian Spartakiad, their home Olympics. (left to right) The Hon. Allan MacEachen, Canada's Minister of Health; Arnie Patterson, then president of the Canada Summer Games.

ever met who not only knew who Aggie Kukulowicz was, but actually knew him personally. I would term the rest of the interview "quite gentle." And on election night I got a telegram saying "A good candidate lost tonight in Dartmouth but congratulations anyway." It was simply signed Aggie.

Another unusual thing happened during the election, and this only about a week before the vote. I won a car at a Rotary Club draw. I had gone to the dinner at the Mic Mac Club, our old bailiwick, and was almost stunned when my name was drawn. I am sure there were Tories in the room who thought the draw was fixed, but no; I don't even remember if the person conducting the draw was a Liberal. I was not all that happy with the publicity, as the papers highlighted my win and undoubtedly turned off a number of voters. It was a small car so I traded in at the dealership for a new, medium-sized Buick for my wife, and a very pretty car it was.

During the campaign rumours surfaced that Fairey Aviation, the riding's biggest employer, was going to be forced to close because the government was not renewing certain of its contracts. Mike Forrestall assured them that this would not come to pass if a Tory government was elected. To help calm mounting fears, Keith Davey, coming to my aid once again, sent Defence Minister C. M. (Bud) Drury to campaign with me. We toured the aircraft plant and later held a press conference at the Holiday Inn. The show of support was of help, but the minister did not categorically say the plant would not lose the government contracts, although he did say that plans for future purchases from Fairey had not been finalized. In that the plant was to close within a year and a half I suspect that he was at least honest.

Two nights before election day, Glo and I headed off to Musquodoboit Harbour for one of our bigger election rallies. En route we had to drive by the K-Mart, which was the site of a major final rally for Mike Forrestall, and it featured Tory leader Robert L.

Stanfield. I suspect other Conservative candidates were there as well, along with the national media. We had to wheel our way through a monstrous traffic tie-up and, as we drove by the K-Mart, I could see that the parking lot was crowded. I knew instinctively that we were in trouble. The turnout was an ominous sign, and the fact that it was being staged in Dartmouth, the site of Stanfield's last appearance in Nova Scotia, indicated to me that this was another major and deliberate blow at our campaign. When I arrived at Musquodoboit Harbour John Young, who seemed to know or sense everything, asked me, "Did you drive by the K-Mart on the way down?" I told him I had. He said nothing more, but I sensed that he had experienced much the same feeling as I upon witnessing the size of the crowds. We had had our own rally at the K-Mart earlier in the election with Prime Minister Trudeau in attendance—and it too attracted a huge crowd—but weeks had intervened since that direct boost for my candidacy and our party. Nevertheless, our Musquodoboit rally was a success; we had one of our largest crowds of the campaign. Dartmouth–Halifax East was a big riding, geographically as well as vote-wise, and we attracted people from a large part of Halifax County, with the bulk from Dartmouth and the Eastern Shore.

It had been a busy, demanding and gruelling two months. So on Sunday I advised my energetic campaign planners that the candidate was going to have an easy day and a drive down the Eastern Shore as far as Musquodoboit Harbour. My sole companion and supporter was to be my wife. En route we visited with a few of our senior campaign workers on the shore and went on to dinner at the Camelot Restaurant in the Harbour, a delightful, sedate place run by Mr. and Mrs. Harry Young. Mrs. Young was a Dartmouth Warner and a distant cousin of mine; her husband, a sportsman, had been a friend of my father. We were the only guests that night and while dinner was being prepared Glo and I watched television in their living room. By coincidence, we caught a thirty-minute show featuring Pierre Trudeau, which had been especially planned by the party to give the campaign a final boost. He was brilliant, and I had the distinct thought (and this was at a time when Trudeau was not all that well-known to Canadians) that we had a Marlon Brando as prime minister. Over the years all Canadians, those who liked him and those who didn't, were to discover that our prime minister was one of the greatest actors on the world stage. We had an enthusiastic sendoff from the Youngs whom we so much enjoyed, but I can't remember—and it has nagged at me since—whether or not we paid our dinner bill. Anyway it was a pleasant way to spend the last day of the campaign.

Election day is a busy day for a candidate. In company with John Young, I set out to visit all of the polling booths to let our own workers know that the candidate was on duty, and to shake the hands of both Liberal and opposition workers at the voting stations. This is not a high-powered exercise, but a ceremonial function, and a considered courtesy. That evening I ate at home with my family. I was in the bath before dressing and leaving for the Mic Mac Club where we were to stage our victory party, or whatever, when Glo called out to tell me that the results were in from Shannon Park, a residential area for naval families in north Dartmouth. We were leading, but only slightly. I knew then that a long night lay ahead; in the past, a Liberal candidate could have expected a massive win in those service family areas. Before I finished dressing we were trailing, and we never caught up. When the night was over I was down by over five thousand votes. John Young, always an optimist, pointed out that we had the biggest Liberal vote in the province, just over eighteen thousand, and we had lots of company in defeat. When I first arrived at party headquarters, all eleven Liberal candidates were trailing, and most by wide margins. Even Allan MacEachen, the cabinet minister, was losing, although he ultimately pulled out a win of less than a hundred votes.

Nova Scotians had given Mr. Stanfield a strong sendoff, but before the night was over he too joined the ranks of the losers as Pierre Trudeau won with a majority government. The Truro native was not to become the fourth Nova Scotian nor the first non-Conservative to be prime minister of Canada. One of my final acts on election night was to go to the headquarters of Mike Forrestall, the victor, shake his hand, and give him the rose from my buttonhole. And I did it again six years later. A difficult task for a losing candidate, but an important courtesy.

The day immediately following the election, Glo and I took Carol and Lori to Prince Edward Island for a golfing vacation with Ross and Pat Mitton and their children, Jeff and Heather. It was a delightful respite after several months of unremitting demands on my time and energies. I repaired from the election loss quickly. And while I would have enjoyed working for Dartmouth in the House of Commons and Ottawa, I nevertheless knew that the sun would come up, and it did that day. My old friend Gerald Regan, himself several times a victim rather than a victor, consoled me with the thought that "in politics victory and defeat are equal imposters." My fling with politics was over. Now I had the challenge of finding a job. It was the first time since my teenage years that I faced the prospect of being unemployed. Moosehead had offered me an opportunity to return to the brewery. I would no longer be general manager but second-in-command to Derek Oland, the son of the owner, who would be moving to Dartmouth. Add this to their proviso that I divorce myself from politics and refrain from doing radio commentaries and the demands became too restrictive. I declined the offer.

While I had a family to support I wasn't really worried. I had contacts with several important power brokers in Toronto, although the thought of leaving home again was not particularly attractive to my wife nor to me. Frank Sobey had suggested that I join his company in a senior capacity in the Halifax area, but the grocery business didn't especially appeal to me. Part of my problem was Nova Scotia offered few jobs as good as the job I had resigned from at Moosehead. Before long I had a call from Al Scott, president of the big William Neilson candy company in Toronto, inviting me up for an interview. We had worked together at MacLaren's years before and were friends. When I got there he offered me a job as the senior vice president responsible for both sales and the management of the big plant. The salary was enticing and there were attractive fringe benefits, including membership in St. George's Golf Club, which I consider even today to be one of the best courses in Canada. I accepted.

We bought a nice home in a good neighbourhood, just a block or so from the golf club with nearby schools for the girls. I enjoyed my job in some respects, although sitting at meetings all afternoon to determine how much chocolate would be extracted from a bar in the interests of economy was pretty boring. I did, however, have a chance to travel the country and again make new friends. Neilsons, part of the Weston food empire, was a good old company with which we had all grown up, its Crispy Crunch, Malted Milk, and Jersey Milk bars Canadian traditions. My difficulty there was that my benefactor, Al Scott, was locked in battle with Weston's powers-that-be who wound up not only firing Scott but his boss, the president at Weston's. Six of the people whom Scott had brought into Neilsons walked the plank. I had a contract, so I was relatively safe. And I was further protected in that, just the month previous, we had sold 36 boxcars full of bars. I was asked to an interview with George Metcalf, the chairman of Loblaws and a key player for the Weston family in its wide-ranging operations. A religious zealot, he was a critical of Al Scott's drinking habits; and while I was a new performer, I was seen as a Scott ally. In the presence of his lawyer, he asked me if I thought I could live with the changes that were being made, and I responded in the negative. He then offered me a generous severance package, which I readily accepted as I was prepared to return home anyway. It was not the happiest experience in my life. Al Scott went back to the advertising business from whence he came, but he never fully recovered from this trauma and died a few years later.

I returned home in 1970 and took a chance on turning CFDR into a profitable business. Up until then, its seventh year of operation, the radio station's financial success had been marginal, though it enjoyed a solid reputation with adults. While I certainly spent the bulk of my energies in that arena, I managed to find time to become active again in Liberal politics. I assumed the presidency of the Dartmouth–Halifax East constituency, and I also took a federal fundraiser in cooperation with Austin E. Hayes of Halifax, who was among other things Allan MacEachen's financial guru in politics. While Trudeau had been favoured with a honeymoon period from 1968 to 1969, a troubling economy had landed his government in grave difficulty by the time he called for a general election in 1972. In addition to economic woes, the political unrest in Quebec was worsening as Parti Québécois leader Rene Lévesque continued to gain converts. Though many Canadians supported the prime minister's actions in the 1970 October Crisis, the temporary establishment of military law gave Trudeau's political opponents plenty of ammunition. The kidnapping of British trade commissioner James Cross and Quebec labour minister Pierre Laporte, and the subsequent discovery of Laporte's murdered body in the trunk of a car, had compelled Trudeau to call in the troops to quell further violence and restore order. Because separatist revolutionaries

A family shot included in literature for the 1974 campaign. (left to right) Carol, Glo, Arnie, and Lori.

were behind the kidnapping and murder, hundreds of known active separatists and others considered a risk to the community were arrested and detained. Trudeau, hitherto viewed as a civil libertarian, was vilified by his political opponents. This blemish added to the Liberal woes on the eve of a general election.

Our job as Liberals in Dartmouth was difficult. The Liberal tide so evident in 1968 had ebbed, and the prospects of victory were dim. Because I had just begun to get my own financial house in order, I declined to offer as a candidate, although I did serve on the nominating committee and later worked as a collector—always the lousiest job in politics. Our toughest task was to find a candidate, almost any candidate, as Mike Forrestall was readying for this third straight win and Bob Stanfield remained on the scene with increased national credibility. We received a blessing when a well-respected doctor, John Savage, offered himself as a candidate. In him we not only had a candidate, but one who exuded intelligence as well as energy. He was not widely known then, but he was articulate, had lived in the city for a number of years, and had in the meantime built up a good medical practice.

I was chairman of the Dartmouth Liberal meeting the night Dr. Savage was nominated. After his nomination was moved and unanimously agreed to (he was the only contestant) he approached the stage through a long corridor that took him out of our view for a few seconds. During this interval I said to someone standing near me, "I hope we don't lose him." Despite our candidate's excellence, it was a disastrous campaign. Dr. Savage lost by more than eleven thousand votes, and the Liberals' national results were poor. The overall election was a cliff-hanger, with Trudeau and his government winning by only a few seats. They were able to survive as a minority government with the support of Ed Broadbent and the NDP, but parliament was dissolved and the prime minister called for an election on July 8, 1974. There was a Liberal resurgence, again in the east, and Trudeau and his government were re-elected—this time with a majority.

A photo of Arnie taken for the 1974 campaign.

Given the crushing defeat suffered by the Liberals less than two years earlier, it again became a task to find a suitable candidate—almost any candidate—for the 1974 election. I certainly had no thoughts of running. When later I was called to the premier's office for a meeting, I went without knowledge of what lay ahead. As soon as I opened the door though, I knew exactly what was going on. Sitting with Gerry Regan were Senator Al Graham and the Honourable Garnet A. Brown. I immediately cried out "no." But I was subjected to the "soft-soap" during which I was told by Graham that they had gone through the list of potential candidates in Dartmouth, and that I was the only one who could win. "Thanks for the compliment, Al," I replied, "but Jesus Christ couldn't win in Dartmouth. In case you have all forgotten, Dr. Savage lost by eleven thousand votes less than two years ago, and the tide is still out."

Back in 1968 I had wanted to run, and I did so with total commitment. Now, in the early summer of 1974, I had no desire or thoughts of running in an election. I said to them, "You can't run a man who is in the midst of a divorce." This shocked my three friends. An incredulous Brown said, "You're not getting a divorce are you?" I replied, "I will be if I go home and tell Glo that I'm running for political office."

Nothing was resolved, although I agreed to think about it and discuss the matter with my wife and family. Amazingly both Glo and my daughters felt that I should run.

My situation was a bit easier in '74 than it had been in '68 when I was working for someone else and had to quit my job to accept the nomination. Should I lose this time out, which was certainly possible, I could return to the radio station where I was working full-time. I also didn't have to face a contest for the nomination but rather won by acclamation. Rather remarkably, however, in a fine show of courage and awakened interest in politics, Dr. Savage offered himself for candidacy. Dr. Max Brennan, a staunch Liberal and a partner of John, asked me if I would bow out of the race as Dr. Savage was waiting in the wings. I declined, but suggested that John seek the nomination if he wished, although I was confident I could beat him. "If he or I can not win the nomination," I told him, "we certainly won't be able to win the upcoming election."

Things were looking up for the national Liberals. While some of Pierre Trudeau's initial glamour had worn thin, 1974 saw the government regain some of the support that had been lost two years earlier, and the polls indicated the Liberals could win the country. Stanfield remained the Tory leader. This was to be his third and final bid for the prime ministry, and that remained a continuing threat to any and all Liberal candidates running in Nova Scotia. We did have two new pluses this time out: Gerald Regan's Liberal government was in power provincially, and all three seats in the large Dartmouth–Halifax East riding were in Liberal hands. The economy was quite strong, and the Regan government had balanced the books, so their help was crucial and important. All three of the provincial candidates, Garnet Brown, Glen Bagnell, and Scott McNutt, campaigned on my behalf, and the premier was a major booster.

John Young, who had been with me in 1968, took on the campaign chairmanship. My friend Joe Zatzman, now with his son Michael, remained active as a fund-raiser. We hired a full-time campaign administrator this time out, and Len Giffen, who had run Glen Bagnell's provincial campaign, was an efficient operator. When you run as a Liberal, particularly if the wind is up, you get lots of volunteers and most of them campaign veterans: Dave Jones, Gloria McCluskey, Judy McKinnon, Henry Bailey, Bob Turnbull, Bob Brown, Merlin Kerr, Johnny Marvin, and many others come to mind. I don't know whether I worked as hard in 1974 as I had in the previous campaign, but I was at it every day and most nights. When we started the campaign, knowing we had eleven thousand votes to recapture, we were a little short on optimism. I myself knew we had an uphill battle. But as the campaign waged on I had the feeling we were gaining ground, and the participation of the provincial cabinet members was indeed helpful. A lot of the Liberal heavies came and offered support, including the prime minister; Marc Lalonde; my favourite, John Turner; and a few others.

On election night we had our workers' party at the Dartmouth Inn. We enjoyed moments of optimism as the early returns showed a gain in strength, but we gradually fell behind and lost by 4,500 votes. Putting a positive spin on things (which politicians tend to do), I could at least take comfort in the fact that we had cut the Tory majority by 6,500 votes. I enjoyed the campaign and I had no regrets. I had had strong support from

Prime Minister Trudeau at a Dartmouth seniors citizens affair. (left to right) Arnie Patterson, long-time Liberal Tom Sliming, and the prime minister.

the Liberal organization, and I myself had worked diligently. I learned from running a federal election that national politics is quite different from municipal and provincial politics. As Gerry Regan once explained, in municipal races both or all candidates are equal, and all have shotguns. In provincial races the candidate has a shotgun but is up against machine-gun fire coming from the party-leadership race. In federal races they break out the cannon fire. The local candidate, while important, is of less consequence because people have a tendency to vote for leaders and parties.

As I think back on these political endeavours do I have any regrets? Honestly, no. Being a candidate was fun, and I would have enjoyed the opportunity to both help my home town and serve the country. The losses may have dented my pride a bit, but in no lasting way. And at least I know that I'm now much better off financially than I would have been had I spent some years in the Ottawa backbenches.

Chapter Twelve: The Birth of CFDR and Q104

In the course of my episodic career, few things have given me more pleasure than my 25-year association with radio stations CFDR and Q104. While I had the assistance of many others, they were truly my creations. I emerged as a radio station owner somewhat accidentally. I had spent a number of happy years in radio, broadcasting horse races, hockey and baseball games, and assorted sporting menus, but my real and primary interest as a young communicator was in newspapers. And though I found these media to be complementary, newspaper reporting was more challenging and in some respects more fulfilling for me. Having said that, radio offers its own rewards. It is a magical medium. It is instantaneous. In many ways, it is the most inventive medium of them all.

It has been my experience that print and broadcast media offer different truth values. Certainly both television and radio put the recipient of the messages on the scene. What can be more vivid, more believable than television news footage showing Palestinian youngsters throwing rocks at the poor, beleaguered soldiers of Israel? It is there for all to see. Yet there are those, and I suspect they are somewhat older, who truly believe only when they can read about such incident, mull it over, and read it again. There is a comfort and a familiarity in the written word that is in itself unique. Even in my years of working away in Toronto I would, on my return to Nova Scotia for vacation, take on the job of editing the *Dartmouth Free Press*. My friend the late Ralph (Kelly) Morton would leave on his holidays, and I would edit and virtually write the paper. Kelly had an outstanding newspaper career, mostly in the United States, where he worked for many years with the Associated Press. He and his wife, Ruth McAulay Morton, were both native Nova Scotians, and like most of us they too were homing pigeons. He quit a good job as a senior deskman with the AP in New York to return to what many saw as a wild gamble; he founded the *Dartmouth Free Press* in 1953.

At that time, Dartmouth had been without a weekly since the *Patriot* had folded under Edmund Morris almost two years before. Then a town of between fifteen- and seventeen thousand (and this before the Macdonald Bridge emerged), Dartmouth had never had a daily newspaper but rather a succession of weeklies dating back more than 150 years. Kelly Morton had worked on the Herald papers in his younger years and was a graduate of Dal Law, although he never practised law. He was well connected in the Halifax community, a son of a prominent Halifax doctor, and his brothers, Allan and Blenus, were respectively the City of Halifax's chief medical officer and the County of Halifax's solicitor. I remember telling my boss, R. J. Rankin at the Halifax dailies that Kelly was starting a new newspaper in Dartmouth. He scoffed and said that he would go broke. Although I was working on the *Mail-Star* as its city hall reporter, I was friendly with Kelly and used to go his Albert Street house on Tuesday nights and write copy for his weekly edition on Thursday. I was sort of picking up where I had left off with the old Patriot although by then my interests had switched from sports to local politics. And though I later left for Toronto and Montreal, we maintained our friendship over the years. Even when I returned to run the brewery in 1964, I periodically wrote articles for his paper. Bob Rankin's prophecy didn't prove accurate. The *Free Press* not only survived but, under Morton's editorship, with a major contribution from his journalist wife Ruth, it became an important factor in Dartmouth life. Some years later it was named the best weekly in Canada. While Morton was somewhat unheralded, I don't think (and this looking back over a long period of time) that there were many people who made a greater contribution to life in Dartmouth than Kelly Morton during that era.

With the newspaper vacuum filled, any thoughts I had about starting a paper in my home town went unrealized. But on a nice summer day in 1961, while I was still living in Montreal, I spied a notification in the *Gazette* that the Canadian Radio-Television Commission was going to grant new radio licenses. With the 1956 opening of the first harbour bridge Dartmouth began a period of remarkable growth. Five years later, on January 1, 1961, the town was given city status by the provincial legislature. I. W. Akerley was the high-powered mayor at the time and he was pushing hard for business and industrial growth. Sitting in my Montreal office on that fateful morning, I made two phone calls to Halifax: the first to Vince Currie, an old friend and former technical hand at CJCH during my hockey broadcast days; and the second to Jack Cruickshank, my brother-in-law. I told them of my plans to apply for a radio station in Dartmouth. Both agreed to participate and would ultimately become shareholders and directors of Radio Dartmouth Limited.

I suspect that, subconsciously, part of my desire related to the ultimate prospect of moving back home, although my old dream of one day being a media owner was part and parcel of it as well. The hearings were slated for late in the summer of 1961, so we had to hustle to get our submission in order. One of our major undertakings was to meet the Department of Transport's demand for more than thirty acres of land for our radio towers. Through a connection of Fred Lahey we found a suitable tract of land owned by the Cooper brothers on Montague Mines Road. It lay just outside of the then Dartmouth boundary, and we paid $9,000 for it. While I was to write the main submission and the city backgrounder, and this with promises of community involvement, we gathered up letters of recommendation from various local interest and business groups. Our printed submission was held up for some years after as a model for applicants, and I had many requests for copies from other aspirants.

A key player in the station's founding, Jack Cruickshank, president of Sackville Downs Limited, was a CFDR director for a number of years.

There were a few people over the years who suggested that we had been successful with the application because of our supposed Liberal connections. I should point out that when we went before the CRTC, the Conservatives under John Diefenbaker were in power. Our team would not have been interpreted as Tory Blue by anyone, for the principals—Jack Cruickshank, Vince Currie, our lawyer Gordon L. S. Hart, our accountant Irving Barrow, and I were all Liberals. We had merit in our application, which I clearly believe won us the license and the day.

Dartmouth, then a new city of 46,500, was by statistical count the fastest growing community in Canada at that time. Further it was the largest community in the country without a daily voice of any kind. That was our thrust. We were not without opposition. CHNS and CHFX, the two old Halifax stations, strongly opposed us. Indeed their manager, Fred Arenburg, appeared before the CRTC on the stations' behalf, arguing that the market (and he portrayed Halifax–Dartmouth as one market) could not financially support another station. Rather kindly, my old boss Finlay MacDonald of CJCH did not oppose the application, although he told me later that he did not think we would succeed. A great disappointment, however, was that my old friend Kelly Morton of the *Dartmouth Free Press* sent a letter to the CRTC, expressing his opposition on financial grounds.

The CRTC hearings were formal and serious undertakings. One had to appear before a tribunal of nine commissioners from various parts of the country, plus their support group of lawyers, accountants, and technical experts. The applicant would speak for fifteen or so minutes, outlining plans for the station, giving emphasis to programming content and community involvement. This was followed by oral submissions from those opposing the application—in this instance, Fred Arenburg. The applicant was then given an opportunity to rebut the remarks of the opponents. I had made our presentation and was called on to do the rebuttal. I must admit that I was helped greatly by the fact that CHNS had strenuously opposed an application less than two years before for a Dartmouth radio outlet, this made by John Funston, who at one time had served as the CHNS program manager. I had a copy of their submission for this earlier hearing and was able to write my rebuttal remarks in advance, knowing that their arguments would be little changed.

Sometimes the decision of the commission is not announced for weeks, but we were back at the hotel for only a few hours and having a drink in the lounge at the Chateau Laurier when I received a phone call from Roy Duchemin, the Nova Scotian member on the commission. He informed me that our application had been approved. We were not to get official notice for some weeks but, I must say, that call put us in a celebratory mood. While we were without so-called political clout, I had made several preparatory trips to Ottawa to call on CRTC officials, including Dr. Andrew Stewart, the chairman, and Carlyle Allison, the deputy chairman, to familiarize them with our plans. Allison, an old newspaperman and a friend of my Ottawa comrade Dr. D. Leo Dolan, another of the newspaper tribe, was particularly open to my approach. Also I had several conversations with Roy Duchemin, the publisher of the *Cape Breton Post*, who had become well-known to me in my capacity as public relations manager of Dosco, and was now a golfing partner when I visited Sydney.

Sometime later, after we had won approval, I happened to run into John Funston, the earlier, unsuccessful applicant, at a Canadian Association of Broadcasters meeting in Montreal. John was then the manager of CFCF radio in Montreal. He was at a loss to understand how we had won the license while he had been rejected. I asked him who he had talked to prior to his appearance before the commission. He said no one. John always gave me the impression that he—and not Marconi—was the inventor of radio, and I suppose he thought it beneath him to solicit support from others. While I did nothing underhanded, I fully admit that I campaigned for the license. In fact I still firmly believe that in sales the more times you shoot at the net, the more times you score.

Giving birth to a new enterprise is always exciting and makes the adrenaline flow. There was much to be done, a staff to hire and physical facilities to be built. I hired Syd Pilkington as station manager. Syd, a former copy chief at CJCH, was a very honourable man and an old radio hand. I sought out my brother Bill as sales manager and Gerry Mulcahy as our second man in that department. Both were to stay with the station for years; Gerry until he died more than 20 years later, and Bill on retirement 25 years later. Another ace acquired during our startup period was Jack Hutchison, a former CBC technical man who became our engineering chief. What a star he was. Vince Currie recruited him, and he stayed with the operation until his retirement 28 years later. Another strong personality in our fledgling operation was Clary Flemming, who came on as sportscaster from his position as race announcer at Sackville Downs and later became the manager of the station for a number of years; he has gone on to major success as a radio and television consultant and producer. My wife's sister Lois, just about the prettiest girl in Halifax–Dartmouth, was the station receptionist–secretary, and a key player in the early days. Most of the original staff of 19 were recruited from local radio, former employees of CJCH and known to Vince Currie and me. I was inundated with hundreds of applications, including many from other parts of Canada. The morning man I settled on was a young broadcaster by the name of Dick Bordeau, who had been working at a station in Sarnia. He was a bright young broadcaster and gave the station a lot of early-morning pep. Our first newsman, a lone figure at that time, was Ben Dalfen, a New Brunswicker who later moved to Israel where he has had a long and distinguished career in radio. He was a novice in those days, but no one put more of an effort into a job than Ben.

Establishing banking credit is always a key element in the founding of any new enterprise, and in this we approached the Royal Bank of Canada at their main branch on George Street in Halifax. This was Sackville Downs' bank, and Jack Cruickshank was well-known to its senior people. Our dealings were with Al Fowler, the soft-spoken, pipe-smoking manager of the main branch. He was receptive and not only agreed to finance our physical startup costs of about $275,000, but gave us personal financing for our shares and established an operating line of credit of $75,000, which we thought sufficient for our needs. While we were to experience ups and downs with finances, I am pleased to tell you that almost forty years later I am still a customer of the Royal Bank. Knowing your bankers and keeping in touch with them, letting them know of both successes and problems, is advice that I give to young friends. A successful banking relationship is one of the most important things in the running of any business. Get to know your bankers. If some young banker at the Royal found the file of my letters written over the years, particularly in the early years, that person would find that I had a remarkable ability to overestimate sales, and underestimate expenses. But I guess that goes with an optimistic nature.

We established station headquarters over Lahey's paint store on Ochterloney Street, in the heart of Dartmouth's old downtown. Our landlord was my long-time friend and mentor, Fred M. Lahey, a prominent Dartmouth businessman and sportsman. We occupied the second floor of his building with a total square footage of about fifteen hundred. While not large the space was nicely finished, and in addition to the main control room, we had a second broadcast studio and a small newsroom. The other space was given over to sales and administration. In the early months of our operation we were permitted to broadcast only during daytime hours, usually from about 7:00 a.m. until shortly after 5:00 p.m. We were sharing a frequency with another station, which was soon to vacate, and when that occurred in the spring we would be allowed to assume a full-time schedule. The station had its launch on December 5, 1962. For us it was an

Lois Hoadley, Glo's sister, was CFDR's first receptionist and a regular feature on station billboards.

auspicious occasion, and we invited half the town to our grand opening. Among the VIPs were Premier Robert L. Stanfield, Mayor John Lloyd of Halifax, and Mayor I. W. Akerley of Dartmouth. Our small premises were jammed, and I recall the booze bill being over $2,000—a princely sum in those days. We were on a high, but it was not to last. By early spring we were in financial difficulty. We had used up our entire $75,000 credit line, and while we had a strong start with Christmas advertising in our first month of operation, the months of January and February were disastrous. I knew how Napoleon must have felt with his armies mired in the snows of Russia.

I had a friend in Boston, Norman Knight, who was the owner of six radio stations and a highly experienced operator. I called on him for some help and he agreed to meet me in Halifax, inspect the operation, and troubleshoot for us. We stayed at the Nova Scotian Hotel during that visit, and on the night of our arrival we had a cocktail party for our small list of clients. Also we had a delegation there from the Royal Bank, and I paraded Norman before them as if he was a show pony, praising him as a financial wizard when it came to radio operations, which he truly was. The next day, after reviewing our financial statements, he said, "If I had known that you were in this much trouble I would not have come up here to Halifax." Anyway Norman stayed at it. He interviewed everyone on our new staff the following day; he gave poor brother Bill and Gerry Mulcahy a lecture they didn't appreciate; and I gather that when he was finished with the entire group some were quaking. That night as we sat in the hotel room with a drink, Norman told me that I had a lot of work to do. He said, "You have lots of friends in business in Halifax and a lot in Toronto, and you are going to have to call them all looking for business. And you may find out that you have fewer real friends than you think."

The other disturbing news was that we were going to have to lay off at least five people from our modest staff of 19. I had never had the difficult task of firing people before, but I arrived at the station at eight the next morning to face it. The first casualty, unexpectedly, was the manager Syd Pilkington, who adamantly refused to take part in the cuts. When I told him the only other option was for him to resign, he did so on the

CFDR goes on the air, December 5, 1962. Premier Robert L. Stanfield officiated at the opening. (left to right) Arnie Patterson, Mr. Stanfield, director Jack F. Cruickshank, Dartmouth mayor I. W. Akerley, Halifax mayor John A. Lloyd.

spot. That was not a very good start to the day for me, but in following directions from Norman I went on to dismiss four other unhappy people before the morning was over. It was an awful experience. One thing I learned then, and many times over since, is that there's no nice or easy way to fire people. However, I rationalized then, as I do now, that the job of management is to keep the ship afloat, and that tough decisions sometimes had to be made to insure the employment of others and your own survival.

Later that day I met with Bill and Gerry. We worked on a sales campaign, offering discounted prices, and we mapped out an approach to a series of potential advertisers. We needed to generate dollars as quickly as possible. The next week I went to Toronto and called on the advertising agencies, particularly my old friends at MacLaren's, Vickers and Benson, McKim's, and a few others, offering what I described as "the best buy in town." I had a fair response. I am pleased to report that by June we were close to breaking even and the blood bath stopped. In desperation we had appointed Clary Flemming, the sportscaster, to be the manager, and this proved a wise choice. He remained at the station for close to eight years and was a very thoughtful programmer. While these were painful days in some respects, the actions taken guaranteed the station's survival, and ultimately its long-term success.

During CFDR's formative years I continued with outside employment by necessity. I had to make money to pay the interest on my loans, and in this way I made more money than the station could pay me. During the years when I was not directly involved in everyday management, I maintained close contact, airing a daily broadcast feature entitled *Round and About*, which allowed me at least to give some editorial direction to the station. When I returned from Toronto in 1969, I became the full-time president and was actively involved in all aspects of the operation. The station had gained a good following and a sterling reputation among the adult population in both Halifax and Dartmouth. Financial success was at best moderate, however, and there was continuing need for the shareholders to put more money into the project. Certainly there were no dividends. But we were on an even keel, and with the continuing growth of the metro area we were confident of the future.

There were many ups and downs during the formative sixties. Major among the problems was our broadcasting signal on 790. Due to the location of the transmitter at Montague, the strongest part of our signal was going in the wrong direction, and at night many of our listeners in Halifax as well as Dartmouth lost us. Because of the costs involved we had to live with it for a few years, but Vince Currie found us a new site on Kearney Lake Road and the subsequent relocation gave us a better signal, although with some continuing problems. We also experienced staffing changes. I think I had been home less than a year when Clary Flemming resigned to form his own production company. Doubtless, even though we were friends, he found my presence frustrating; we had differing views on certain matters and he moved on.

In 1970 I decided it was time to seek new quarters for CFDR. I wasn't all that happy with the physical facilities over the paint store so I bought a nice two-storey office building at the foot of Queen Street, only blocks from our old location, and a hop, skip and jump from the ferry terminal. It was of solid brick construction, and we quickly converted it to suit our purposes. Among other things it gave our morning man, Gerry Parsons, and other on-air announcers a view of the harbour, and this became a daily talking point. We built an enlarged newsroom on the second floor, where all broadcast facilities were located. The ground floor was occupied by the business offices, including my own and those of the sales and accounting staff. Engineer Jack Hutchison and I were seriously thinking of expanding to 50,000 watts. This was a major move involving a substantial expenditure of monies. My partners Jack and Vince, who had got little out of their investment up until that time and who were surely convinced that I was leading them to bankruptcy with expansion plans, decided to bail out. I was sorry to see them sell. They had been very patient and faithful to the operation, but their involvement was not as deep as mine, nor was their commitment, so the sale was consummated. I became the sole owner, although I transferred minority shares to brother Bill, who was a key player in the station's operations.

The early 1970s were good years for both the Canadian economy and the Halifax area, and we gained and grew with it. Sometime in the mid-seventies, we made a bid for a 50,000-watt station and a change in signal to 680 on the dial. We had to battle Ottawa technocrats for the approval but ultimately we got the first 50,000-watt license in Nova Scotia. While we were able to greatly expand our reach, there continued to be holes in our signal, which remained weaker than those of CHNS, established in 1926, and CJCH, established in 1944, both of which had fewer stations to protect against. Nevertheless we were happy with our improved position and made much about it in the market. Our revenues continued to increase but so then did our expenses. And, in business, you always have the need for further growth and expenditure to keep up with the competition. Unfortunately, being privately owned, our pockets (which were really my pockets) were not quite as deep as those of the opposition. CHNS was owned for many years by the Halifax Herald Limited and later by Maclean Hunter, one of Canada's communications giants. CJCH was equally endowed, being owned by the CHUM organization in Toronto. Both local operations were well-run and staffed by veteran operators. Despite the older competition, we were able to cut out a strong niche for ourselves in the market; and while we seldom led in overall numbers, teens, or the audience under 35, we had a good hold on the older segment of the adult audience. I always found this an easy audience to sell, as it had money and spent it.

Veteran CFDR morning man Gerry Parsons on the penthouse balcony with its spectacular view of the harbour. A major figure in the Halifax area, Parsons broadcast for close to forty years.

As time went on, increased revenues allowed us to expand our staff. While we were conscious of the overall market and had a large audience in Halifax (perhaps it was even a more significant audience in that it was richer, older, and a target for our sound), most of our community endeavours were on the Dartmouth side of the harbour. And even though Halifax brought us more in advertising dollars, we continued to identify

On top of the town, CFDR had a spectacular view of Halifax and the harbour from its perch above Dartmouth's Queen Square.

ourselves as the voice of Dartmouth and to carry far more Dartmouth content on our news and community affairs programs than did the other stations. I had critics in that regard, who felt that my focus on the younger and smaller city was restrictive and reflected the prejudices of my growing-up years in Dartmouth. But we broadened our reach as time progressed. We had reporters at the Dartmouth and Halifax city halls, the legislature, and the Halifax courts. We were becoming "metropolitanized," if there is such a term (and, if not, I just coined one). Anyway our attraction was our music format, and this was clearly directed to people at least over the age of 35, and getting older. Our morning man, always the key job on a radio station, was the veteran Gerry Parsons, who before joining us had worked at both CHNS and CJCH, and who incidentally had been in college with me. He was a bit of a curmudgeon, difficult to work with and the subject of complaints from both engineering and sales, but he was a broadcaster with a unique and at times masterful music touch. Gerry joined the station in its first year of operation and stayed with us until after I myself had retired. Despite bad arthritis he was out of bed every morning at 5:00 a.m. and never late for his 6:00 a.m. startup. He was a legend in Halifax radio and remains so today. Sadly he died about ten years ago.

The station had been on its Queen Street site, just off Alderney Drive, for close to ten years when I got "moving fever" again. Queen Square, an imposing and ambitious 18-storey office tower, had just been built across the street from the radio station. It was suffering a slow start and its occupancy rate was less than twenty percent when Kirk

McCulloch, the building manager, approached me to see if I was interested in taking space. I must say that I was immediately tempted. I had visited the building many times, and had gone to the still-vacant penthouse and admired its spectacular view of Halifax and the harbour. From the easterly corner of the top floor you could see down the vortex of the harbour; from the western corner you had a commanding view of north Dartmouth and even Brightwood golf course; and from the centre the City of Halifax, the dockyard, and the whole of its waterfront sprang into panoramic view. There was no better outlook on these cities. At night it was like living in a magical kingdom, and the daytime view was staggering.

By comparison our building on Queen Street was comfortable but getting a bit cramped, and while we had modernized it, the building could not be called a prestigious site. The penthouse at Queen Square offered only about 3,800 square feet of space, and we needed at least 10,000 feet to cover our needs and provide for future expansion. I met with Kirk and we made a deal in which he included (reluctantly, I suspect) the sign rights on top of the building. As well I pushed him for a ten-year rather than a five-year lease, arguing that the presence of the radio station would add immeasurably to the building's exposure and prestige. He agreed to the terms and, although the timing wasn't great with a recession setting in, in 1980 we moved to our new quarters. The penthouse housed the actual broadcasting studios, the library, and the newsroom, while on the floor below we rented about 7,000 square feet for sales and administration.

Halifax architect Keith Graham designed the layout, in concert with our chief engineer Jack Hutchison. On Keith's advice much of the area was finished in oak (costwise it might as well have been gold) and when it was finished we had what I thought was a remarkable effect. *Canadian Broadcast* magazine did a feature on the new station, describing it as one of the finest setups in Canada. Of course, we had several advantages that would be available to very few stations in Canada. First, we had a view from the eighteenth floor, overlooking majestic Halifax Harbour, with a breathtaking view of the capital city in the foreground. Second, most of the floors below were not yet occupied, so we were able to throw an official opening that comfortably accommodated several thousand guests, including Premier John Buchanan who spoke at the opening. I did not time the move as well as I'd hoped, however. In our first year at the new studios, the country struggled through a major recession and sales slumped. After just a few months, I had to cut staff, although by only four people, and three of these were able to return within a matter of months.

In 1983, with business quite buoyant, we applied for an FM license (we had been refused earlier) and this choice was rather bizarre in some respects. We decided to go for a "rock"-designated license, which we thought would add muscle and strength to our overall audience by attracting teens and those in their early twenties. With only an AM station, and one catering to mature adults at that, we had been at a disadvantage in the market. Both CHNS and CJCH had FM arms (CHFX and C100, respectively) and, like FM stations throughout North America, they were gaining ground. Those in senior positions at CFDR were somewhat older and none of us had even heard of most of the top tunes on the "rock" charts. Clearly it was time to learn. When we had appeared before the CRTC seeking an FM license a few years earlier, our lack of knowledge about this type of programming had cost us the license. In fairness, the programmer scheduled to give the main thrust of our presentation had come down with the flu a day or two before, so program director John Cunningham, the trusty Jack Hutchison, and I appeared before the commission. John made the presentation and when he got in trouble, I tried to jump in. It was as if the Marx brothers were doing the honours. I wasn't going to let that happen the second time around and I sought out expertise.

One of the top "rock" stations in the country at that time was Q107 in Toronto, so I went to see owner Allan Slaight, whom I knew, and he turned me over to his son, Gary, the manager and a young radio hot shot. Gary agreed to serve as our consultant and was most helpful in music selection and things of that nature. Boy, was this the discovery of a new world! Q107's morning man went by the name of "Scruff" Connors, and his show was a series of sexist jokes, punctuated by a morning visit from "Baby Doll." Gary recommended was that we pay big bucks in hiring our morning man, and he even suggested the man for us: none other than "Brother Jake" Edwards. Jake was then hosting a similar show in Winnipeg but could be lured east, Gary said, for a fat contract. The Brother, when he was in the real world—and this was not often—was Vernon Mozerolle, a native of Moncton, New Brunswick.

I listened to audition tapes and there was no question that the Brother was zany if not wild, but he was at the same time a real talent, particularly in that "rock" element. In fact he could have been highly successful in any format. He was a well-seasoned broadcaster, had trained on smaller stations and was on his way to making a name for himself. He agreed to join us and became our major player. My daughter Lori, who was promotion manager of the stations, did most of the hiring, doubtless with input from the eerie Jake. Together they came up with a starry crew, which among other personalities included a saddlemate for Jake by the name of Hal Harbour. Hal was actually Doug Barron, who had worked in Halifax radio for a few years and who turned out to be almost as talented as the Brother. There was a bit of sanity behind them. The mid-morning show was anchored by Bob Powers, who was a more conventional broadcaster and added stability to the overall programming. Another up-and-coming star was J. C. Douglas, who did the afternoon show. While he was young at the time, he also proved highly popular.

At the time I likened the new station addition to that of a torpedo in the water—headed straight for C100. While the competition in the market was always polite and somewhat friendly, Jake added a new dimension to the market. Compelled by his roaring ego, he hurled a barrage of threats at the competition, mocking them on the air with such comments as "You guys had better start looking for new jobs for the Brother is

The opening of our new studios atop Queen Square. (left to right) Bill Patterson, vice president of sales; Halifax mayor Ron Wallace; Premier John Buchanan; Dartmouth mayor Dan Brownlow; Arnie Patterson.

taking over the market." Even though we took extra footage when we had moved to our new studios a year or so before, we had to enlarge our set-up with the arrival of our new baby. We were able to fit most of the programming side on the penthouse level, though no more than fifteen feet separated the two studios: one presided over in the early morning by the sedate and sane Gerry Parsons; the other by Brother Jake and Hal Harbour, who at times sounded as if they were escapees from a mental institution. About fifteen feet, I said, and about thirty years in both temperament and age. Parsons, usually happy with his own company, acted as if they had never arrived. He used to look at me as if I had gone out of my mind. It was, however, great radio in both instances.

Q104 had success in building an audience of its own, and quite quickly, although the advertising revenues lagged and the losses in the early months were staggering. Fortunately CFDR was doing well and was heavily subsidizing the new operation, which was more draining than anticipated. Jake was a brilliant programmer, but he knew little about financial management and couldn't have cared less. After about six months, with the red ink continuing, I cut a few bodies, including one in a three-person community-programming unit that produced an editorial-content package to satisfy CRTC requirements. When this cutback was announced, Brother Jake came storming into my office, telling me that I could not let Andrew X go. I explained the financial problem to him as patiently as possible but, while a bit taken aback, he did not retreat fully. He said, "You will make Barb Anderson [the head of that unit] very unhappy with this move." I said, "Jake, she will be very happy. She will have a job." Fortunately we were able to re-employ Andrew at a later date, and he has since gone on to be a solid broadcaster.

We had Jake for about a year when our original benefactors, Q107 in Toronto, stole him to replace their "Scruff" who must have created a riot or something, for they let him go. I have often thought that the Slaights farmed Jake out to us while they awaited the moment when they could insert him into their own line-up. I might have been angry, but we simply moved Bob up to the early morning slot, and he was a more than suitable replacement, although not the madman his predecessor was. I liked Jake. While I understood little of his style of broadcasting, I did appreciate his talent. I am sure that it will be a long time, and it has been already, since the Halifax market will see his like again. He was one of a kind.

Despite these early problems, I felt that ultimately Q104 would not only be highly profitable, but would strengthen our overall operation. For its part, CFDR had a great reputation and was loved by those who listened. Even now, 13 years after I retired, I still get comments from people who miss it and contend that it was the best radio station ever. Toronto experts deemed, however, that it could win a larger audience by going country. In many ways though the old CFDR was a very good radio station for we won many awards; even as late as 1984, CFDR was named the top community station in Canada for its many public works. But we had an aging problem. Each year our audience got a little older, and advertising agencies were looking for audiences between the ages of 25 and 39 and even a little younger. The average age of our audience by 1985 was somewhere in the vicinity of 45 and it was growing older. With Q to attack the younger end of the demographic, I felt that we could stay pretty much where we were with our music policy while endeavouring to introduce some new music at certain periods of the day. For one thing I refused to allow any of the programmers to touch the breakfast show presided over by Gerry Parsons. His audience was so loyal, and largely a strong one, that any experimentation would hurt the station, I felt. That, however, was not a unanimous opinion throughout the station, as a number of the programmers and others felt we should be making changes. I stuck to my guns though, and in 1986 CFDR had the best year in its financial history, and while Q was still a loser, it was gaining ground.

Over the years I had many offers to sell the stations. There must have been at least ten suitors in the last ten years that I was there. I had no intention of giving them up and thought that, with my health being good, I would not sell for many years, if ever. One day I received a letter in the mail from a consulting firm in California that specialized in appraising the commercial value of radio stations. For the fun of it I answered the inquiry and was sent a series of questionnaires by the firm. They requested information on the financial history of the station for the previous five years, our current financial position, and financial forecasts for the three years ahead, plus certain financial information on our market and on our competition. Because all of our facilities, including equipment at both the AM and the FM transmitters, were new, and because I had sent photos of our facilities, with details of our technical equipment and with their estimated values, the consultants felt there was no need for an on-site inspection. They informed me that they would soon be making an assessment.

One day a letter arrived on my desk with a California dateline. When I opened it I was nearly floored, for the value they indicated was much higher than what I had personally anticipated. I called the consultant and told him that I was pleased with their effort, although I said I thought his estimate was on the high side. "It could be that it is low if your sales estimates are correct." he said. "Radio stations are attracting very high prices at the moment." I didn't show the report to anyone else at the time and simply dismissed it; the sale of the station was not something I would consider.

My long-time golfing friend John Randles, Sr., had bought a place a few years before at Isla Del Sol in Florida, and had suggested I come down with Glo for a vacation. We did it for three years, renting at various places around his golf course at Isla and generally falling love with the magnificent setting. There was not only a pristine golf course, but the island itself was surrounded by water and joined to St. Petersburg by a bridge. I grew up with golf, had caddied at Brightwood as a boy, and one of my ambitions was to own a nice place on a golf course in sunny Florida. The bug had bitten me, and I bought a condominium at Isla and joined its golf club. On returning from one of these vacation trips I found a letter from a broadcast representative of the Irving companies in Saint John, expressing an interest in buying the stations and asking to meet with me. A month or two earlier Bill Mingo, a prominent Halifax lawyer, visited me at the station with the same request for an unidentified buyer. I always assumed it was the Sobeys, although this was just a guess. Within the year, I had two other offers: one from Harry Steele of Newfoundland Capital, and another from a Hamilton radio owner.

While it is nice to own something that other people obviously think is of value, I was really not thinking of selling. But prompted by these inquiries, I went to see Rollie Jamieson, my accountant and financial adviser. We discussed the inquiries, and I suggested writing three of the suitors and expressing an interest. I said the letter should indicate that all inquiries be made through Rollie rather than me. After some thought we decided to enclose the California consultant's assessment of the stations; though I thought it inflated, I really was not that keen on selling so I had nothing to lose. We sent

Special guests at the opening of CFDR's new studios at Queen Square. (left to right) Premier John Buchanan, Arnie Patterson, and hockey personality Allan Eagleson.

our package to the Irvings, the Hamilton station owner, and Harry Steele, and heard immediately from all three. Although our letter clearly named Rollie as the contact person, I had a call at home that night from Harry Steele. We were friends and had served together on the board of Eastern Provincial Airways, and later he had asked me to join the board of the Halifax *Daily News*.

Aside from being engaging, Harry is a very candid and direct operator. "Arnie," he said, "if you're not too busy I thought I might drop out and see you tonight. Will you be home?" I said I would be, and he said, "Perhaps I'll come out now?" He was at my place within thirty minutes. He joined me in our family room and I got each of us a drink. In the meantime he passed me an envelope, which I assumed was an offer of some kind. I casually placed it on the arm of my chair and resumed our conversation. Then he said, somewhat quizzically, "Aren't you going to open it?" In a few brief paragraphs he'd outlined his offer, which basically was acceptance of the consultant's valuation with the addition of monies to cover whatever accounts receivables were on our books. "What do you think?" he said, leaning towards me. I replied, "I think we have a deal. I'll talk to my brother, who is a shareholder, and my accountant tomorrow." Our negotiations took all of forty seconds.

By mid-June of 1987 the deal and the details were finalized with only minor alterations to my verbal agreement with Harry. The document signing took place at Newfoundland Capital's office on Windmill Road, and when Harry presented a cheque to me. It was for $5.1 million. I passed it over to Dave Stewart, my lawyer, for deposit in the Royal Bank. I was now, at the age of 58, retired.

When I got back to the station I packed my personal belongings and had a visit from the new manager, Pat Cairney. He had been the manager of a Standard Broadcast station in St. Catharines, and I had known him slightly. We had a cup of tea at my conference table, and I gave him a bit of advice. I suggested that if I were him I would do nothing drastic for a few months, simply get to know the market and find out why we did things a certain way. I don't think I was down to the main floor on the elevator before the music changed on CFDR. Pat, doubtless acting on instructions from his Toronto mentors, implemented the country music format and initially at least, the station went into a tailspin with both a loss of audience and revenues. Pat Cairney was to leave the station six months later. The station went through the hoops and jumps before regaining some health in recent years—as a born-again country music station. Q, in the meantime, has been a great success. My radio heydays ended with an official banquet at the Holiday Inn, attended by several hundred people at $100 a head. The proceeds went to the Victorian Order of Nurses for which I was grateful; my mother had been a V.O.N. nurse during the depression years. It was a heady affair with old friends Dick O'Hagan, Finlay MacDonald, Pat Connolly, and Senator Al Graham gilding the lily as head-table guests. Glo was presented with a beautiful flower bouquet, and we received two airline tickets to anywhere in the world.

We went to Vienna in late October. I had been an amateur student of the Hapsburgs and their old empire for many years but had never been to Austria. Now with money in my back pocket, and no job to go to, we didn't spare the expenses. We reserved a first-class room at the famous Imperial Hotel in Austria, described as Queen Elizabeth's favourite hotel. On October 27, 1987, a date few investors will ever forget, we were lying in bed watching television when a newscaster reported that disaster had struck the world stock markets. Everything was tumbling. Another world depression lurked, according to some analysts. Glo said to me, "What does that mean to us?" I replied, "Nothing. All we have is cash." I had left the money from the sale on deposit in the Royal Bank and was too busy playing golf, planning our trip, and conveying small favours on my family to take the time to invest. When we got back to Canada and I made my investments, I bought stock for substantially less than prices offered in mid-October. Sometimes you are lucky!

Before I leave off this radio tale I have a confession to make. This is too good a story to be left untold, although it reveals a long hidden secret about Q104 and our introduction to the airways. The new crowd we brought in—Brother Jake, the very bright Ray Plourde, and others of that ilk—were pretty "cool," and they knew a lot

The brilliant Jack (Jock) Hutchison, chief engineer for CFDR and Q104. A man for all seasons, he was also the host of the popular "New and Old Scotland" radio hour.

about radio promotion and how to make a dent in the market. Jack Hutchison (day-in, day-out, one of the smartest guys ever to work in radio) joined me for a beer one day and was complaining about the new crowd and how different they were from our sober souls on the CFDR side. I don't know whether it was his Machiavellian mind or mine that concocted the idea, but the two of us became joint villains in a mischievous plot to drop a big rock on the parking lot at our rival station, CJCH-C100.

We went up to the Steed and Evans Quarry, beyond the Mic Mac Mall, and toured the site, looking for a suitable rock. I found one that was about five feet high. I forget the weight but it was considerable, something in the area of seven hundred pounds. I was a director of the quarry company at the time, and they were able to put us in contact with a trucking firm that would deliver the rock to our intended target. In the meantime we went to Lahey's for paint and brushes, and Jack went back to the quarry and emblazoned on the side of the rock: "Q104–The Rock of the Atlantic." Next we went to CJCH to "case" their property. I was concerned, as their employee parking lot had been newly asphalted. With a seven-hundred-pound gift to render, I didn't want to be responsible for any undue damage. So we went to Burgess Transfer, where we obtained a number of large cardboard boxes with the thought of using them as a landing pad.

This was a "hush hush" project. We didn't want Jake and his boys and girls to know. We did, however, let my brother Bill in on our ploy and invited him to join us at 2:00 a.m. the next morning when we planned to plant our rock. In the dead of night, 1:30 a.m., Jack and I met up with our truck driver and assistant in the parking lot of the Dartmouth Sportsplex. I told them our plan and said that if we encountered any problems, I would take responsibility. I am sure they thought we were a bit nuts, but they laughed and agreed to the mission. There was no sign of Bill. We called him and got him up out of bed. A bit groggily he said, "You guys aren't serious are you? This is a joke." Jack assured him that "Project Big Rock" was about to be put into action, and we urged him to hurry to the parking lot. He was still unbelieving when he arrived, but the sight of the rock in the back of the truck, the very size of it, made him gape. "You're

CFDR's Tony Beech and Gerry Parsons, two stars of radio, prepare to take part in the Dartmouth Natal Day parade.

both nuts," he asserted. I travelled to CJCH in the truck with our drivers, while Bill and Hutch followed in an unmarked car. My big hope was that we wouldn't encounter the police en route.

I had let one other person in on our mad scheme—Alf Hollingsworth of the *Daily News*—promising that we would get a photo to him. Hutch, an inveterate photographer, had his camera with him and planned to take the film back to the station and develop it in our dark room that night. The big concern was whether our rock would drop right-side-up and show the Q104 slogan. The truck was equipped with a power hoist, and as it went up the rock came shooting down the metal surface. The noise was shattering; enough to wake up the whole of the north end. In fact almost immediately lights went on in several houses along this quiet street. Fortunately the rock landed perfectly, just off the entrance to the parking lot, not to be missed by any CJ-C100 employees when they arrived for work the next morning. Pulling a balaclava over my face, and sporting gloves and dark clothing, I jumped along side the rock and Jack quickly shot the photographs. Mission accomplished. We returned to the station in a gleeful mood.

Bill and I had coffee in our employee lunchroom while Jack went to develop the photos. We were hardly seated when he came back in a violent mood. "I left the bloody casing on the camera," he announced. No photos. I insisted we had to go back. Bill said, "Now I *know* you're crazy. The whole street has been alerted after all that noise, and the police will be there." But Hutch agreed, and he and I drove back and surprisingly found no one astir. We did our dirty deed and returned—this time with a photo, which we had couriered to the *Daily News*. When the sun came up on June 4, 1983, our photo appeared on the front page of the paper with the following cut line: "Obviously the masked man shown above is a fan of Q104 radio and is today the subject of an extensive police search. Sometime in the middle of last night he and an accomplice dropped a 1,000-pound rock on the parking lot of CJCH-C100 radio. Evidently they play rough in the radio wars around here." The next morning the prank was the talk of the stations. As soon as he got off the air, Brother Jake came rushing into my office with a copy of the *Daily News*.

" I had nothing to do with this," he said, "nor did any of our crowd." "Jake, I don't mind a bit of fun with the opposition, but this is going a bit too far. That rock is enormous," I said, as I scanned the photo. He was at a loss to explain, suggesting that only demented minds could come up with such a scheme. I put out a staff memo saying that if we found the culprits they would be expected to apologize to CJCH management in person, and cover any of the costs involved. Later that morning I received a call from Bill Bodnarchuk, the manager of CJ and one of the great fellows in radio. He rather apologetically told me of the incident, adding that they had to get a backhoe to remove the rock from the parking lot. I assured him that if we caught the offenders they would be dealt with severely. To this day no one has discovered who the perpetrators were, and I say to my friend Bill Bodnarchuk, it was all done in fun.

Do I miss radio and CFDR and Q104? Occasionally—although I have had thirteen years of enjoyable retirement and have played 2,400 games of golf, both winter and summer, since. Also, I have had good health (which is a blessing) and many things to occupy my time. I'm like the guy who said, "I'm so busy now that I'm retired, I don't know how I had the time to go to work." I think I did a clever thing in signing on with my friend Doug McKay to write that Sunday column for the *Daily News*. I think I have written over a thousand since I joined the paper. It has been an interesting experience and one that has allowed me to keep abreast of developments in and around our town. I must admit too that I love being in the company of reporters, even now, 53 years after I started in the trade. They are a special breed. Do you know what I miss most about running the radio stations? I miss the opportunity to promote good local causes. And strangely, I miss writing obituaries about special local people who have gone on to their greater reward. But what great fun it was!

Chapter Thirteen: The Central Trust Debacle

I thought I might entitle this sad tale "*Sic Transit Gloria*," for the rise and fall of Central Trust and its affiliated companies was a calamitous happening that saw a billion—yes, a billion—dollars in assets evaporate overnight. In 1992 thousands of shareholders were victimized by the collapse of this once solid financial institution. And while they were major losers, the big loser may have really been Atlantic Canada. Created here, an amalgam of a host of Maritime trust companies, Central was in the late 1980s the third largest trust company in Canada, and growing.

At a more promising time, this in 1987 when Central Trust marked its hundredth anniversary, author Harry Bruce wrote: "The creation in the Atlantic Provinces of a financial institution that serves tens of thousands of Canadians from coast to coast is as rare as rich uncles or gold on the beach." In a company-sanctioned book, *A Century at Central Trust*, Bruce said that while the Royal Bank and Bank of Nova Scotia had been founded in Halifax, their affairs had long since been run from central Canada, and the expanding power base of Central Trust made Atlantic Canadians a major player on a financial scene that was one of their own making. Within two years, this venerable, largely Atlantic institution was crumbling, and by 1992 it no longer existed as a corporate entity. The better part of its bones were acquired by the Toronto-Dominion Bank, and other remnants were scattered as financial vultures made bargain buys.

What happened? This was a company that, at the time of its hundredth anniversary, just five years before its demise, had assets of $3.4 billion and that added hundreds of millions more shortly thereafter. In fact, that was probably the key element in its spin out of control. High up on the list of ailments, however, was reckless and spendthrift management by those on a glory ride. The man who must take the biggest share of the blame for the company's dramatic decline was the new hired gun Peter Cole, who became the CEO of the newly created Central Capital Corporation in 1986. With its formation, control of Central Trust and its affiliates shifted from Halifax and the Maritimes to Toronto. The cautious, careful ways that had guided Central and its acquired and predecessor companies for most of their existence were ignored.

Under Cole and Tom Hodgson, his executive vice president brought in from Canada Permanent Mortgage, the new capital company went on a spending spree that would have made Daddy Warbucks blush. And it seemed that they not only bought the wrong properties, but paid outrageous prices for them. In the space of a few years, Central Capitol acquired Toronto-based Guaranty Trustco for $400 million. Then these high-rollers bought Capel-Cure Myers, a capital management company in Britain. Next came a major purchase of stock in National Trust, another prestigious Toronto financial institution, with a view to acquiring control of the company; this plan failed to materialize. Their craziest move was paying $300 million for Financial Trust, a company facing imminent collapse. During their borrowing spree, Cole and Hodgson borrowed more than $500 million from Japanese banks and Canadian lenders. I had a front row seat for this wild ride as I had a fairly intimate knowledge of the company. I had been associated with since 1965.

I had moved back to Dartmouth in 1964 to run Moosehead Breweries' new operation and to involve myself with our operation at CFDR. Donald Grant, the president of Nova Scotia Trust, invited me to lunch, and John Walker, a company director and prominent Halifax lawyer, joined us. They asked me to serve both as the chairman of the new advisory committee that they were establishing in Dartmouth for the trust company, and as a director of the company itself. I agreed on both counts.

Nova Scotia Trust was a solid and highly respected local trust company, which had been founded in 1812. When I joined the board its numbers included many distinguished Nova Scotians, including Harry P. MacKeen, a former lieutenant governor of Nova Scotia; W. H. C. Schwartz Limited; Gordon Archibald, president of Maritime Tel and Tel; and Ronald G. Smith, president of National Sea Products. President Donald Grant, a handsome man in his late fifties, was a native of Sydney and a graduate of Dal Law. I found him charming, a man of prudence as well as caution. Donald Grant's serene world was challenged in 1967 when Central Trust of Moncton, New Brunswick, a reputable but smaller trust company, started wooing the Halifax-based institution. Nova Scotia's directors met these advances with a stern rebuff. They were not prepared to allow control of the company to move out of the province.

But there was a fox in the hen house. The controversial New Glasgow industrialist R. B. Cameron owned ten thousand shares of Nova Scotia Trust and he offered them to Reuben Cohen of Central for an inflated $35 a share. Then in a bid to raise the price even higher, Cameron withdrew his offer and extended an offer to the directors of Nova Scotia, who couldn't come up with enough money to satisfy him. Cohen and his partner returned a bid of $70 per share, startling not only the directors but also the shareholders, and the bid succeeded. On January 1, 1974, the two companies disappeared into the Central and Nova Scotia Trust Company. Donald Grant retired, and Halifax lawyer Harry Rhude became president of the merged force. With this early coup, growth for Central was still in its infancy. In 1976 it acquired the Eastern Canada

Savings and Loan Company, another venerable Nova Scotia financial firm whose Halifax roots went back to 1887. Unlike the acrimonious takeover of Nova Scotia Trust, the joining of eastern Canada to the growing Central family was done without hostility. Central was also to acquire control of Nova Scotia Savings and Loan in the late 1980s, and this after several years of bitter battling.

I had served as a director of Nova Scotia Trust, and carried on with Central Trust until 1979 when I resigned to avoid a conflict of interest, as I had accepted the post as chief press secretary for Prime Minister Trudeau. Central was then registered as a federal company and I didn't want to cause any embarrassment to the government or myself. I did, however, stay on as chairman of the Dartmouth advisory board until it was disbanded in the late 1980s. All told, I had more than a twenty-year involvement with the companies. Much of the growth in Upper Canada, as well as most of the troubles, were to come long after I had resigned as a director. I stayed in touch through my connection with the advisory board, as a shareholder, and as a friend to many of the senior employees in both the Halifax and Dartmouth branches.

Most of those who followed the downward spiral of the Central Trust companies faulted Peter Cole as the shareholders lost hundreds of millions of dollars, and thousands lost their jobs. Hired by Leonard Ellen and Reuben Cohen, Cole was an ex-banker. I met him only once, and this was at the annual Central Trust cocktail party in the new Halifax convention centre. Always a big occasion, it attracted the business elite of the province. Darrell Kennie, the manager of Central's main Halifax branch, introduced me as a former director and a client. Cole, obviously well into the sauce, looked at me and said, "You worked for that bastard Trudeau. He was a fairy and a flake." When I went to dinner late that night with a number of the senior people from the Halifax office, I suggested that they were in deep trouble with that mad man running the company.

It is difficult for me to understand, years later, how two men as smart and as wily as Reuben Cohen, whom I very much admired, and his partner Leonard Ellen could have missed the boat in hiring such an arrogant man as Peter Cole. While he had held a senior vice presidency with the Canadian Imperial Bank of Commerce, he had had a reputation as a playboy and big spender. It was a mistake in judgement that was to cost them their company, and with it their fortunes—jointly estimated at more than $150 million. I felt bad at the time, and still do, for Reuben Cohen, who was always considerate and thoughtful, not just to me but to everyone he encountered. A soft-spoken, basically quiet man, he would often sit by me at the directors' meetings, although at the time I was one of the youngest directors. I was flattered.

Reuben Cohen deserved a much better fate. While it was for the most part a sad tale, I enjoyed his autobiography *A Time To Tell*, which recounts in detail the collapse of the empire that he and Leonard Ellen built. A self-made man who grew up in Moncton, where he practised law for more than 55 years, Reuben Cohen has been much honoured over the years, and among other distinctions served as chancellor of Dalhousie University. He is now 79 and continues to practise law in his home town. I was so touched after reading his book that I called him. I had difficulty finding him, as his home phone number was not in the book. When I reached his law office a male voice answered. I told the party on the line that I was looking for Reuben Cohen. The reply: "You are talking to Reuben Cohen. Who is calling?" When I told him how much I enjoyed his book he expressed his pleasure and thanks. He went on to say that he had two great regrets: first, that the shareholders lost money; and second, that the loss of his fortune would not allow him to fulfil his plans for a charitable foundation, which was to provide enhancement for post-secondary education.

Cohen's book cites two factors that contributed significantly to Central's demise: the regulators and the media. He said that when you are their darling, the media can be effusive with their accolades; but if they perceive you on the ropes, they can be ruthless and hasten your destruction. As for the regulators, he said that with a degree of federal cooperation, the trust company could have been rescued, but they acted too quickly in forcing the takeover of the company by its lenders. I cannot pass judgment on his second argument as I have little knowledge of the regulators' role, but I question Cohen's accusation that the media were responsible in any way for the company's problems. The media reports and the news surrounding Central in its final days did little to evoke optimism, but the company's shareholders and the general public had every right to know of the tragic tale that was unfolding. The big problem was simply poor and reckless management. And as much as I like him, I am afraid that Reuben Cohen has to share much or at least some of the blame as one of the company's principal players. As I said earlier, the Atlantic Canadian provinces, particularly the Maritimes, are the big losers in this. We have lost four strong lending agencies that contributed much to the growth of our region: Central Trust of New Brunswick, Nova Scotia Trust, Eastern Canada Savings and Loan, and Nova Scotia Savings and Loan. For homeowners seeking mortgages, and for small businessmen in this area, their departures have constituted a major loss.

Ironically, in re-reading Harry Bruce's hundredth anniversary book on Central, I came across a line which read, "Their first and biggest catch was 49 year-old Peter Cole, the number three man at the Canadian Imperial Bank of Commerce, and a fellow of such talent and reputation he'd been rumoured as a candidate for the bank presidency." This was written in reference to Harry's earlier outline of the proposal in which Central Trust, with Cohen and partner Leonard Ellen as the leading advocates, created a new company, Central Capital Management (CCMI). This sister company to Central Trust, whose formation was announced in January 1986, would allow Central to participate in a broader range of activities. CCMI would function chiefly in the areas of commercial banking and commercial lending. At the time few people realized that saddling this tough old Maritime trust company with this new stepchild was going to lead to the elder's demise. What a roller-coaster ride it had for the next four years with Peter Cole in charge of the controls. I would think, in light of the circumstances and the tale of woe that developed, that the CIBC and its brass were thanking the Almighty for the loss of Central's so-called "biggest catch."

Let me close this sad chapter on a light and happy note. For all the responsibility and problems that he faced throughout his business life, Reuben maintains a great but quiet sense of humour. One tale in his book gave me a good laugh. While dining with Rollie Frazee and his wife, Marie, in St. Andrews, New Brunswick, Rollie witnessed an amusing exchange. Rollie was the retired chairman of the Royal Bank. When he began dating Marie, she had another boyfriend, a rugged fellow with a physique more strapping than Rollie's. The former boyfriend had also gone into the Royal Bank and had spent his lifetime there, retiring as the manager of some small-town branch. Over dinner, in the heat of a spousal argument Rollie said, "And where would you be if you had married your previous boyfriend, Mr. X, instead of marrying me?" Her reply: "I would have been the wife of the chairman of the Royal Bank, but where would you have been?" One of the great retorts of all time.

Chapter Fourteen: Life with Pierre Trudeau

If offering as a Liberal federal candidate in the elections of 1968 and 1974 were unexpected events in my life, the decision to move to Ottawa in 1978 to become Prime Minister Pierre Elliott Trudeau's chief press secretary was even more inexplicable. We were at our summer house at White Point Beach, ninety miles from Halifax, when I received a phone call from my friend Dick O'Hagan. Dick was serving as Prime Minister Trudeau's chief press secretary after spending a few years in Washington as the press chief at the Canadian Embassy, and had earlier served as chief press secretary for Prime Minister Lester Pearson, both in and out of office. We exchanged pleasantries, asked about wives and families, we probably even discussed the weather. It was a sparkling sunny day at White Point and I was about to depart for the golf course. This was not, however, simply a random call from an old friend but rather a somewhat staggering request. He wanted me to take a leave of absence from my businesses, radio station included, and spend a year in Ottawa as press secretary to the prime minister. He had been offered a vice presidency, corporate affairs, at the Bank of Montreal, and they were pressing him for a decision. He said that he felt an obligation to both the prime minister and our friend Jim Coutts, the principal secretary, to get a replacement before he departed.

"It is essential that I get someone senior and someone who knows the media business, and unquestionably you are the man," he said. He had talked to both Coutts and Senator Keith Davey, another friend, and both had endorsed his choice. O'Hagan is one of the most sophisticated people I have known in my life, and I have always been susceptible to his charm. But I knew it would be impossible for me at that point to pack up and leave Nova Scotia for a year or so, even for a job as exciting as press secretary. "Dick, you know I would love to go but if I did I would come back bankrupt. I have several new operations under way that need my input," I said. We wound up that day with a promise that we would talk again, but I knew that it would be impossible for me to accept this challenge. It was not until early December that I received another call from O'Hagan, asking me if I would come to Ottawa for a meeting. I told him that I had not had a change of heart and that my coming would be a waste of his time. He said to come on up anyway; we could have dinner and talk about old times. I agreed to fly up on December 13.

Glo, privy to these discussions, said, "You're not going to take that job, are you?" I said no, "I'll just go to Ottawa and see a few old friends, let them down easily, and then come home." I should have known better. Oh my, was I set up! The prime ministerial offices were, at that time, in the Langevin Block just below Parliament Hill while the East Block offices were under repair. The six or seven press offices were on the main floor, and were well-furnished and modern. I was greeted by Lois Webb, Dick's private secretary, who must have been privy to the negotiations because she looked me over, not critically but with a friendly, discerning eye. Dick was all smiles. Fashion plate that he was and is, he was sporting a pale blue shirt with an enlarged, white collar, a smart, military-striped tie, and a natty pair of white braces. We had hardly exchanged greetings when he said, "Let's go upstairs and see if Jim [Coutts] is in." I assumed from the remark that Coutts didn't know I was coming to Ottawa. Again, I should have known better.

Glo at White Point with daughters Carol and Lori in the mid-1970s. White Point has been the family's summer base for more than forty years.

We found Coutts huddled in conversation with Senator Davey, who was to be co-chairman of the expected fall election campaign. Both jumped to their feet, and Jim walked over with his hand out, "I think it's great that you're going to join us for the campaign," he said, smiling broadly. Now, if you follow hockey, you know that Wayne Gretzky was a slickster. Well, Jim Coutts was the Wayne Gretzky of politics. On top of that he was a mastermind. With a confirming nod of his head, Coutts said, "We are delighted that Dick has been able to enlist your support." I told them that it would be impossible for me to move to Ottawa at that juncture, as much as I would enjoy the battle that lay ahead. I even used the same line I had used before with Gerry Regan when he and others prevailed upon me to run in the 1974 election: "You can't hire a guy who'll be in the midst of a divorce." Coutts, as always, was way ahead of me: "Oh, we don't have to worry about Glo, she's too good a Liberal to push for the divorce until the election is over." You can't kid a kidder.

Anyway the discussion got serious, as it was bound to do with three fervent political junkies. They knew where to strike, and my will was fully tested. They told me that a thrilling campaign was in prospect with Trudeau seeking a fourth consecutive mandate. It would be great challenge, and fun; it would present an opportunity for me to see old friends. When I mentioned I had read that the Liberals were trailing the Tories by twenty points in the polls, this was quickly dismissed: "Arnie, you know what polls are like. You can never trust them." "I know," I replied, "they're always right." Anyway after about an hour, or perhaps less, I was like a beached whale: my only option was surrender. But then I asked, "You know, if I'm going to do this I should talk to the prime minister himself because he may not be as receptive as you are." They assured me that he was and that he was waiting in his office on Parliament Hill to welcome me aboard. The time involved would be less than a year, they said. The election would probably be called in the late summer, and I would be home long before Christmas. At least no one produced handcuffs, I thought. Glo, how was I going to explain?

Dick and I walked up the hill to the House of Commons. This is one of the most imposing buildings in the world—much more impressive than Capitol Hill in Washington or the Parliament buildings in London. On that day my heart beat a little faster as I marvelled at the scene and realized the decision that I had made. I was viewing my new playground. I knew the prime minister, of course, having been his candidate in two previous elections, and I had talked to him a year or two before at a Liberal convention. If I had not known him, I would have suspected he was in on the conspiracy, for he too came walking from his desk, his hand extended, a smile on his face. I thought they must have been having a tough time getting someone to take the job. Anyway we had a pleasant talk, and he spoke glowingly of Nova Scotia and of how he had spent a week there the summer before, visiting the Murder Point compound of well-known Liberal Don Johnston, a member of the Trudeau Cabinet. Trudeau and Margaret were then separated, so I assumed that he had gone with his three sons. He was interested in the fact that Dick and I had known one another since college days, and that we had worked together on a Toronto newspaper and maintained our friendship for all these years. He said, "It is nice to have an old and intimate friend." I didn't think much of that remark at the time, but I later learned that the reserved Trudeau was not a man with many close friends—a handful at best. I, however, liked and admired him and was prepared to serve. Before leaving I said, "There is only one thing that bothers me prime minister, and that is I don't think you really like reporters." I had seen him scuffle with a reporter on a television interview only months before. "Arnie, Arnie, that is not true. I like you very much." Even all these years later, I am not sure I was wrong in my assessment.

Dick was able to leave and join the Bank of Montreal, where for the next 17 years he had a highly successful career. And, given the increase in bank share prices, I assume he accumulated quite a bit of money. I, in the meantime, with the approval of my wife, was to depart for Ottawa and my new job in late January. My brother Bill took charge at the radio station.

Walking into a new job and a new set of circumstances is sometimes difficult, but I had been through the exercise many times and it was not a frightening proposition. As it turned out the people I was to work with were pretty special, and I developed a good working relationship with them. I was ultimately to make a number of good, new friends. The deputy press chief was an Ontario francophone. Jean Charpentier, who was movie-star handsome in an elegant French way. Indeed prior to his recruitment by O'Hagan he had been a major television newsman on the CBC French network. He was a charming fellow and exceedingly well-liked and respected by the media, both French and English. His judgement remained that of a newsman, which I found refreshing; it was a trait that would serve us well on the campaign trail. Jean and I were compatible from the start, and while I think he questioned my partisanship, we worked well together. In one of the early staff meetings I gave what he thought was a Liberal campaign speech. In my mind, however, we were there for one purpose and that was to elect the prime minister. We weren't hired as objective reporters, for when we each accepted our job at the secretariat we became partisans in every respect.

There were four other press officers in the group: Ralph Coleman, Jim MacDonald, Suzanne Perry, and Patrick Gossage. Ralph Coleman was actually an army major on special leave to the Prime Minister's Office. He was a quiet man in his early thirties, with an infectious laugh and a good sense of humour. Ralph did not have the extensive journalistic background of Jean Charpentier, but he was a solid thinker and a highly efficient organizer. He played the role of lead logician as we moved into campaign mode. Jim MacDonald was a specialist in preparing background notes for the prime minister's press conferences. These were thoughtful and well-written, and while his role, by his own choosing, seemed limited, he was valued. A more recent addition was Suzanne Perry, whose background in television and media, as well as her movie-star looks, proved her a major hit with the press corps when we hit the road. She was a very savvy young lady. She later married television newsman Keith Morrison and moved to Los Angeles where her son, Matthew Perry, has become a popular television star. The fifth officer was Patrick Gossage, who was the unofficial office comedian. A little light for heavy work, Patrick's main role in the campaign was to give the prime minister time signals during his speeches.

There were several others in the office doing research and secretarial work. I would be remiss if I didn't make mention again of Lois Webb, who was my secretarial inheritance from Dick. A tried and true Ottawa hand of French-Canadian descent, she was one of the most efficient people I have met in my lifetime, and her ability and background knowledge of Ottawa and the PMO proved invaluable to me as a newcomer.

I moved into a small suite in the Delta Hotel in downtown Ottawa. As I was hopeful of being there no more than nine or ten months, Glo and I decided I would commute between Halifax and Ottawa on weekends. I think I fulfilled that promise about three times in the months that lay ahead. The learning curve had to be short with an election just months away. Things moved along at a hectic pace, and I had two or three meetings a week with the prime minister, Jim Coutts, and Michael Pitfield, the principal clerk of the Privy Council. The regular business of government continued while plans for the campaign were left on the back burner. Every day there were requests from the Ottawa press corps and others throughout the country looking either for statements from the prime minister or interviews. Indeed there was a backlog of more than a hundred such requests. It was going to be a long time before we made everyone in the media happy.

There was also some travel involved in that "phony war" period leading up to the election. We went with a family of journalists to Washington to meet with President Carter, whom Trudeau admired, then travelled on to New York for the prime minister to attend a Carnegie Hall appearance of the Winnipeg Ballet. There were other trips to Vancouver and Winnipeg, although the real cross-country marathon was not to start for a few months. Several all-media press conferences took place in the media centre near Parliament Hill. These were full-dress rehearsals with more than a hundred journalists present, all shooting questions at the prime minister. My own relationship with the prime minister was certainly pleasant enough, although he was not the "hail fellow, well met" politician whom I had known throughout my lifetime. I was slowly catching up on the issues, and this was the most difficult part of my job. In that regard both Coutts and Jean Charpentier were helpful and gave me many quick briefings. While some knowledge of policy was important, my focus was dealing with the media and getting to know the principal players. Few days went by when I didn't lunch with journalists from the *Toronto Star*, *Montreal Star*, the *Montreal Gazette*, the Ottawa papers, or with television reporters for the CBC and CTV. I also encountered a cadre of Maritimers, including Mike Duffy, whom I knew as a teenager and budding radio newsman; Jim Munson, a Bathurst boy then with CFRB radio, Toronto; and Steve Kimber, a freelancer who had worked with me at CFDR.

If Trudeau had certain reservations about the media this feeling was returned. I found that, while there was respect for the prime minister and certainly for his intelligence, he was not really well liked. The zealous Trudeau fans across the country would have been surprised, even shocked, to find that most of the reporters were at best only lukewarm to the prime minister. Part of this, of course, was due to his long tenure in office; over a period of eleven years there were many moments of disenchantment on both sides. Unlike Lester Pearson, who had many friends among the media, and several who were unofficial close advisers, Trudeau's relationship with them was largely polite and civil but never intimate. Craig Oliver, the veteran CTV commentator, was one of the group that took summer canoeing trips with the prime minister but even he was not considered a close friend. One day while returning from New York on a small government aircraft with the prime minister, his executive assistant Allan Lutfy, and Jean Charpentier, I passed the prime minister a list of interviews that I thought important. It was some time before the election call, but as I mentioned, there was a backlog of requests. My list of twenty names was prioritized relative to importance, with some regional weighting. He shrugged and turned to Lutfy, saying sarcastically, "Well I guess we can forget about the business of the Privy Council. The press secretary wants me to devote my full time to the attentions of the media." Poor Charpentier was waiting for me to break my front teeth, but I wasn't to be cowed. I said, "Prime Minister, the PCO is not that important any more if getting elected is a priority." He, however, unwilling yet to concede my point and waving the list, said, "Why would you include the *Montreal Star* on the list?" He added, "We are going to get every anglo vote in Quebec anyway, and they are not important."

The *Star*, which had long been one of the best newspapers in Canada, had just come off a long and paralyzing strike, which had resulted not only in a major financial bath and an even more vital loss of circulation to the rival *Gazette*. I had had lunch a week or two earlier with Bill Wilson, the veteran *Star* parliamentary reporter, and Ray Heard, the managing editor of the paper, and both had made a strong pitch for an interview with the prime minister, thinking that an exclusive of that nature would help their ailing fortunes. I was sympathetic and promised to make a representation on their behalf. I told the prime minister that the *Star*, a faithful and staunch supporter of the Liberal Party, and of Trudeau personally, was in danger of extinction and would certainly benefit from the proposed interview. He said that we could discuss the matter as the election approached. They never got their interview. And sadly, the *Star* went out of business six months later. Canada lost a great newspaper and one of its few major English voices in a hostile Quebec.

One night after the National Press Club dinner I went back to the Ottawa Press Club with Allan MacEachen, then minister of health. I had been close to Allan for a long time and had travelled to Russia and Australia with him years earlier, but I had not talked to him before taking the job as press secretary, assuming that either Coutts or Davey had advised him of my move. It seemed to have irked him that I had not advised him of my intentions. This evening, however, we were enjoying a companionable walk across the square from the House of Commons when Allan asked me, "How are you getting along with the prime minister?" I replied, "Quite well, although I don't really know him all that well yet." He said, "If you ever get to know him let me know what he's like."

Trudeau and MacEachen had been cabinet members together for close to 14 years, and both were key players in government during that period. The relationship between Trudeau and MacEachen changed, however, when Allan as House Leader engineered the defeat of the Clark government in the Commons in January, 1980, forcing a new election and opening up Trudeau's return to the prime ministry. They became closer. In time

MacEachen was assigned the finance portfolio and later the deputy prime ministry. In the former role, he came close to being a latter-day R. B. Bennett (the prime minister during the Great Depression), as interest rates soared to 21 percent and the country recorded the greatest number of bankruptcies since the early thirties. The government was then in the fifth year of its mandate, and as we got to March speculation about a pending election call increased. Every day callers to the press office asked me to confirm rumoured dates. If Trudeau knew, however, he was keeping it close to his vest. Even Coutts seemed to be in the dark, although we were gearing up each day for the battle that was sure to come.

One night I invited four or five Maritime reporters over for a light dinner and a few drinks. We were sitting around in my hotel when I got a call asking me to report to 24 Sussex as soon as possible. The election call was less than an hour away. My reporter friends suited up and departed as quickly as firemen responding to a major blaze, no doubt racing to the nearest phone with news of the election call. My job was to escort the prime minister to the media theatre, where he would announce an election for May 20.

Although that day was more than eight weeks away, we hit the road within a week. Senator Keith Davey and the Honourable Marc Lalonde were named co-chairmen of the campaign, and I was named to the committee. We continued to trail in the polls, but Coutts indicated that there was a slight movement upward, and given Trudeau's forceful speaking style there was the expectation that we could catch up. Tory leader Joe Clark was not highly regarded by our troops, and we believed that Trudeau would outgun him on the trail. Federal elections are exhausting. There was a constant crossing of the country from the Northwest Territories to Newfoundland and back again and again. We travelled in style aboard a chartered Air Canada airplane, its staff at our service, and we stayed in the best hotels. We had a weekly routine, we would leave for the road on Monday or Tuesday, staying out until late Saturday night, and then returning to Ottawa. Usually we made two and three stops a day, taking in about four events in total. The major speech typically was given at night at a rink or big hall, and visits to schools, industrial plants, and shopping malls occupied our days.

We were accompanied in our travels by a full complement of media people from all of the bigger papers and television and radio networks. It was not a free ride for them as their companies were charged an overall fee for the duration of the campaign, and some of the smaller media companies signed on for shorter periods. Journalists occasionally switched between campaign planes, as Clark and the Tories were also out in full force. While I don't ever remember the two opposing parties campaigning in the same city or town on the same day, we did run into the Tory campaigners and its press entourage at the airports. We never saw a trace of the NDP who were apparently travelling more modestly and with a smaller press corps. As I mentioned, we left Ottawa early in the week and returned Saturday night, usually after a major rally in Toronto. There is no question that Toronto with its 23 ridings, a Liberal stronghold, was the number one target. There was always a lot of whooping joy when our rag-tag crew landed back in Ottawa, for the reporters too had been out on the five day grind. Completely bushed, we all looked forward to a weekend of replenishing.

Sometimes I would go back to the hotel and have a quiet dinner with Coutts, and we would replay the week's events. He thought we were gaining ground and was encouraging to me, saying that I added strength to our small team. Sunday morning I would sleep until 10:00 a.m., and then run off to an 11:00 a.m. campaign meeting. The Ottawa ground troops, which included chairmen Davey and Lalonde, and others from the offices of senior cabinet ministers, would be there to hear our reports and give us their analysis and assessments.

One thing I learned was that the English and French campaigns, if I may call them that, were somewhat distinct entities. Actually, I had experienced that in the past at national conventions. In 1975 when I served as co-chairman for Senator Al Graham's successful bid for the federal Liberal presidency, the Quebec wing operated on their own and, while they largely supported Graham, we had few communiqués from them. In the 1979 election Lalonde was the Quebec supremo and, while he also contributed to the more general planning, he left most of the planning and implementation for events outside of Quebec to the Davey team. We were several weeks into the campaign before we even got to Quebec. This was bothersome to me in that I wanted to expose the media to this old Liberal stronghold. I felt that the "rouge" factor and the enthusiasm with which it was greeted by the people of Quebec would be so evident that it would convince the media that we were no longer simply underdogs. Strangely when we got to Quebec we wound up touring communities that Lalonde and his strategists felt could give us trouble, and for this reason we seldom experienced the enthusiasm that I was looking for. So all the early tour of Quebec did was shore up the belief that we were in mortal combat.

Ultimately we made about four forays into Quebec. We visited Chicoutimi, the Beuce, Rimouski, Valleyfield, Quebec City, and other towns distant from Montreal. We went to a big rally at Granby; this, if I remember correctly is about forty miles outside Montreal. It was the first occasion on which I had an opportunity to hear Jean Marchand speak. He was one of the celebrated "three wise men" of Marchand, Trudeau, and Gerard Pelletier whom Lester Pearson had attracted to Ottawa and the Liberal Party in 1965; all became cabinet ministers. There was a huge turnout in a big fire hall; the crowd was virtually hanging from the rafters. While the speech was in French (little understood by me) it was one of the most remarkable performances I have ever witnessed. Marchand was in full flower and what a firebrand! With his hands flailing, his foppish hair covering one eye, he had the crowd in a constant thunder. After one monstrous roar, a reporter from the *Toronto Star* asked me what Marchand had said. I responded, "He just said Joe Clark was surely going to hell for lying about the Liberals." This Marchand meeting reflected the Liberal Quebec that I was so keen to show to the English-language reporters.

Marchand, of course, had been a famous labour leader in Quebec as president of the Confederation of National Trade Unions. He was courted by the Pearson Liberals for the 1965 election but refused to run unless invitations were also extended to Pelletier and Trudeau. The three had become friends during the violent and highly-publicized labour strike at Abestos and Thetford Mines in 1949. Marchand was then leader of the union involved in the bitter dispute, which saw Premier Maurice Duplessis' Quebec government ally itself with the company forces. Pelletier, a reporter with *Le Devoir*, covered the strike and was patently pro-union. Trudeau, just returned from an extensive tour of Europe, Asia, and China, went with Pelletier to explore the situation. Through Pelletier he met Marchand and became engrossed in the battle, winding up as a legal adviser to the striking mine union. While Trudeau had misgivings about running for the Liberals, he consented to join Marchand and Pelletier as a candidate for the party in Quebec. There was misgiving on the other side too. Many Liberals saw Trudeau as a dilettante and a maverick, but he was nominated and won the Montreal Mount Royal seat. It was probably the most Liberal seat in the whole country, and remains so today. Trudeau was to hold it during his entire stay in politics, running and winning his last election in 1980.

When we went back to Ottawa that weekend and had our weekly campaign committee meeting, Marc Lalonde announced that, other than a final big rally in Montreal, there would be no need to focus on Quebec because the party would win between 68 and 70 seats. At the time I thought this an arrogant boast but it turned out to be right. In the May 22 election, we won 67 seats, the Tories 2, and the then Social Credit 6.

Before leaving this topic, and Quebec, I should comment on the Quebec media. During most of the campaign about a dozen Quebec media members travelled with us; I think at one time the number may have peaked at twenty. While one might expect them to be Liberal-leaning (as I somewhat naively did), I found to my dismay that the majority, almost all, had separatist leanings. Individually and collectively, they were among my favourites on the plane, and I developed a warm friendship with a number of them. The prime minister commented that my relationship with the Quebec journalists was unusual in that I did not speak French. Jean Charpentier, the deputy press chief, was immeasurably helpful in this area. On a number of occasions he invited the Quebecers to our rooms for a nightly drink, and in this way I got to know and like them. One night (when we were in Rimouski, I think) there was a party in a local restaurant—about 18 journalists, all male, and all Quebecers, save me as the only anglo. Before the night was done we had toasted one another many times over; it could have been a scene from a Russian banquet. Many expressed their separatist leanings and a number showed me their membership cards in the Parti Québécois, but they all thought that a successful new relationship could be worked out with Canada. I read somewhere later that the majority of journalists in Quebec are separatists. No one needed to tell me that, as I had experienced it first-hand.

Arnie Patterson and Prime Minister Trudeau leaving Parliament Hill to attend a media conference at the Media Center in Ottawa.

In the course of our travels the French reporters gave me a nickname: *Ton Ton.* When they would enter the plane coming back from a meeting they would pass by my seat, near that of the prime minister, nod and say, "Bonjour, Ton Ton." Charpentier later told me the English translation: "favourite uncle." I was flattered.

The pace was unrelenting as we continued to penetrate deep into all parts of Canada. Trudeau was brilliant and addressed many issues, most especially national unity and expansion of Canada's quest for oil and gas, and hence independence from outside sources. Every day we would have four meetings of varying kinds and, no matter what town we were in, interviews with the local television and radio personalities. Trudeau would complain to Coutts and to me that we were having too many press conferences. He felt that his "set" speeches to groups in the different towns provided enough fodder for the media. In contrast, Coutts and I felt that press conferences complemented the prime minister's speeches, which were often versions of the same theme—necessary when one must do four appearances in one day. As is their wont, the journalists preferred to hear new ideas and approaches. And too they wanted their turn at bat, the opportunity to ask tough questions. I encouraged the prime minister to have more casual contact with the reporters, but this he was reluctant to do. I can't recall him ever walking to the back of the plane, as I often did, to talk to "the boys." In fact when my wife Glo came on the plane for a trip from Sydney to Saint John (one of the few occasions that I saw her during that two month period), the prime minister said, "I am glad you are on the plane, Mrs. Patterson. It may keep him back here with us for awhile."

The setup in the plane had Trudeau occupying the first two rows on the right, and Coutts and I sharing a double seat directly opposite. Trudeau ate alone at times although he would invite Coutts, myself, and other senior staffers to join him on most occasions. If cabinet ministers came on board they would join him for lunch or dinner. I thought it would be a nice gesture for us to invite a few of the more senior and key journalists to eat with him every now and then. He reluctantly agreed and the first experiment went well. The reporters seemed pleased and Trudeau was at his charming best. A week or so later we decided to repeat the exercise, and I went back in the plane to invite Mary Janigan of the *Toronto Star* and Geoffrey Simpson of the *Globe and Mail* to join the prime minister. Simpson, who I thought even then was one of the best reporters in Canada (and he has long since proven that), refused to take part when he learned the conversations were "off the record." Anyway Tom Axworthy, a brother of the cabinet minister and a senior aide to the prime minister, overheard this and volunteered to get another guest. He arrived back at Trudeau's seats with Mark Phillips of the CBC. If Geoff Simpson was one of my favourites on the plane, Mark Phillips was one of my least favourites. A brash and arrogant redhead, and a native of Montreal, Phillips was one of those reporters who was constantly in search of embarrassing angles. Whenever I talked to my wife, she would tell me that Phillips was sabotaging us with his nightly features. I never thought him to be a particularly good reporter. Anyway he and Axworthy were standing in front of me and I had no choice but to welcome him to the table.

Mary Janigan and Mark Phillips sat on one side of the table, the prime minister and I on the other. There was a wide-ranging discussion on many of the current issues; nothing said that was new or earth shattering. The prime minister reiterated his stand on bilingualism, saying that the aim was to allow both English and French an opportunity to speak to their government in the language of their choice. The discussion turned to whether the prime minister was expecting to win a majority government. He said that it was up to the people to decide. Mark Phillips then asked if the election was close—say if the Liberals trailed by a seat or two—would he endeavour to form a government. The prime minister treated this as a hypothetical question, giving one of his famous shrugs and saying that we would have to wait and make a judgement on whatever circumstances prevailed after the election. As I recall we were on our way to Vancouver and a rally for the Honourable Iona Campagnolo, but we stopped at Winnipeg for refuelling and other refurbishments. Phillips got off the plane and, as soon became obvious, called the CBC, airing a story that Trudeau would cling—yes cling—to power even if he fell a few seats short of a minority government. The next day Mary Janigan's banner headline in the *Toronto Star* said: "Trudeau Will Cling to Power." And the rest of the Canadian media went with that line.

I had sat through the discussion and I knew that Trudeau had never made such a claim. Phillips had quickly conferred with Mary after the dinner, and she agreed with his read on the story line. I don't think she ever heard the conversation in full as she was a nervous flyer and was distracted by the turbulence. It was a shoddy piece of journalism. I think Mary was hoodwinked.

This ended my grand plan for lunches or dinners with the prime minister. I had a gun-shy candidate on my hands. I was also ready to boot Tom Axworthy off the plane, and this while in full flight. It had been a very down day for me when we reached Vancouver. I recall having lunch with a consoling Senator Ray Perreault, one of the principal British Columbia campaign people, who suggested that these things happen in campaigns. Nevertheless I felt personally responsible for the damage that had been done. After a few days in British Columbia we returned to Toronto, stopping en route in Winnipeg, where cabinet minister Lloyd Axworthy boarded the plane. We were planning a full day's campaign in Winnipeg on his behalf the following week. He told me that he wanted the prime minister to do an interview with John Roberts, then the host of a widely-viewed television show. He assured me that Roberts was friendly to both him and the Liberals, and that such an appearance would help his campaign. I knew Roberts slightly when he had been a sportswriter with the *Montreal Star*. He was a journalistic maverick and always on the lookout for the sensational. Given the shell-shocked response of the prime minister to the "clinging" story, and this only a few days before, I had immediate reservations.

The following Monday morning in Ottawa I sat next to Keith Davey at a campaign committee meeting. Among the list of recommendations for our activities the next day in Winnipeg was the television interview with John Roberts. I told Keith that I believed the interview could be dangerous, that Roberts was a highly controversial guy and that, given the shaky trip and bad press we had just encountered, it would be my recommendation—Lloyd Axworthy or not—to pass up the invite. He suggested that I fly out to Winnipeg that day, talk to Roberts and then, if I still felt that he had a hidden agenda, I could cancel the appearance. I caught a noon-hour flight. When I got to Winnipeg I called Roberts at the television station and told him I would drop by to give him some background on the current issues. When I arrived we had a friendly chat. We had a mutual friend in Al MacNeil, who had coached the Montreal Canadians when Roberts was writing sport in Montreal. We talked about hockey and finally got to politics. He was an intelligent fellow and seemed to hold no grudges towards the prime minister or the party, although there was no direct questioning in that regard. He even came back to the hotel with me and had a drink. I felt comfortable with him and decided to allow the interview to take place. The next day we trooped over to the station in the company of at least a dozen of the regular press corps from the plane. Trudeau was in fine form, and Roberts was gracious enough as they went through a rather polite interchange about the campaign in general and certain of the issues. As the interview neared its close, always a danger point, Roberts fired the assassin's bullet.

"How come you're out here campaigning for Lloyd Axworthy," he asked, "when he voted for John Turner at the leadership campaign and is a known Turner supporter?" I wanted to throw the TV camera through the window. The prime minister handled his response with equanimity, giving Roberts a lecture on free choice in politics and speaking glowingly of Axworthy's contribution to Canada. I knew he was seething underneath. After leaving the studio I walked with Trudeau back to the hotel. He was annoyed. He said, "Why would you subject me to that type of sheer rudeness?" I told the prime minister that I had been opposed to the interview in the first place, and that the reason I had not been on the campaign plane coming to Winnipeg was that I had had reservations about the interview and had gone on ahead to talk to Roberts. I said I had earlier recommended we not do the show. He said, and pointedly, "As my press secretary I expect you to protect me against that type of situation, and in the future I expect you to say no to the campaign committee, and anyone, who exposes us to that kind of risk." Another down day. It was not that this interview would hurt us much, for Trudeau had taken command of the show and performed well. Further there would be no national reverberations as Axworthy's past support of Turner was well known. This was dead news. The next day Roberts was quoted in the *Winnipeg Free Press* as saying that I came out to "spook" him.

Despite his aplomb, with two media setbacks in a row I felt our man was getting a bit brittle. I later expressed my concerns to Jim Coutts, the most all-knowing of men.

He agreed with me, suggesting that we cut back on our "openness" and noting that we had already covered more interviews and media contact than our predecessors in the 1972 and 1974 campaigns. Furthermore the polls showed new Liberal strength in eastern Canada, although the west remained a major problem. We just could not afford major mistakes. While I thought Trudeau was the smartest guy in any room he entered, he nevertheless had competition from Coutts. A native of Manton, Alberta (the home of the Paliminos hockey club), Jim was a business and law graduate for whom almost every waking thought centred on politics. He had been president of the Young Liberals and had served some years before as principal secretary to Lester Pearson. His chief concern was politics, rather than policy, and the main thrust of his actions and thoughts was to re-elect the prime minister. He was a source of strength to me throughout the campaign and gave me full support.

I am not suggesting that we pulled back from media contact totally, just that we planned to be more cautious in our approach to exposing the prime minister. He was not privy to this, but since he complained regularly that I was subjecting him to too many interviews and press conferences, we didn't expect a complaint from our principal, and we didn't get one. There was one interview ahead that was causing me concern. I had agreed that the prime minister do a television interview with Peter Debarats, although a year or two before they had been involved in a nasty exchange. If I remember correctly, it related to questions about the prime minister's estranged wife. I think Peter was among those who had reported that Margaret, on a rare visit with her husband to the Ottawa Press Club, had gone into the women's washroom and smoked marijuana. Needless to say Debarats had not made a friend of the prime minister. Indeed Coutts was quite surprised when the prime minister agreed to the interview. As an old reporter, I knew that it was never prudent to suggest any limitations on the questions to be asked, but late in the campaign, particularly if we were in a smaller market where the reporters were not totally attuned, I would sometimes suggest they stay away from questions about his wife. I said this would end the interview, as the prime minister would simply walk out. Trudeau seldom talked about his wife, and never publicly. It was tender ground, and awkward for us as she was at the time making a cross-country tour to promote her new book and was sometimes in the news. One of my most embarrassing moments came in another fuel stop at Winnipeg. It seemed an unlucky place for me. It was customary that local newspapers delivered to the plane would be given to the press secretary, and on this occasion they presented me with the *Free Press* and the *Tribune*. I reached across the aisle to give the *Tribune* to the prime minister, and as I held it in mid-air, I read the headline: "Margaret Admits to Affair with Teddy." The story referred to Madame Trudeau and Senator Ted Kennedy, and was apparently taken from her new book. If I could have cut my arm off at that juncture I would have. A painful moment even now. The prime minister made no comment then or after.

The interview with Debarats went along well and in the closing moments the journalist said, "Prime Minister I want to ask you a question which you may consider private." I nearly had a heart attack. Then he went on to say, "How are your sons taking the contest? Are they rooting for their dad?" A smiling prime minister, so proud of his boys, answered fully and said that they were not only rooting for him but expected that he would win. I think the prime minister sometimes thought that I didn't approve of how he treated journalists, and as we walked from the room he said, "Well, how would you judge my behaviour today?" I told him I would give him a star.

On one occasion, and this midway through the campaign, we made a weekend stop in Vancouver. We had come out of Winnipeg, where it was freezing, and flew into Vancouver, where it was not only rain-free but sunny. The flowers were out and as we bused our way into the harbourside hotel, the Bayshore Inn, we saw nothing but greenery and delicately landscaped gardens. It was as if we were on a holiday cruise, for when we got to the hotel many of the reporters took advantage of the outside pool and went for a dip. We had scheduled a press conference for Saturday and a big dinner rally on Saturday night. A light schedule. Everyone was in a relaxed mood and ready for a little fun.

I went out that Friday night for dinner and a few drinks with Don MacNeil of the CBC and Bruce Garvey of the *Toronto Star*. Garvey was an old friend and was in my opinion one of the best reporters in the country, although unquestionably an assassin. Whenever he came on our plane I would say "Garvey, please go with Joe Clark." He was the reporter who first used the word "wimp" in connection with the unfortunate Clark. MacNeil was an outstanding television broadcaster, who later moved to one of the American networks. At the next morning's press conference, the good mood was reflected and the reporters threw nothing but soft pitches at the prime minister, who gave mostly smiling responses. On leaving the room the prime minister said to me, "I must say your boys and girls were well behaved today. I even enjoyed myself." I said, "Well, I think the lectures are helping." He stopped abruptly and said, "What lectures are you talking about?" I told him that at night I gave a series of talks to the media on etiquette and how they should deal with the prime minister, stressing politeness. He seemed astonished. "I can't believe it. Does anyone show up?" I told him that we had twelve at the meeting the night before. When we got on the elevator who was there but Garvey and MacNeil, my previous night's companions. Both stepped aside as we entered. I said to the two of them, "Say 'good morning' to the prime minister, gentlemen." Both immediately said good morning, and as an afterthought Garvey added "Prime Minister." As I walked the prime minister to his room he shook his head saying, "I find that hard to believe." I never told him that I was funning.

We made only two sorties into my home territory of Nova Scotia. On one visit we stopped in Halifax and Yarmouth, and on a second trip in Sydney. Before arriving in Halifax I told the Quebec reporters that they would love Halifax and that it was a part of the Canada that they as Canadians owned. I added that Quebec City was also theirs, and mine as well. We stopped first at the Bedford Institute of Oceanography before taking a ferry down the harbour. It was a spectacular day, and I stood with the cadre of Quebecers, pointing out the sights. They were impressed. Dr. John Savage, who was the Liberal candidate in Dartmouth that year, was aboard, and I spent some time with him as well. He was optimistic, although he was again to lose his sword on election night, with Mike Forrestall posting another victory for the Tories. Dr. John was persistent, however, as he came back later to become first the mayor of Dartmouth, and later the premier of Nova Scotia.

A platform had been erected wharfside at Historic Properties from which Trudeau was to make his remarks. There was an overflow crowd present although in-part hostile, for placard-carrying members of the postal union were present and shouting obscenities. (In private files, the RCMP indicated that a small militant and communist-leaning leadership controlled the union.) In such moments of confrontation Trudeau was perhaps at his best, because he would take them on without hesitation. The crowd there was largely Liberal, and so he got resounding cheers when he called them "slackers."

Funny things happen on your way to the forum. I had a few moments to say hello to my wife and daughter Lori after the rally, and while walking with them to the awaiting press bus, I passed Buff Mahony, one of the protesting postal workers. I knew him to see him, although I don't think he could have said the same of me. As I passed I said, "It's good to see you here, Buff. I didn't realize that you were such a fervent Liberal." With that I walked on, leaving an angry postal worker in my wake.

We were then on to Yarmouth, which sits on the southern tip of Nova Scotia and which is one of the main tourist entry points from the United States. We stayed at the Grand Hotel, an old Yarmouth institution which had been rebuilt and which, on that occasion, provided us all with two-pound lobsters. Trudeau joined one of the press tables and enjoyed himself. The following day we went to Wedgeport, a fishing village, where the prime minister spoke to a group of workers, men and women, at a fish plant. It was one of the most inspiring speeches of the campaign. He extolled the Acadian people of Nova Scotia for their courage and resilience, and for the great contributions they were making to Canada, despite their earlier and tragic setbacks. The workers were almost exclusively French speaking, and he spoke in both languages. I wish I had kept a copy of the remarks because they were so moving. I was standing next to Henry Geller of the *New York Times*, and when Trudeau concluded I said to him, "Now I know why I am, at 51, out here on the campaign trail." I was elated. Trudeau had never been in better form. On our second trip to Nova Scotia we went to Sydney, where Russell McLellan was our hopeful. It was a late night meeting, fully attended. Knowing how the television reporters had to hustle to catch the late evening news, and knowing of the importance of this exposure for the prime minister, I always warned the local speakers to be brief. On that occasion I spoke with Russell McLellan and asked him to keep his remarks to no more than ten minutes so as to accommodate the prime minister. Caught up in the enthusiasm of the big crowd, he went on for 25 minutes and we missed the late news. Anyway, there is a happy ending to this story, for Russell not only won the election but held that seat for 19 years before vacating it to become the premier of Nova Scotia.

The final days of the campaign were spent in the bigger cities, and on the Friday and Saturday before Monday's election, we barnstormed Toronto with its potential reward of 23 seats. The prime minister spoke to a big Italian gathering somewhere in North Toronto, which I am sure broke every fire department regulation in the books; the audience was standing, shoulder to shoulder, shouting and waving. I have always loved Italians, and never more so than during an election campaign, because they are almost all Liberals—buoyant, enthusiastic Liberals at that. Like the Acadians, they had a special kinship with Trudeau and it showed. I am not sure whether it was on that trip or not, but he also spoke to a meeting in Forest Hills, an affluent township with a large Jewish population, and again mostly Liberal. Robert Kaplan was our candidate, a member of the cabinet and a shoo-in to win his election. In the midst of his remarks, however, the prime minister said that he would not support Israel's call to make Jerusalem the capital of Israel. He said it would inflame an already unstable situation in the Middle East. It was a good thing that it was a safe seat because the prime minister did not win any friends that night, and apparently Kaplan was greatly annoyed. Fittingly Toronto was also the site for the final major meeting of the campaign. The O'Keefe Centre was packed, and the prime minister, striking his famed "gunslinger's pose" with head and shoulder thrust forward and hands tucked in on his hips, gave what I thought was the best speech of the campaign, with continuing cheers and applause from an admiring crowd. He was more than just an outstanding speaker, he was a great performer. These days when I watch the other leaders, including the recent American presidential battlers, Gore and Bush, I think them amateurs alongside of Trudeau.

The Sunday campaign meeting in Ottawa was alive with nervous tension. The news from the west was not promising, although there was continuing hope that we would win a few seats in British Columbia and maybe make a breakthrough in Manitoba. Alberta's adamant hatred of the National Energy Policy, made the winning of a seat there a distant prospect. While Alberta is now Alliance–Reform country, it was no less alienated in Trudeau's time. I remember that in the remote areas of that province it was like travelling in Ku Klux Klan country; their hatred for the Liberals, and for Trudeau and Lalonde particularly, was so pronounced. The Liberals had rented the big ballroom at the Chateau Laurier as a gathering place for the faithful on election night. Several big television screens were placed throughout the room, and we awaited the results there. The prime minister was going to watch the returns at 24 Sussex and come to the hotel later as results confirmed either victory or defeat. While the polls commissioned by the various media indicated a close election, they nevertheless showed that Joe Clark was going to win with an overwhelming tide coming in from the west. Coutts had told me that our own party polls indicated that we could make it, and he remained confident, pointing out that we had a good campaign and that the prime minister had widely outperformed Joe Clark and Ed Broadbent of the NDP. So we were hopeful, although I said to Coutts, "Are you sure about the polls? I am the press secretary. You shouldn't lie to me." I said it largely in jest, but I meant it. I knew he wanted to keep me pumped up so that, in my dealings with the media, I would put a confident spin on things. And this I did unfailingly.

As the early returns came in, the roomful of Liberals was gleeful. Newfoundland and New Brunswick produced significant Liberal wins. Nova Scotia, with lingering memories of Robert Stanfield, went Tory as expected, but Allan MacEachen held his seat. We came out of the Atlantic Canada with twelve seats, down one from 1974. There was general elation as the Quebec vote came in: the Liberals, 67; the Tories, 2—a net gain of seven for us. The media hordes were there, of course, and after each result they would interview me as to my interpretation. Jean Charpentier was working with the Quebec media, Ralph Coleman was also busy handling inquiries, and Pat Gossage was working behind the scenes. Doubt and some despair evidenced as the Ontario returns came in. We all knew that Ontario was the key battleground, and in the previous election the Liberals had won 55 seats to the Tories' 25. When the big Ontario count was finalized a loss of 23 Liberal seats was realized—catastrophic unless miracles were produced in western Canada, and this was unlikely if earlier polls were to be believed. Going in to Manitoba, and with the results from the Atlantic Provinces, Quebec, and Ontario, we had a lead over the Tories of 111 to 87. Having stood in the back of halls in rallies at Camrose, Moose Jaw, Regina, and other western centres I had a forlorn feeling, although I kept smiling as press inquiries continued. The west turned out to be a disaster with our party winning 3 seats to the Conservatives commanding and overwhelming 59—a loss of 10 for us, a gain of 9 for them. When the battle was concluded Joe Clark became prime minister with 136 seats to the Liberals' 114. Of minor consolation was the knowledge that we had 39 percent of the vote to the Conservatives' 35.6, but the deepening alienation of western Canada had sealed our fate.

As the tide continued to turn in the west, the buoyancy that earlier had existed in the ballroom turned to gloom. I held the fort as best I could but it was clear that we were facing defeat. I saw Pat Gossage slip silently out of the room, although the other press officers stayed on and gave support. The prime minister did not arrive until late. Like us, he had waited, hoping that British Columbia would treat us more kindly; but with a shutout there, all hopes were dashed. When he mounted the podium at the hotel I thought for a minute that I was mistaken and that we must have won, for he was all smiles. It was not, however, to be a long speech. He said that he and other Liberals had been true to their traditions and had campaigned for social justice and for a stronger and united Canada. He paid tribute to Mr. Clark and wished him well with his new government. His final remarks were directed to Liberals everywhere who had given him such strong support over the years. There was no suggestion that he would step down from the leadership. The campaign, however, was over. Exhausted I went back to my hotel and went to bed. It had been a very trying night; and while the campaign itself had been exhilarating, it also had been a physically challenging exercise, with the constant flights through time zones leaving me almost continually drained. I went to bed saddened but awoke happy with the knowledge that I would soon be home, back to family and my real life. I had enjoyed it, but I had promised Coutts and Davey, as well as Dick, now safely ensconced in the arms of the Bank of Montreal, that I would stay only for the election and then I was off. I had put all of my financial holdings, including the radio property, in trust, and among other things I was anxious to see how they had weathered in my absence.

As I write these words, it has been only months since Pierre Trudeau died at his home in Montreal at the age of 81. In the days following his death, the tribute on television and in the papers was overwhelming. The victory in the Second World War got less media play. I recall the words of Allan MacEachen after a tour of the Lenin tomb in Moscow in 1967: "Our tribute to Christ is modest by comparison." While more subdued, it was Trudeaumania all over again. The whole country seemed captivated, and the outpouring of love and tributes was unending.

The PMO was kind enough to call me in Halifax and invite me to the funeral, with a seat in the basilica. I immediately made a reservation with Air Canada to fly up the night before the funeral and was planning a reunion with Dick O'Hagan, Jim Coutts, and Ralph Coleman, who was working on the invitation list for the funeral. When I called Dick to make sure he was going, I found in talking to his wife, Wanda, that he was in hospital. He had fallen down a day or two before and "blown his knee." This was a major disappointment as I looked forward to seeing him. I was suffering from bronchitis at the time and Glo sensibly, as always, prevailed on me not to go, suggesting that the hustle would be a bit too much when I wasn't feeling well. With O'Hagan not to be present, my enthusiasm had ebbed. I probably got a better view of things by watching television, and I thought the CBC, and in particular Peter Mansbridge, did an outstanding job in the coverage. I was sorry to miss paying tribute, and seeing old friends, but I did write a column in which I saluted Trudeau's many accomplishments and his significant contribution to Canada. When I talked to Dick O'Hagan on the phone during one of the tear-filled tributes I said, "Are they talking about the same fellow we knew? Everyone seems to love him, but I can remember loggers, postal workers, and a host of others who wanted to hang him from the nearest tree."

A day or two after the funeral I was delighted to get a call from my grandson Ian who is attending King's College here in Halifax. He is 18, and recently returned to Canada with his family after a long stay in Moscow. I was amazed when he told me that he and his roommate, Jay, a Toronto boy, had flown up to the funeral and had stood with the mourners outside Notre Dame Basilica. They listened to the Mass, broadcast over the loudspeakers. I thought, what a wonderfully Canadian thing to do. It will be an event that they will think about all of their lives. A few months later, with the general election called, Ian and Jay were out knocking doors for the NDP candidate. Well, at 18, it's okay to have a social conscience and to be involved in the affairs of the nation. I was proud of both of them.

Over the years I have had many people ask me what Trudeau was like and whether he was difficult to work with. I never gave them a complex answer, but said simply that I thought he was "the brightest guy in the room," and I meant all rooms because his intelligence was so penetrating. I also said I liked him very much but I never claimed an intimacy with him, as few who knew him could. Even Coutts, who worked with him so closely, once said, "You will never really get to know him." But as a public figure and as a servant of Canada we got full value, for he was not only the most exciting Canadian of our time, but one of the ablest.

That's my mission statement, and now if you will allow me to elaborate, and this after many years, I will attempt to give you a further insight into this very complex man. The label "arrogant" was probably the most-used adjective when Pierre Trudeau's name was mentioned, either in print or in conversation. Yet I must say that I never found him arrogant, and I always thought it a wrong label. He was without question an elitist, a natural aristocrat. His instinctive combativeness, exhibited many times, may have won him the label "arrogant" because he never backed down from a foe. In one of our cavalcades through downtown Vancouver, I remember a group of loggers shouting obscenities as we passed. Trudeau had the car slowed, stood up, and waved his fist. His theatricality was one thing that set him apart from many of our past, drab leaders. In this regard he was almost un-Canadian, for he was at times a showboat. The night he attended the Winnipeg Ballet performance at Carnegie Hall he wore a cape and a wide-brimmed black stetson. Jean Charpentier shook his head and said, "Let's hope he doesn't go to a nightclub tonight and get his photo in the morning papers."

In his biography on Trudeau (and this one of the early ones) author George Radwanski told an interesting story relating to Trudeau's first nomination as the Liberal candidate in the 1965 election. Because he was somewhat forced on the party as a condition of Marchand's running, there were those in the constituency who were unsure that they wanted him, perceiving him a radical. Radwaski wrote:

> Trudeau almost compounded their misgivings by turning up for a crucial pre-nomination meeting [Mount Royal] with Liberal organizers, dressed in an open-collared sports shirt, a suede jacket, a beat-up old peaked hat, muddy corduroy slacks, and sandals. He was intercepted as he stepped out of his Mercedes SL-300 and sent home to change into more conservative attire before others could see a further display of unconventionality.

Pierre Trudeau was different from you, from me, from Canadians. Many saw him as a semi-dilettante. As a man of inherited wealth, he had few of the problems or worries of the average Canadian, and he was able to pursue his quest for adventure and knowledge. He had been superbly educated at the University of Montreal, Harvard, the University of Paris, and the London School of Economics, and through his world travels and wide reading he had gained a unique view of the world. I suppose you could say that he worked a little bit—he taught law for a few years, wrote articles for *Cité Libre*—yet many of his early acquaintances wondered whether he would ever settle down and do something meaningful with his life.

I can remember a conversation with him one day in his office on the Hill when he said that he had never given thought to being prime minister before joining the government, and that he really had little inclination to seek election to any political office. His pursuits were simply intellectual and his writings and commentaries almost rebellious in tone. And yet despite his early disdain for politics, although not political thought, he became one of the most memorable prime ministers in the country's history. Listening to him, which I did on countless occasions, I was totally aware he was a man who wanted to make an imprint on his country, not necessarily a personal one, but one of ideas that would forever change the way Canadians thought and acted. I think he opened the country and the eyes of our people to the diversity that exists among us. Dalton Camp, one of the most enlightened pundits in the land, commented in the Halifax *Daily News* after the 2000 election that the strength of the Liberal Party, reflected by Jean Chretien's third straight majority government, was in large part due to its occupation of the centre of the political-philosophical spectrum. He said the Alliance, as a right-wing party, did not have enough room to woo the majority of Canadians; much the same was the fate of the NDP, who occupied too narrow a philosophical space on the left. The Liberals, he said, had the privilege of moving either to the right or the left, always leaving a toehold in the centre, which guaranteed them a solid vote. The Liberal party has traditionally been the party of the centre, and the party (as it styles itself) of change. Pierre Trudeau with his continuing thrust for change, for policies that veered both left and right, narrowed the divide, and his legacy was to leave the Liberals with an even broader-based vote.

In my epitaph to this great but complex man I steal a line from the movie *Citizen Kane*: "he was one and at the same time the most loved and hated man" in the country. We hope he was more loved than hated.

Chapter Fifteen: The Present and the Past

As I write this I am 72 years old, and thus I have more room to look back than ahead. I am undaunted by this prospect, as life has been good to me and I have enjoyed every phase of it. I find it difficult at times, however, to imagine that I am an older man because memories of running down the wharf and jumping in the war canoe at the Mic Mac Club in Dartmouth don't seem that far removed. Where have 55 or so years gone? In the preceding chapters I have chronicled events from my past life. For me they were great experiences, rich and rewarding for the most part, but not without the occasional setback. But that is life, as I now understand it being a member of the senior gentry. The real purpose of this chapter is to tell you a bit about this survivor as he is today.

I reside with my wife, Glorena, as graceful today as she was when I first met her fifty years ago. We live in a great old house in Bedford, Nova Scotia. It is located on a relatively large secluded lot and was built in 1919 by the legendary Halifax architect Andrew Cobb. It is a unique house and we love it, and often I say a silent prayer for Andrew who, of course, has long since departed this earth. We have been blessed with two lovely daughters: Carol, a lawyer, now resident in Toronto with her husband Malcolm, sons Ian, 19, and Colin, 13; and Lori, in public relations, resident in Bedford, just up the street from us, with husband Patrick, son Liam, 11, and daughter Andrea, 8. Few days or nights go by that we are not invaded by our Bedford grandchildren, and for this we are eternally grateful. And as well, despite the distance, we remain in continuing and close contact with Carol and her family. Visits are frequent now that they are back in Canada after living for ten years in Moscow, where she practised law and Malcolm was the resident bureau chief for *Maclean's* magazine.

I must pause when I mention Carol and Malcolm's ten years in Russia as it always provokes questions. "What are your children doing in Moscow?" A bit unusual I would agree, but for them a particularly rewarding time. I think I played a small role in this, although I may be taking more credit than merited. I have had over a period of years special interest in Russia, Czarist times, the revolution, and in Leon Trotsky particularly, who in some respects was one of the most formidable personalities of our times. I think in part my avocational interest sparked my bright daughter Carol's attention. She pursued Russian history and language in her undergraduate years at Dalhousie, and later spent a year studying at the Pushkin Institute in Moscow when she was just out of her teens. At the same time it was incidental; the move that took them to Moscow for their ten-year stay was husband Malcolm's transfer there as a *Maclean's* correspondent. Doubtless this was encouraged by Carol's background in Russia and its language and furthered when she was able to join Baker McKenzie's three-lawyer legal staff in the Russian metropolis. My own modest roots in Russia's past and history were greatly surpassed as the Gray family became firmly implanted in the real life of Russia, and were first-hand witnesses to the dramatic change that has taken place over the past decade or so.

A skilled and thoughtful journalist, Malcolm through extensive travels to all parts of that magical and immense land is today probably one of Canada's foremost experts on the new Russia. Carol for her part became joint manager of the Baker McKenzie firm, which has more than 125 employees and is the principal foreign law firm practising in the country. Having returned to Canada, she is now a partner at the Toronto office of Baker McKenzie. While they went to Russia with the thought of perhaps two years service there, they got caught up in life there and stayed for ten. Glo and I, of course, as parents and grandparents, are happy to have them back in Canada, and they too, despite their rich experiences, find it refreshing after the years away.

Lori has also had an interesting career although hers was practised at home. After graduating from Dalhousie, she joined me at CFDR in a public relations and promotions capacity. And a busy job it was, for radio stations are endlessly caught up in promotion of all kinds. We sponsored regattas on the harbour, a fifty-piece community concert band, endless stage concerts by noted artists, and commercial activities that demanded a great deal of effort from our public relations officer. One of her most lasting credentials, however, rests not with our flagship, CFDR, but rather with the new kid on the block, Q104.

While it is now a well-established station in the city's mix, Q was probably more Lori's baby than that of anyone else involved in bringing it into existence. She did the hiring, the talent search, and a lot of the early creative promotion. She stayed with the stations for about a year after I sold and retired, and then moved on to a position as public relations officer for Metro Transit, a busy and fulfilling job that she has enjoyed. Her husband Patrick is one of the busiest fellows in town. He operates an industrial real estate sales and development company and while he has some ups and downs (an appropriate term for the skier that he is) recent years have brought him great success in the burgeoning Burnside Industrial Park. Theirs is a family of skiers, with Pat, Lori, Liam, and Andrea spending most winter weekends at their ski house at Wentworth. Both of our girls have opted to couple business careers with the rearing of children. This is so common today among young people, who expect a certain degree of material

(left to right) Arnie Patterson, hockey star Al MacNeil, and CFDR manager Clary Flemming, at a Nova Scotia sports banquet. A close friend since his junior days in Toronto, MacNeil was named top athlete for the year 1969.

comfort. I have perhaps old-fashioned and mixed feelings about this lifestyle. On the one hand, I think that in the past we have wasted so much of the talent available to us in bright and able women who years ago opted to stay at home and rear a family. And yet I am concerned about the heavy responsibility taken on by career women who have other major responsibilities waiting for them at home too. Glo, like most women of her era, ceased work shortly after our marriage and spent her life as a homemaker. Given her intelligence and abilities I am sure that she could have had a highly successful commercial or professional career had that been her option, but I think both she and I are comfortable and satisfied with her choice to remain at home for she has been of strong support to me in my various pursuits. This is perhaps too deep and too complex an area for me to expound on. Let me simply bow out by saying that it is my experience both in the workplace and in observing from afar, that women are as bright and as capable as men in most areas, and it is my expectation that we will see continuing upward mobility and advancement by the feminine gender in the workplace. Now, back to safer ground.

Since my retirement Glo and I have had a highly enjoyable life centred largely on family and golf and travel. I sometimes find it difficult to realize that I have been retired for fourteen years, having sold my business interests at 58, and yet I have managed to keep myself busy with other pursuits. As a guy who worked hard most of his life, I often feel a little guilty basking in the sun in Florida with my only assigned tasks as golf, bridge, and the enjoyment of friendships. I have often thought that, but for the grace of God, I might have been catching rivets at the shipyards, and here I have gone through life doing things I enjoyed.

At this writing, after fourteen consecutive years of winter residence in Florida, I often think we have the best of both worlds. In 1985, prior to retiring, I bought a lovely one-bedroom condo at Isla Del Sol, a golf-residential development created by General Electric. I had first visited there in 1983 with my long-time golfing associate John Randles, Sr. I knew on my initial visit that it was a special place and that it would be my retirement home away from home. In 1987 I bought a much larger unit overlooking the water and situated right off the fourth hole.

Isla is situated on an island, joined by a bridge on one side to mainland St. Petersburg and by a bridge on the other side to St. Pete Beach. The golf course is cradled in the centre of the island with condos running down the sides of the fairways and a little beyond. The focal point of our settlement, which in most respects is like a small town, is the club, which includes not only golf but tennis and yachting as well. Its total membership is close to 750, almost all island residents. When asked how I liked Isla, I used to say, "Going to heaven will be anti-climatic. I want to stay right here." About eight to ten percent of the membership is Canadian. We seem to share the same interests, hopes, and aspirations of our American cousins, and by and large there is close accord. A friend of mine once asked me which life I enjoyed most—life in Nova Scotia, or our Florida sojourn. I love Florida, our new friends, the golf, and the social life, but there is no place like home. It is not only where the heart is but, for the mature person who lives with memories, it is where the head is as well. I often feel that I have been reincarnated, with two separate and distinct lives, sets of friends, and enjoyments. Going to heaven may be anti-climatic after all.

I have enjoyed writing this book. Strangely it has made me relive my life. Many of the events recorded in the preceding chapters deal with the past, and in some cases the long past. And yet, those events are so fresh in my mind, and my remembrances of the people who paraded through these pages so clear to me. The toughest task I have faced in writing this work has been to write it in a way that engages Nova Scotians, my principal audience, and to record with both feeling and clarity some of the more significant national events. It has been just as challenging to write about people who walked upon the local or national stage many years past and, I hope, present them in a manner that captivates people of all ages. The style has been reportorial, largely factual, although I have at times expressed an editorial or "personal" opinion. In this final kick at the can, the final chapter, I speak from my own opinion. I have long held fairly firm positions on politics and business. Earlier from my own pulpit at CFDR and over the past fourteen years in my column in the Halifax *Daily News*, I have had an opportunity to express them.

As a director of Sackville Downs, Arnie presents a championship pacing trophy to Dr. and Mrs. Mark Browman of Montreal whose horse won the Nova Scotia pace.

Anyone who has read my column with any regularity would conclude without question that I am both liberal and Liberal. In regard to small "l" liberalism, I am probably not as consistent as I am relative to governmental Liberalism. This may sound like a contradiction. Yet if I were to examine my own thinking and political philosophy closely, I think I would conclude that while I without question am liberal and Liberal—a firm and consistent advocate of social welfarism, a government role in most aspects of our life, and such specific things as government health care and aid for the have-nots in society—I am at the same time an unrelenting believer in the free enterprise system and most of its capitalistic overtones. If you read the chapters "Dosco Days" and "The Bull and Dief the Chief," you are probably familiar with Albert L. Fairley, Jr., who was president of the steel and coal company. While I was young and somewhat idealistic in my days at Dosco, I learned that things that don't make money are of little use to anyone in the long run. Mr. Fairley used to preach this message to me: "No profits, no raises, and ultimately no jobs." I was party to a lot of tough business decisions in my Dosco days, particularly as they related to the mining interests. There seemed to be trouble on every front. I was with Fairley when, representing the company, we the closure of the mine at Springhill. I was also with him when we closed the more than sixty-year-old iron ore operation on Bell Island. In both instances the communities were totally dependent on the mines. Periodically there were layoffs at the shipyards, the Trenton Works, and other units within the company. These were hard, old decisions. And yet as difficult and as soul-searching as they were for me, I thought then, and as an older man think now, that those decisions were necessary and just. Although I was never to encounter anything like the massive layoffs experienced in Dosco, in running the radio stations I was called on several times to lay people off, which was never a pleasant task. But in every instance this move was motivated and necessitated by economic conditions, and my rationalization was that the boat had to be kept afloat for the good of the majority and that certain sacrifices had to be made.

Al Fairley would comment, after I had given him clippings of some sharp newspaper attack on layoffs or certainly closures, that those things would be carried out in the United States without fanfare. He would suggest that Americans were far more attuned to capitalism than were Canadians, and that they more readily accepted cutbacks as simply part of the game. I can't say that I ever accepted his statements at face value, but I think that we in Canada have a different entrepreneurial code than that of our neighbours. I think the decision-makers in business are far more conscious of the social impact of their actions, and indeed those who aren't often have to deal with governments that in most areas of Canada have a social-welfare bent. There are examples, however, in which our social instincts have caused us as a collective society to make mistakes. The most glaring is right here in our own Nova Scotia backyard, and I refer to the tragic and costly manner in which we have handled things at the steel plant in Sydney. When Hawker Siddeley announced the closure of the mill in 1967 they were denounced as cold-hearted buccaneers. The provincial government under G. I. Smith stepped in and assumed ownership. That was 31 years ago and Nova Scotians in the interim have absorbed losses of close to $3 billion, and there is no end in sight as the current government stumbles along seeking new owners. The sad thing is that the mill should have been closed following the Hawker announcement. Perhaps the government should have kept it going for a year to ease the situation, and then softened the blow to its workers with some form of compensation. Hindsight is a great thing. Happily I was long gone from Dosco when disaster struck at Sydney, for in my day the steel plant was relatively profitable but steel fortunes throughout North America were already on a downhill track.

While I am on my soapbox I will close with two themes that I have dwelt on many times in my column over the years. First, we Canadians are the luckiest people on earth, and while the United Nations has voted Canada the world's best country in which to live, and this for six successive years, those of us living here already know that. I think too that Nova Scotians have a better way of life than most of our fellow Canadians. Supposedly we are a "have-not" province, but I would suggest that given the growing revenues from offshore natural gas production at Sable, and the promise of so much more, we will experience our greatest period of growth and prosperity over the next twenty years. When I hear the complaints of protest groups of various stripes and causes, I sometimes wonder what the problem is. I am not suggesting that they have no legitimate concerns, but for most people in Nova Scotia, and I could add the whole of Canada, life has never been better. We have more security than any other nation in the world, and our freedom as a people is unequalled. There is a car in every driveway, shining new houses springing up like mushrooms, a television in every abode, computer technology revolutionizing most, and certainly food in just about every belly. My second thought to end this sermon is: save some money. It is not impossible, it just requires a bit of discipline. There will come a time with advancing years when you will love the independence that being financially secure will give you. Today with medicare, the Canada Pension Plan, the Old Age Pension, the baby bonus, and compulsory company pension plans we as a people have never had a better opportunity to build in comfort for later years.

Chapter Sixteen: Potpourri

There are so many things heretofore left unsaid in this tome that I thought I would add a rumble seat. For those too young to know from experience, the rumble seat was a small, two-seat affair built into the rear end of a car. They were fun to ride in, unless in winter, for you rode in the open air much like a convertible with the top down.

I never talked hockey in this epistle. It would be sacrilegious for any Canadian writer, particularly for an old hockey broadcaster, not to touch on his love for the game. While I, along with other Canadians, suffered through many a spring as the Russians beat our amateur hirelings (a contradiction in terms), I fervently maintain that hockey is our game and no one in the world plays it better. As a wintertime resident of Florida for the last thirteen years I have become a sporadic fan of the Tampa Bay Lightning. While I am convinced that the Americans are out to steal our game, I marvel at how quickly it has spread and how popular it is in such sunny climes as Tampa, Phoenix, Nashville, Miami, Atlanta, and California. This is a remarkable phenomenon, and while I worry about the Americanization of the sport my wife says, "Well, look at all the well-paying jobs it gives Canadian hockey players." I suppose there is some truth to that—sixty percent of the players in the NHL are Canucks, although there is annually an increasing number of Russians, Czechs, and other Europeans breaking into the ranks. American college hockey too has produced an influx of good, young players, and they now account for close to twenty percent of the current crop. We can take comfort in the fact that our game now enjoys worldwide popularity, and as a nation we made it all happen. I had an opportunity to introduce members of the Czech national team some years ago at a function in Halifax. At the affair the president of the Czech hockey union told me that when they played hockey as youngsters the game was called "Kanada." He said they would run to the lakes yelling, "Let's play Kanada!" It's the game we gave to the world.

Back on hockey with my second love thrown in. Last summer I had the privilege of being the chairman of the volunteers (370 in total) at the first Wayne Gretzky and Friends golf tournament held at the Glen Arbour course just outside Halifax. This two-day event, which attracted capacity crowds, featured three of our legends, Gretzky, Mario Lemieux, and Brett Hull in a best-ball event against Mike Weir, our latter-day hero. It was a marvellous event in which the golf pro, pitted against the NHL's trio, won on an extra playoff hole. The crowd, myself included, was so impressed with the way our Canadian boys deported themselves on the course. As big an icon as he has become, Wayne went out of his way to sign autographs and chat with the kids in attendance. In watching our hockey stars in television interviews, and in drawing on my own experience as a broadcaster, I can see that our guys are far more engaging, gentlemanly, and natural than most of the American athletes. National prejudice? Possibly.

Now that the task of writing this 80,000-word tome is drawing to a close, I am alarmed at having left many things out. There are four associations that come to mind, all directorships: Steed and Evans, an Ontario and Maritime road building concern; Eastern Provincial Airlines; Ferguson Industries (the Pictou Shipyards); and the Atlantic Development Board.

If I were to think of the best day's work I ever put in, it would have to be the day I spent at a directors' meeting at Ferguson's in Pictou. Jim and Allan Ferguson, the owners of the yard, were two of the nicest men I have known in business, and they had operated the yard, the town's major industry, for more than forty years. I had known Jim in my Dosco days when I would go to Ottawa to call on the Nova Scotian MPs, sometimes in the interest of our Halifax Shipyards. He would be there, with the support of Pictou MP Russell McEwan, seeking work for his yard. In this respect he was highly successful. Sometime around 1975 or thereabouts, Jim called me and asked me if I would like to join Ferguson's as a director. While it was a family affair, there were four outside directors: Frank H. Sobey, the Stellarton grocery king; William Flemming, a former superintendent of Dosco's railcar plant at nearby Trenton; a provincial government appointee by the name of Clarence Ivey; and me. A few years later, on a bright summer day, I was asked to go to Pictou for what Jim classified as "an emergency meeting." As it turned out, the August holidays for the workmen were only weeks away and substantial monies would be required for their holiday pay. Caught in a serious cash flow problem, with no further help coming from the banks, Jim explained that there were no monies available and the operation could be facing bankruptcy.

Earlier that day we had toured the yard and had viewed two fishery patrol boats being built for the Department of Fisheries. From my Dosco days I knew the feds had a program in which they paid a portion of their fee as each stage of the work was completed. Quite innocently I said to Jim and Allan, "Has the government advanced any money for the construction of the Fisheries vessels?" The answer was no, that policy had been discontinued several years before. When we got back to the office, I put in a phone call to a man named MacIntosh (if I remember correctly his first name was Henry) who was responsible for the administration of vessels being built for the government agencies. I had met him a number of times in my days with Dosco when we would both be in Ottawa on Halifax Shipyards business. When I reached him he was most receptive, but explained that the policy had indeed changed. He did add, however, "Arnie, if you can get someone high enough in the government to give the okay, we might be able to do something." Presto. I called minister of health, Allan MacEachen, and explained the yard's dire straits and the threat of closure. Three days later two cheques arrived from Ottawa, totalling something in the area of $800,000. A good deed was done. The Fergusons carried on for several more years and later sold to Nickerson Brothers, who sadly went into bankruptcy.

The other directorships were equally interesting and rewarding. In Steed and Evans, I not only enjoyed a 25-year relationship, but remain today close friends with the company's two principals, Roy Steed and Dennis Evans. While they are now both largely retired, under their leadership the company met with outstanding success. My airline experience brought me into contact with Harry Steele, another director, who was to buy my radio stations some years later. My involvement with the Atlantic Development Board was a heady exercise in that we spent million of dollars in the Atlantic area on behalf of the federal government.

I will close with one other anecdote and this on the day when the federal government announced the closure of the last coal mine in Cape Breton. While this decision is totally justified, I can't help but feel sad because my own involvement with the coal towns was for the most part highly enjoyable. Certainly their citizens are special people. In the early 1960s, during the time of the Rand Commission inquiries into coal operations, I attended a banquet at Morrison High in Glace Bay. One of the featured performances was that offered by four miners, led by Jimmy P. MacNeil, a former mayor of New Waterford. The men entered the darkened room, their miner's lamps shining, and sang a number of songs. It was a most impressive performance. Some years later Mrs. Cohen of Sydney organized a campaign to raise funds for the construction of a miners' museum in Glace Bay. The campaign met with success and the museum continues in operation to this day. At the time I was running the Moosehead Brewery in Dartmouth, and she asked me to serve as the mainland fund-raiser in conjunction with the project chairman, the Honourable L. D. Currie. At one meeting I suggested we organize a miners' choral group, and within a matter of days Mrs. Cohen advised me that she was acting on my idea but that they would need a sponsor. I offered the support of the brewery, and the "Moosehead Men of the Deeps" came into existence. All the original equipment, clothes, lamps, and other such apparatus were provided by the brewery. Their Canadian debut took place in Montreal at the 1967 Expo when, under Moosehead sponsorship, they sang at the Nova Scotia pavilion. I was later to tour with the group as the master of ceremonies for inaugural concerts at Glace Bay, Sydney, and New Waterford. I am still delighted when I hear them all these years later.

Chapter Seventeen: Ten Most Memorable Men

In the foregoing chapters you have met many outstanding personalities, and I have always felt that one of the gifts of my episodic career was that I was able to encounter people in just about every walk of life. Now in compiling this list let me tell you the simple rules that have guided me in choosing these ten most memorable people. First, I will deal with men only, simply because until recent years there were only a handful of women in the front ranks of business. Fortunately this has changed as women now are moving into senior jobs in hundreds of corporations. Second, I will exclude sports personalities, although my early life was centred in this world. Third, while accomplishments and attainments are a factor in my judgement, the influence that those named have had on my own life is also a major consideration.

One—**Crawford Gordon, Jr.** While his final years were tragic, and his talent and capabilities unrealized, Crawford was a brilliant man, who at the peak of his career as president of A. V. Roe Limited commanded a work force of thirty thousand men. I think too that his unrealized dream of bringing the Avro Arrow to final development was a great loss to Canada and Canadians. He was a man of immense personal charm.

Two - **Fred G. Gardiner**, the dynamic first chairman of the metropolitan government of Toronto. As chairman in the fifties, Gardiner gave Toronto the push it needed to development into the world-class city we know today. He was a commanding figure, a masterful speaker, and a clear thinker. While his name is little known to Torontonians today, one of the city's major arterial roadways—the Gardiner Expressway—is named in his honour.

Three - **Harold M. C. Gordon**, the vice president of Dominion Steel and Coal Corporation. Harold was a real mining boss, tough, arbitrary, difficult, and seldom wrong in his own mind. And yet he was one of the finest and certainly one of the most courageous men that I have known. An imposing physical presence, Harold should have lived in an earlier age when he could have led kilted Scottish troops into battle. There would have been no retreat.

Four - **Pierre Elliott Trudeau**, Canada's prime minister, 1968–84. He was perhaps the most intellectually brilliant man I have known in my lifetime. Much like *Citizen Kane* in the movie by that name, he was the most loved and hated man in Canada at one and the same time. But he too had immense charm when required. A great speaker and a clear thinker, he will be remembered as one of Canada's all-time great prime ministers.

Five - **Allan MacEachen**, Cape Breton's gift to politics. No one in the history of Canadian politics did more for the "common man" than Allan. In his almost forty-year career he was a leader in social-welfare legislation, including labour law and medicare. He held just about every portfolio in federal politics, he was a deputy prime minister and finally became a senator. Basically a modest man, MacEachen was a gifted speaker who kept the Liberal Party on course, usually left-of-centre.

Six - **I. W. Akerley**. This is a choice from my own home town. Ake led Dartmouth to city status in 1961 and was later a highly effective minister of highways in the provincial government. Of much the same mould as Fred Gardiner of Toronto, Ake was an able administrator and a natural leader.

Seven - **John M. Turner**, another prime minister. Perhaps reflecting some prejudice, I feel that he could have been one of our great prime ministers. While he was a complete liberal and Liberal, he had a good feel for business and the economy. Sadly, Trudeau buried him with his outlandish and lavish senatorial and ambassadorial appointments when he left office. Above all things, he is a thoroughly decent man.

Eight -**Albert L. Fairley, Jr.** A perfect gentleman and a Southern charmer. Many of the economic principles that I learned and cling to were taken from his reservoir of wisdom. He was not a "tough guy" like Crawford Gordon or Harold Gordon, but he was intelligent and thoughtful and a man who won respect easily.

Nine - **Roy G. Steed**. In selecting my top ten personalities, I excluded all close, personal friends. While Roy fits into this category, he is somewhat older than me and was a mentor. He is one of the most remarkable men I have known. A good engineer, a wily financier, and a brilliant mathematician, he also had the ability to charm people in all walks of life. His is a friendship that I very much cherish.

Ten - **Dr. Horace J. Fraser**. While I was subject to his presence and guidance for only a year, he was one of the ablest and brightest men whom I have ever encountered. He was a strong leader for Falconbridge Nickel and is remembered today as one of the major figures in Canadian mining. An additional plus for him was that he had a wry sense of humour.

There it is. There are so many more whom I could add: Al MacNeil, our hockey stalwart; Allan Eagleson, another hockey boy; Dick O'Hagan; Jim Coutts; and Pat Connolly. They were friends and not necessarily mentors, I have admired them all. As I review my list it would appear that I have a tolerance for drinkers in that three of my top ten, Crawford Gordon, Gardiner and Akerley could be two-fisted participants at times.

Bibliography

Bruce, Harry. *The Story of R.A. Jodrey, entrepeneur.* Toronto: McClelland & Stewart, 1979.

Bruce, Harry. *A Century at Central Trust: the story of its growth.* Halifax, N.S.: Nimbus, 1987.

Le Bourdais, Donat Marc. *Sudbury Basin: the story of nickel.* Toronto: Ryerson Press, 1953.

Martin, John Patrick. *The Story of Dartmouth.* Dartmouth, N.S.,1957.

Newman, Peter Charles. *Flame of Power: intimate profiles of Canada's greatest businessmen.* Toronto; New York: Longmans, Green, 1959.

Phillips, Nathan. *Mayor of all the People.* Toronto, Montreal: McClelland and Stewart, 1967.

Radwanski, George. *Trudeau.* Toronto: Macmillan of Canada,1978.

Stewart, Greig. *Arrow through the Heart: the life and times of Crawford Gordon and the Avro Arrow.* Toronto; New York: McGraw-Hill Ryerson,1998.